Christian Women and Modern China

Christian Women and Modern China

Recovering a Women's History of Chinese Protestantism

Li Ma

LEXINGTON BOOKS
Lanham • Boulder • New York • London

Published by Lexington Books
An imprint of The Rowman & Littlefield Publishing Group, Inc.
4501 Forbes Boulevard, Suite 200, Lanham, Maryland 20706
www.rowman.com

6 Tinworth Street, London SE11 5AL, United Kingdom

British Library Cataloguing in Publication Information Available

Library of Congress Control Number: 2020947620

ISBN 978-1-7936-3156-5 (cloth : alk. paper)
ISBN 978-1-7936-3158-9 (pbk : alk. paper)
ISBN 978-1-7936-3157-2 (electronic)

∞™ The paper used in this publication meets the minimum requirements of American
National Standard for Information Sciences—Permanence of Paper for Printed Library
Materials, ANSI/NISO Z39.48-1992.

For my daughter Mercy, the Future

Contents

Acknowledgments

The genesis of this project lay in the limitations of my previously published book *Christianity, Femininity and Social Change in Contemporary China* (Palgrave MacMillan, 2020), which offers oral history accounts of ordinary Christian Chinese women who were born in post-reform China. I soon realized the need of further historical research on Chinese Christian women. A second prompt came from the hostile attacks I received from male scholars in the field of Chinese Christianity after publishing *Religious Entrepreneurism in China's Urban House Churches* (Routledge, 2019) which uncovers a range of power abuse including alleged sexual assaults against women. These moments of reckoning brought me to penning this current volume.

In short, I feel the need to write this book as a female scholar who changed her mind about how a history of Chinese Protestantism should be presented. As long as the stories and history of women are not integrated into this history, narratives and traditions codified by men will remain oppressive to women. Almost every book of mine in the past engages in "advocacy" scholarship. This one is no exception.

This project is the fruit of encouragement and support from many friends and colleagues. I am also deeply indebted to Kristin Du Mez, a social historian on Christian feminism. It was through her book *A New Gospel for Women* on Katharine Bushnell that a lot of changes coalesced in my mind. While Bushnell switched from her missionary career to retranslating the Scripture for the sake of honoring women, a similar sentiment made me transition into writing this women's history. I also feel indebted to another female scholar Kwok Pui-lan, whose works reoriented me to another level of theological reflection in how women's history can be presented. It is due to the scholarly contributions of both these female scholars that I came to a full reckoning about the history of Chinese Protestantism.

My husband Jin Li has been a persistent supporter of all things I do, especially in the creation of this project. As a historian himself, he helped gather historical archives and materials that I would otherwise have no access to. A few of his friends, including economic historian Qin Fang at Fudan University, also helped me gaining access to some important materials. I have also consulted with long-term church affairs observer Chris Gu who offered a lot of insights on the history of the Three-Self Patriotic Movement and many other issues.

I dedicate this volume to my daughter, Mercy Minyue Li, with the hope that she can continue the storytelling and reconstruction.

Li Ma
Grand Rapids
During COVID quarantine, summer of 2020

Abbreviations

CCP   Chinese Communist Party
CNP   Chinese Nationalist Party (or Kuomingtang, KMT)
PLA   People's Liberation Army
PRC   People's Republic of China
PUMC   Peking Union Medical College
SFPE   Sino-Foreign Protestant Establishment
TSPM   Three-Self Patriotic Movement
USSR   Union of Soviet Socialist Republics
WTO   World Trade Organization
YMCA   Young Men's Christian Association
YWCA   Young Women's Christian Association

NOTE ON CHINESE TERMS:

When it comes to personal names and locations, I use the contemporary, internationally recognized *pinyin* system of romanization. For some names that are widely known in former usage, such as Chiang Kai-shek or T. C. Chao, I made an exception by using its most common forms. I also provide Chinese characters for the main women figures in this book.

Chronology

	China & World	Chinese Christian Women (in this volume)
1807	First Protestant missionary Robert Morrison came to China	
1851–1864	Taiping Rebellions	
1894–1895	Sino-Japanese War	
1898	Hundred Days Reform	
1899–1901	Boxer Rebellion	Shi Meiyu trained nurses in her new hospital
1905	Imperial Exam system abolished	
1912	Republic of China established; Chinese Nationalist Party (CNP)	
1916	Yuan Shikai restored monarchy	
1915–1925	New Cultural Movement; Warlordism	Zeng Baosun returned from England to found the Yifang Girls' Collegiate School
1919	May Fourth Movement	Xie Wanying became famous for her novels
1921	Chinese Communist Party (CPC)	Shi Meiyu began Bethel ministry in Shanghai
1922–1927	Anti-Christian Movement	Ding Shujing joined YWCA training in New York
1925	May 30 Incident	
1926		Ding Shujing became YWCA General Secretary
		Xie Wanying returned from America to teach literature at Yenching University
1927	Exodus of foreign missionaries	Zeng Baosun and her school suffered mob attacks by radical communists
	Chiang Kai-shek purge communists in Shanghai	Wu Yifang became president of Ginling College

(Continued)

	China & World	Chinese Christian Women (in this volume)
1929		Lin Qiaozhi became the first indigenous female physician in the Department of Obstetrics and Gynecology of Peking Union Medical College hospital
1933		Zeng Baosun published short novels on Chinese women
1937	Japanese invasion	Wu Yifang joined the People's Political Council
1940		Lin Qiaozhi opened a home clinic in Beijing
		Xie Wanying published a short story *About Women*
1944		Zhao Luorui pursued a doctoral degree at the University of Chicago
1945–1949	Civil War between the Chinese Nationalist Party and CCP	Wu Yifang represented China in the founding of the United Nation
		Xie Wanying taught at Tokyo University
1949	People's Republic of China	Zhao Luorui began teaching in Yenching University
1950–1952	Land reforms	Wu Yaozong led the Three-Self Patriotic Movement
		Christian colleges were closed down
1951	Korean War	
1953–1957	Nationalization of industry and commerce	Zeng Baosun represented Republic China at the UN commission on the Status of Women
		Gu Shengying was awarded by the Polish government for her musical performance of Chopin
		Cao Shengjie participated in the first China Christian National Conference
		Lily Hsu was part of the Local Church where Watchman Nee was arrested
		Lin Qiaozhi became the vice chair of Chinese Medical Association and a deputy director of the Chinese Academy of Medical Services
1957	Anti-Rightist Movement	
1958–1961	Great Leap Forward; famine	Gu Shengying won top prize in piano for China at a contest held in Switzerland
1962		Zhao Luorui began translating Walt Whitman
		Cao Shengjie was appointed the secretary of China's Three-Self Patriotic Protestant Movement Committee
1964		Gu Shengying won top award in the Queen Elizabeth International Piano Contest held at Belgium

(Continued)

	China & World	Chinese Christian Women (in this volume)
1966–1976	Mao's Cultural Revolution	Zhao Luorui's husband Chen Mengjia committed suicide
		Gu Shengying committed suicides
		Lin Qiaozhi was appointed the vice chairwoman of the National Women's Federation (1973)
1976	Death of Mao	
1977	National College Entrance Exam reinstituted	
1978	Rural de-collectivization; reform began	Xie Wanying translated works by Rabindranath Tagore
1980		Lin Qiaozhi published *Gynecological Tumors* and other books
		Cao Shengjie was appointed the vice general director of the China Christian Council
1989	Tiananmen Movement	Chai Ling became "commander" of the Defend Tiananmen Square Headquarters
1992	Deng's reform and opening up policy	Lü Xiaomin began composing Canaan Hymns
1995		Chai Ling was featured in documentary *The Gate of Heavenly Peace*
1997–1999	Hong Kong's and Macao's handovers	Yuan Li became one of China's most well-known actresses
2001	China joined the World Trade Organization	
2003		Lü Xiaomin was featured in the documentary *The Cross: Jesus in China*
2004	Private property rights written into the Chinese constitution; housing market boom	Cao Shengjie represented the China Christian Council in six Bible exhibits in Hong Kong, the United States, and Germany
2008	Beijing Olympics	
2011		Lily Hsu published *The Unforgettable Memoirs: My Life, Shanghai Local Church and Watchman Nee*
2012	Xi Jinping's rule	
2014		Chai Ling released public allegations of sexual abuse against evangelist Yuan Zhiming
2016		Yuan Li set up her own charity foundation in in Shanghai
2017–1918	#MeToo movement around the world	Lily Hsu published her sequel book *For Whom the Siren Wails: Watchman Nee and the Local Church in China*

Introduction

In recent decades, more and more female scholars have tried to write women into history.[1] Scholars of Chinese history are placing women back at the center of China's past in order to gain a renewed understanding of it.[2] In her book *Women and China's Revolutions*, historian Gail Hershatter writes: "A history that neglects gender and the role of women in a profoundly gendered society is going to miss or misperceive some of the most fundamental ways that people made sense of their tumultuous environment."[3] She adds that the symbol of the "Chinese woman" has helped to "hold the empire together, bring it down, and underwrite nation-building, socialist construction, and capitalist growth."[4] It has always been "a flexible symbol of social problems, national humiliation, and political transformation."[5] Women's issues were used to strengthen each movement's need for legitimacy, but when the movement was consolidated, women were again encouraged to double up the labor, both at home and work, and to sacrifice for the larger common good. Almost at every turn of China's modern history, women found their rights for equality come in second to another more sublime goal. Nevertheless, even these failures to fulfill gender equality need to be integrated into a coherent historical narrative.

In the subfield of the history of Chinese Christianity, however, scholarly efforts at restoring the role of women have been scant. One primary reason is that for over a century, the most prominent narrative in the history of Chinese Christianity (in the English-speaking world) has been that it was the foreign missionaries, including men and women, who made history. The indigenous Chinese remained largely a faceless multitude. Feminist theologian Kwok Pui-lan writes that "the relation of women to the unfolding drama of the missionary movement in China has never been recognized as the *problematik* of serious scholarly study."[6] In his 2012 book *A New History of Christianity in*

China, historian Daniel Bays recalls that in the early 1980s, studies in the history of Chinese Christianity mainly focused on the foreign missionaries and what they did in China.[7] Bays's own work did include some female figures, but it largely perpetuated the existing narrative.[8] Women's experiences have been trivialized, fragmented, insufficiently documented, and ignored.[9]

The task of writing Christian women into the history is important also for tracing the beginning of modern China. Some historians propose that it was the arrival of Protestant missionaries after the Second Opium War.[10] Given the centrality of the woman's question to China's modernity, the date should be around the 1880s, when an influx of Western women missionaries mingled with indigenous women to push for substantive and institutional reforms. At different times, Christianity has acted as a catalyst to raise women's consciousness of their social and religious exclusion. Consider the following assessment by two Chinese women scholars:

> Despite the missionaries' teaching of conservative family values and women's submissive roles, their women converts and students excelled in life and work outside their homes. They became the first Chinese women evangelists, teachers, nurses, and doctors, and ironically, many modeled themselves after the single women missionaries and chose to remain single . . . a quiet gender revolution took place in society. There were not only escalating demands for women's education but also for women's reading materials such as women's magazines, family handbooks, and women's fiction, which addressed the many adjustments that women needed to make regarding their new added responsibilities.[11]

There is a reason why the challenge of modernity in China began with "womanhood." As historian Jessie Lutz argues, although missionary education projects emerged out of the needs of the missionaries rather than a result of the demands of the Chinese,[12] the timing was perfect. As historian Philip A. Kuhn also puts it, "A dynasty already weak was confronted with a radically new challenge in the form of militant Western expansionism."[13]

Another reason that the history of Chinese Christian women lapsed into obscurity is that even when the topic of Christian indigenous leadership is introduced, scholars tend to favor the narrative that it was a select group of Chinese men who made history. Whenever indigenous leadership in the Chinese church is discussed, names of well-known male leaders are the first to be mentioned.[14] Take revivalism, for example. Silas H. L. Wu once asked, "Why were the major Chinese revivalists before 1927 predominantly women, and why after that date did female Chinese revivalists suddenly recede into the background in the next stage of Christian revivalism in China?"[15] She points to a "marked shift of gender selection," which elevated male figures such as Watchman Nee, Wang Mingdao, and John Sung to the forefront. Even some male leaders' sexual abuses of women coworkers were ignored. The most illustrative example is that of Watchman Nee.[16] Although in the 1950s the allegations of sexual abuses were tried by court, evidences exhibited to the public, and Nee himself was excommunicated by his own church, house churches continued to sideline this story about Nee.[17] As a result, new converts to the house church tradition tend to defend Nee on the ground that the abuses were fabricated by the communist regime. Even when they were brought to light again in the 2010s by ethnographer-historian Lily Hsu's new book, *The Unforgettable Memoirs: My Life, Shanghai Local Church and Watchman Nee*, there was a lot of heat in the Chinese diaspora defending Nee. Hsu herself received criticisms and fervent attacks.[18] The same pattern repeated itself when it comes to other prominent house church leader who either allegedly abused women or covered up abuses.[19] Recent scholarly works concerning contemporary leadership figures in China also named only men.[20] Therefore, until today, the stories of Chinese Christian women have suffered the same lack of scholarly attention. As historian Janet Moore Lindman writes, "Institutional church histories may mention particular women, usually noted for their piety or wifely connection to a famous divine, but women in general are not central to the narrative."[21] The current history of Chinese Protestantism is deficient because it marginalizes women's lives and contributions.

Nevertheless, a more careful examination of this history reveals that many important male leaders of the indigenous Chinese church were first nurtured in some women-founded ministries. For example, the well-known evangelist John Sung, before becoming known as the most well-known charismatic preacher in all East and South Asia, was first recruited by Shi Meiyu (Mary Stone) into her Bethel Mission team. The story of how Dora Yu's ministry led to Watchman Nee's conversion in 1920 has been widely told. The renowned Chinese theologian T. C. Chao (Zhao Zichen) was from early days mentored by female educator Zeng Baosun. Likewise, Christian literary critic and scholar Wu Ningkun returned from America to teach at Yenching University because of a job offer extended to him by leading English literature scholar Zhao Luorui (also known as Lucy Chao, daughter of T. C. Chao). While the names of the men were later elevated or even enshrined in the history of Chinese Christianity or Chinese intellectual history in general as iconic figures and household names, the names and stories of their female mentors faded into obscurity.

When it comes to the more contemporary scene, women are pushed even further to the margins, despite Christianity becoming relatively feminized in mainland China and in diaspora Chinese communities.[22] Whether in popular media or scholarly works, the role of Chinese Christian women has largely been minimized.[23] Chinese Christian men have increasingly become the gatekeepers of the institutional church, theologies, and even scholarship.

Consequently, the history of Chinese Christianity has formed its own boundaries, canon, and iconic figures that continue to exclude women. To a certain extent, the paucity of Chinese women scholars or their marginalization has contributed to the lack of research on women's history in the Chinese faith community.[24]

In her 1983 book *Women and Ideas and What Men Have Done to Them*, Australian scholar Dale Spender recovers the lost intellectual history of women and explains that the absence of women's voice is fundamental to the perpetuation of patriarchal power.[25] If one integrates women's history, some of the most dramatic transformations need to find more thorough, nuanced explanations, not only in politics, but in employment, family life, and religious activism. In other words, writing a women's history would often be a game changer in certain spheres of power. But as Harvard religion scholar Catherine Brekus claims, "if historians do not become more self-conscious about who is included in their stories and who is not, they will perpetuate the fiction that male leaders alone have made history."[26] In explaining the same neglect of women's role in American religious history, Brekus offers several reasons, one being the fear that "women's history will contribute to the fragmentation of older narratives, making it difficult to tell coherent stories about the past."[27]

This book attempts to retrieve and recover a women's history of Chinese Protestantism.[28] Seeking to interrupt a hegemonic and positivist framework of writing the history of Chinese Christianity, it is largely a reconstruction which has been much needed in academia and the life of the Chinese church. As previously argued, although Chinese Protestantism has been feminized, historians have mostly written with an exclusive focus on prominent male heroes or institutional developments without doing justice to mentioning women, who sometimes were mentors and founders to these heroes and initiatives. The prejudice against female figures and movements has, at times, turned ideological. On another account, the social world of Chinese Christianity scholars has been dominated by men who are attracted to macro, binary frameworks such as church-state relations and civil society.[29] Motivated by a general illusion of Western-imported Christian nationalism, expressed in the assumption such as "Christianity may democratize China" or "China would become the most Christian nation," their narratives and analysis lack nuances and depth of thought.[30] The critical lens is often directed at the communist regime, not the power structure of the church itself. They instinctively frown at inconvenient issues such as abuses of women by prominent leaders in the Chinese church.[31]

Reconstruction of this history raises difficult contextual and historical problems. First of all, a frame of reference is needed to discuss the available historical evidence. "Historians who pretend to record nothing but pure facts while refusing to acknowledge their own presuppositions and theoretical perspectives succeed only in concealing from themselves the ideologies upon which their historiography is based,"[32] as Harvard feminist theologian Elisabeth Schussler Fiorenza declares. I explore formal institutions and rules as well as social networks and social norms. Thus, gender is not the only analytical lens in this book. For example, in presenting how Christian women responded to Marxism, it is important to understand what the political, economic, and cultural context meant for them, and how the roots of ideological antagonism played out in Chinese women's lived experiences. In today's China, the heat of this encounter has not dissipated. As another scholar observes, "No other worldview shook world Christianity more seriously, and no other movement has had a profound an impact on so many. . . . Unless we struggle toward an understanding of the Christian encounter with Marxism, the entire Christian self-understanding in the late modern world will be inadequate."[33]

Secondly, my approach is different from a secular feminist stance which risks becoming politicized. This book does seek to provide a coherent narrative which challenges the Christian religion, or more specifically Protestant mission, as legitimization of the patriarchal order and status quo. But I do not argue that biblical religion is inherently sexist. As Elisabeth Fiorenza says, "such a postbiblical feminist stance . . . too quickly concedes that women have no authentic history within biblical religion and too easily relinquishes women's feminist biblical heritage. Nor can such a stance do justice to the positive experiences of contemporary women within biblical religion."[34] A secular feminist stance sometimes challenges that Christian women ought not to socially comply and as a result they should relinquish their spiritual heritage. I would argue that this stance does not do justice to the positive experiences of Chinese women within their faith tradition. I also challenge the binary thinking of putting secular and sacred, or liberal and conservative on opposite ends. Reality is much more complicated. In this volume, the experiences of every Chinese woman had some liberation elements, but other themes (such as filial piety, patriotism, and even right-wing radicalism) exist too. It would be a form of oppression to deprive people of their history and the complexities that come with that particular history. In *History and Social Theory*, Gordon Leff offers some criteria for what makes a "good history." He considers historical "objectivity" to consist of the dynamic interrelation between the information gleaned from the sources and the "unifying vision" of the interpreter. "To make the past intelligible," the historian ought to go beyond the events in an act of "intellectual recreation."[35]

A reconstruction of a women's history and Chinese Protestantism is needed in order to reclaim this history as the history of women and men.

Admittedly, the personal experiences and social location of a historian determine her assumptions and narrative rhetoric. I come to this work not only as a female scholar but also as a woman in the Chinese church for the past two decades. As a female scholar, I propose that a more fruitful scholarship is possible when we decenter past narratives and re-center trauma and abuses suffered by women and women's agency into the historiography of Chinese Protestantism. I write as a Christian woman who has witnessed the harm of male-dominated historiography which sometimes contributes to false public images of male leaders. But as long as the stories and history of women are not integrated into this history, narratives and traditions codified by men will remain oppressive to women. I believe that the history of the church, in general, will look quite different if we place the most vulnerable group and their agency at its center. This is an analytical lens for this entire project. Compared to the orthodox approach of traditional historians, cultural historians have tended to favor more nuanced and diverse presentation of who makes history. By exploring the lives of those who were once ignored, whether slaves, women or immigrant laborers, scholars are able to reshape the norm of historical narratives. Such efforts are driven by the common belief that "historical change does not only come from the top down, but also from the bottom up."[36] Consequently, stories of the marginalized do count as history. Social historians also favor this approach because they found quantitative data and social theory insufficient when trying to answer the most pressing question about how individuals made sense of their lives in certain historical contexts.

This book bridges the gap by presenting a social history of Chinese women pioneers in Chinese Christianity since the 1880s. A longitudinal evaluation of Chinese women's changing roles in the church needs to examine the deployment of gender in the narration of identity, the negotiation of power differentials between the powerful and the marginalized, and the reinforcement of patriarchal control over spheres such as family and culture. This book presents how indigenous Christian women created change in Chinese society, dealing with power structures in family life, professional work, and Christian ministry. It is time not only to challenge the traditional "master narrative" centered around indigenous male leaders, but also to diversify it, because histories that recognize the female presence are bound to be richer. Rather than placing either women or men at the center of my narrative, I hope to allow a more complex understanding of gender, power, agency, and institutional change. This multi-level landscape is more inclusive and more representative of the real lives of the Chinese people in the past. I also seek to contribute to a broader transnational women's history, helping our understanding of the impact Chinese Christian women have crossed national boundaries. Overall, this study is crafted to reintroduce Chinese Christian women pioneers not only to women's history and the history of Chinese Christianity, but also to the history of global Christian mission and the history of many modern professions, such as medicine, education, literature, music, charity, journalism, and literature.

Women in Chinese society have lived through political upheavals that traumatically affected their lives. In the kaleidoscope of social change in China since the late Qing dynasty, when Protestant Christianity began to affect the lives of more ordinary Chinese, women as a social demographic group have experienced the most dramatic ups and downs. As historian Jessie G. Lutz says, it is important to understand "gender entanglements with politics, social structures and values, nation building, and even the economies of agricultural and industrial societies."[37] It is an attempt to recover the stories of indigenous women and to restore the historical significance their lives deserve.

This study assumes first of all that women have indeed participated in the creation of Chinese Protestantism. Secondly, it assumes that gender has affected the shape of Christianity in China. Finally, it affirms that a history of Chinese Protestantism includes the motivations, goals, theological assumptions, and reflections that Chinese women employed as they participated in this development. Thus, this book demonstrates how Chinese Christian women have at main points in time "made history" that matters for Chinese Christianity. By inviting the presence of these women pioneers, historical contours are enriched because "women's history demands that historians ask questions about the construction of gender and the political and social realities of women's lives and in relation to the religious community."[38]

The stories in this volume span one and a half centuries, examining stories of Chinese women who lived across historical eras from late Qing dynasty, Republic of China, a totalitarian Mao era, to a post-reform China and then a globalized Chinese diaspora. Outlining social change within distinct historical phases is important because each phase poses unique challenges while offering unprecedented opportunities for Chinese women. These historical contrasts offer a broader picture of social change for the role of women in China. For example, in the late nineteenth century, I examine Chinese women who were mentored by Western women missionaries and accomplished pioneering work in medicine, girls' education, and social reform. They pushed through social hurdles such as foot-binding, illiteracy, domesticity, and equality rights for workers. After the founding of the communist regime, however, the focus shifts to politicized struggles along partisan lines. Challenges for Christian women came from a regime that discouraged elitism and foreign connections. Taking each historical period as one laboratory of institutional change for Chinese women, this approach helps to highlight the contrast within Chinese society during these periods. Despite these changes, there have been enduring themes in these women's pursuits—an identity that is not simply defined by a woman's familial roles of daughter, wife, and mother, but rather as gifted individuals who can contribute to the common good. As historical actors, these Chinese women had diverse experiences, interests, and talents. Within various structural constraints that were characteristic of their times, these Chinese women pioneers achieved extraordinary levels of social and cultural participation.

I also ask challenging questions about traditional narrative frameworks that tend to be male-dominated: How did home-bound Chinese women, who were mostly illiterate, embrace Christianity when Protestant mission spread further into China in the mid- to late nineteenth century? How would historians have written about mission pioneers in the 1920s in China if they had explored the lives of women as well as of men? What would have been their main themes? What made Chinese Communism appealing to many Christian women pioneers in the first half of the twentieth century? How should the story of Christian women under Maoism be told? What expectations did women have for the New China that proved false in the 1960s? How did the professional skills of Christian women contribute to society despite the communist regime? How did the demarcation between Three-Self churches and house churches affect the Chinese church and women's experiences, including before and after the economic reform? What role did Christian women in the Chinese diaspora play after the 1990s, an age of transnational migration and globalization? How are Christian women finding opportunities to serve in the 2010s with China becoming the world's leading economic power? Lastly, did their gender make these women into political, cultural, and ecclesiastical outsiders in their society, or were they able to carve out new ways of engagement with public life? In all these attempts, the recovery of women's stories should lead to new narratives. Such knowledge is likely to transform our understanding of the historical landscape of Chinese Protestantism.

This study does not seek to offer an exhaustive history of Christian women leaders in China. Rather, it tells the stories of ten generations of significant yet under-recognized historical female figures. Each of the women selected occupied a unique position in a specific historical phase and left a legacy or a wider social impact. My selection was guided by archival availability and the significance of leadership in her way of life. Within each historical phase, particular women stood out as the pioneers and trailblazers of their time. I qualify such selectiveness by a few measurable criteria. First, each woman was baptized as a Christian believer and participated in faith communities. Secondly, during her lifetime, she enjoyed a national and global reputation in either professional expertise, evangelistic influence, or institution-building. For this reason, I exclude historical figures such as Lin Zhao whose influence came decades after her story was written.[39] Thirdly, among the married women, they achieved pioneering status in various fields quite independently, without relying on the reputation of their husbands.[40] Therefore, I do not include women leaders such as Soong Mei-ling, whose life has already been covered by many China studies monographs.[41] Apart from choosing figures whose contributions have been widely recognized, I have tried to select women whose life and faith journeys represent larger and complex issues at the crossroads of Christianity and the Chinese society.

On a deeper level, the recovery of women's history in Chinese Protestantism also allows us to rethink many assumptions about the crises of modernity in Chinese society. At the center of these women's stories is power relationships with the state, patriarchy, and social norms as the Chinese society transforms from imperial order to modernity, communism, postmodernity, and then global diaspora. These women acted as cultural interpreters between East and West as well as between old and new. In their explorations of selfhood, gender roles, nationalistic consciousness, and Christian identity, many were cross-cultural synthesizers who formulated their own distinct expressions of the Christian faith. Because of these multifaceted processes, the women in this volume did not live without controversy. Their stories can reveal both the promises and perils of Protestantism Christianity in the Chinese society.

This book is structured to include an introduction, three main parts including ten historical chapters, and a conclusion. The chapters that follow are organized more or less chronologically. Each offers historical background which situates the women's stories in their political and social contexts. Although the periodization largely maps onto how historians perceive Chinese history, the re-centering of women's experiences may also challenge or even subvert previously held narratives. Within each historiographical chapter about women who belonged to a particular generation, there are three parts. First, I locate the main figures in the social context of one specific historical era. Exploring the setting from which the history of Chinese Christian women emerged is essential to understanding their stories. Next, I give historiographical accounts of their lives, drawing extensively on materials written by the women themselves and by their contemporaries in both the English and Chinese languages. The research materials include newspaper and magazine accounts, personal memoirs and diaries, and ministry reports. I use their biographical accounts as "case studies," integrating historical examination of the larger social forces that shaped their understanding and pursuits. Although being active agents of change, their lives also bear the indelible imprint of the ideas, practices, and movements of their times. Lastly, I resituate and evaluate the significance and implications of these women in the broader historical trajectory. I discuss how their agency interacts with broader currents in each historical phase.

Part I spans the Era of Revolutions from late Qing to early communist China (1880s–1953). Missionaries, physicians, and reform-minded educators are the main focus in this section. Under the section title, I offer a short summary of major institutional change in this phase. The first two chapters explore life in China during the final phase of the Qing dynasty. Chapter 1, "Foreign Devils and Heathen Sisters," explores the lives of Western missionary women and Chinese indigenous women like Shi Meiyu to trace the common ground as well as tension in their work and community building. Chapter 2, "A Confucian Christian Feminist," describes a time of continued missionary expansion and domestic unrest in which women like Zeng Baosun found a middle path between Westernization and Chinese tradition. Girls' schools became "an alternative social universe" to the one provided by the family.[42] It was during this time that "the Chinese woman question" emerged as central to the forming of a Chinese nation. The two chapters that follow examine the activities of Chinese women pioneers during the tumultuous decades leading up to the communist revolution. Chapter 3, "China's First 'Christian Republic'," looks at the role of YWCA in China when the tension between elitism and populism divided local mission work. Women became a major part of a modern industrial working class during this period. Chapter 4, "Life and Death of Christian Colleges," focuses on the institution-building efforts of Western missionaries in Christian higher education. Many of these projects promoted women leadership. The Nationalist government tried to redefine women's role through its New Life Movement, but these efforts were ineffective and counterproductive, leading to more popular resistance against elitism. Meanwhile, both the YWCA and Christian colleges gradually became training grounds for progressive students who sympathized with or embraced communist thought. At this time, the conceptualizations of the New Woman and the Modern Girl operated differently.

Part II covers the Era of Militant Communism (1954–1979) and the following recuperation years in the 1980s. The main characters in this section include Chinese intellectuals, resisters, and accommodators. Under the section title, I offer a short summary of major institutional change. Next, Chapter 5, "Patriotic Intellectuals and the New Regime," examines the transitional period of China's independence, and from socialist construction to radical politics under Mao. Although the new regime did radically rearrange women's lives in marriage, work, and society, new forms of inequality also emerged along class lines, especially against intellectuals. Chapter 6, "Does the Motherland Love You Back?," explores an often ignored phenomenon of mass suicide during Mao's Cultural Revolution. Chapter 7, "The Party Could Still Use You," describes the lives of two professional women, Lin Qiaozhi and Xie Wanying, who contributed to medicine and literature, respectively.

Part III examines the Era of Developmental Communism (1992–2008) and the following decade of China as a globalized economic power.[43] The main characters in this section include influencers, whistleblowers, and celebrities.

Under the section title, I also provide a summary of major institutional change. Next, Chapter 8, "Bibles, Hymns, and Competing Influences," discusses through the lives of two women church leaders, Cao Shengjie and Lü Xiaomin, how the antagonism between two systems of Chinese Protestantism led to the branching out of two competing influences in the Chinese diaspora. The last two chapters explore recent trends in Chinese Protestantism in the 2010s. Chapter 9, "Exposing Abuses, Changing Narratives," depicts the stories of two women, Lily Hsu and Chai Ling, who advocated against sexual violence against women by church leadership. Their efforts subverted some long-held narratives. The topic of sexual abuse in the church remains not just relevant to but central to women's experiences. Chapter 10, "Consumerism, Censorship and Christian Celebrities," turns to a new public phase of the way celebrity Christian women engage in popular culture and public sphere that is both consumeristic, heavily censored, and intensely divided.

The conclusion brings this volume to a close with a historical evaluation of several generations of Chinese women's experiences. I revisit themes such as gender, power, and women's agency. Lastly, I also include an Epilogue as a personal note on the experience of writing this book.

I am well aware that this research has many limitations. By recovering the stories of Chinese women pioneers, this book is still too elitist to be inclusive. Almost all the Chinese women in this book enjoyed privileges of classism. Though it seeks to restore to Chinese women the status of a "historical subject," it has imitations by selecting only a dozen or so women pioneers while ignoring a vast number of female contributors. An elitist approach is a necessary step but remains incomplete and inconsistent with its inclusive principle if it continues to leave out other voices. Collecting these other conversations would be a difficult task, as Kwok Pui-lan describes in the following excerpt:

> Even if they have "spoken," their speech acts are expressed not only in words
> but also in forms (story-telling, songs, poems, dances, and quilting, etc.) that
> the academic and cultural establishments either could not understand or deemed
> insignificant. These knowledge have been ruled out as nondate: too fragmented,
> or insufficiently documented for serious inquiry.[44]

The difficulty with Chinese historiography of women is that the society as a whole has lagged behind in embracing cultural pluralism. Pervasive exclusion of women from the realm of public symbol formation and decision-making has meant that women were subsequently subordinated to the imagination and needs of a world designed chiefly by men. Historians of Chinese Christianity often work mostly from printed sources while leaving out experiences of relationship dynamics, changes in faith communities, disillusionment, and cognitive dissonance on the part of Chinese Christians.

Using a social history approach that appreciates a multiplicity of local and nontotalizing histories may interrupt master narratives. But this is why we need a multifaceted lens of race, class, gender, and sexual orientation that destabilizes the routine categories of historiography.

Another limitation of this work is probably lack of engagement with discussions about the female body and sexuality, other than foot-binding and reproductive health. When it comes to the female body, feminist theologies have embraced embodiment as a women-centered value. First, embodied morality takes emotions seriously. Kwok Pui-lan writes that "Too often, the memory of multiply oppressed women is inscribed on the body, on one's most private self, on one's sexuality. We have yet to find a language to speak in public how the body in such circumstances remembers and passes on knowledge from generation to generation."[45] Secondly, the concept of "bodily integrity" is central to issues of not just abuse against women, but also gender roles dictated by pregnancy, lactation, physical bonding, and care in long-term child-rearing. Theologically speaking, there has also been little discussion about the use of inclusive language in the Chinese faith community when referring to women or to God. As Elizabeth A. Johnson writes as an ending to her book: "What is the right way to speak about God in light of women's reality? . . . a more inclusive way of speaking can come about that bears the ancient wisdom with a new justice."[46]

In recent years, there have been contemporary works on marginalized subgroups of Chinese women, but very few of them dealt with women's religious practices.[47] Little scholarship has incorporated the lives of ethnic minority women who bear layers of multiple marginalization in a predominantly Han Chinese society. This book serves as a preliminary account and an invitation to more research in the future.

NOTES

    1. Jane Lewis, "Women Lost and Found: The Impact of Feminism on History," in Dale Spender, ed., *Men's Studies Modified: The Impact of Feminism on the Academic Disciplines* (New York: Pergamon Press, 1981), 73–82. Catherine A. Brekus (ed.), *The Religious History of American Women: Reimagining the Past* (Chapel Hill: University of North Carolina Press, 2007).

    2. Gail Hershatter, *Women and China's Revolutions* (Lanham: Rowman & Littlefield Publishers, 2018). Vivienne Xiangwei Guo, *Women and Politics in Wartime China: Networking Across Geopolitical Borders* (London: Routledge, 2018). Wang Zheng, *Finding Women in the State* (Oakland: University of California Press, 2017).

    3. Hershatter, *Women and China's Revolutions*, xv.

    4. Ibid., xix.

5. Ibid., xiii.

6. Kwok Pui-lan, *Chinese Women and Christianity, 1860–1927* (Atlanta: Scholars Press, 1992), 1.

7. Daniel Bays, *A New History of Chinese Christianity* (Hoboken: Wiley-Blackwell, 2012), 1. A secondary theme, according to Bays, is the "cross-cultural process" by "the creation of an immensely varied Chinese Christian world in our day."

8. Bays acknowledges that he seeks to present "a coherent narrative" which would "strike a balance" across different periods of Chinese history. He focuses on a "basic tension" between (foreign) mission and (Chinese) church over a century and a half with attention to their often-contentious relationship with the Chinese regime. But this still appeared to largely a continuation of the Westerner-centered approach.

9. Kwoi Pui-lan, *Postcolonial Imagination and Feminist Theology* (Louisville: Westminster John Knox Press, 2005), 30.

10. Jonathan D. Spence, *The Search for Modern China* (New York: W. W. Norton & Company, 1991). Immanuel Y. Hsu, *The Rise of Modern China* (New York: Oxford University Press, 1999).

11. Wai Ching Angela Wong and Patricia P. K. Chiu, *Chinese Women in Chinese Society* (Hong Kong: Hong Kong University Press, 2018), 7.

12. Jessie G. Lutz, *Pioneer Chinese Christian Women* (Bethlehem: Lehigh University Press, 2010), 22.

13. Philip A. Kuhn, *Rebellion and Its Enemies in Late Imperial China: Militarization and Social Structure, 1796–1864* (Cambridge: Harvard University Press, 1970), 1.

14. Leslie T. Lyall, *Three of China's Mighty Men* (London: Hodder and Stoughton, 1980). John Sung, *The Journal Once Lost: Extracts from the Diary of John Sung* (Singapore: Armour Publishing, 2007). Lim Ka-Tong, *The Life and Ministry of John Sung* (Singapore: Armor Publishing, 2011). Leslie T. Lyall, *A Biography of John Sung* (Singapore: Armor Publishing, 2015). Thomas Alan Harvey, *Acquainted with Grief* (Grand Rapids: Brazos Press, 2002). Stephen Wang et al., *The Long Road to Freedom: The Story of Wang Mingdao* (Lancaster: Sovereign World, 2002). Lian Xi, *Redeemed by Fire: The Rise of Popular Christianity in Modern China* (New Haven: Yale University Press, 2010). Lee-ming Ng, "An Evaluation of T. C. Chao's Thought," *Ching Feng* 14 (1–2) (1971): 5–59. Winfried Glüer, *Christliche Theologie in China: T. C. Chao 1918–1956* (Gütersloh: Gütersloher Verlagshaus Mohn, 1979). Chen Yongtao, *The Chinese Christology of T. C. Chao* (Leiden: Brill, 2017). Daniel Hoi Ming, *A Study of T. C. Chao's Christology in the Social Context of China, 1920–1949* (New York: Peter Lang, 2017).

15. Silas H. L. Wu, "Dora Yu: Foremost Female Evangelist in Twentieth-Century Chinese Revivalism," in Dana L. Robert, ed., *Gospel Bearers, Gender Barriers* (New York: Orbis Books, 2002), 86.

16. Joseph Tse-Hei Lee, "Watchman Nee and the Little Flock Movement in Maoist China," *Church History* 74 (1) (2005): 68–96. John Dongsheng Wu, *Understanding Watchman Nee: Spirituality, Knowledge, and Formation* (Eugene: Wipf and Stock Publishers, 2012).

17. In 1953, Watchman Nee admitted to the rape allegations during a court trial. Watchman Nee was known to have taken video recordings of a woman coworker he had alleged raped. Negative films and video clips were put on the spring 1956 public exhibit of Nee's crimes. Over 130,000 people went to the exhibit. Lily Hsu

was among many members of the Local Church who reluctantly went. Three decades later, Hsu interviewed the women survivors and confirmed the validity of these allegations.

18. Another biographer-historian of Watchman Nee is Dana Roberts. See Dana Roberts, *Understanding Watchman Nee* (North Hollywood: Haven Books, 1980). Dana Roberts, *Secrets of Watchman Nee: His Life, His Teachings, His Influence* (Newberry: Bridge-Logos Publishers, 2005). Lily M. Hsu and Dana Roberts, *My Unforgettable Memories: Watchman Nee and Shanghai Local Church* (Maitland: Xulon Press, 2013). Lily M. Hsu, *For Whom the Siren Wails: Watchman Nee and the Local Church in China* (Maitland: Xulon Press, 2018). The last two books received attacks which are included in chapter 9 of this volume.

19. In the 2000s, it was Gong Shengliang, pastor of the South China Church, whose name means devotion and persecution in the English-speaking world but pops up sexual abuse in a simple Chinese-language Google search. In 2019, it was Wang Yi, pastor of Early Rain church in Chengdu, who covered up allegations of rapes committed by men in his second-tier leadership. In the English-speaking media, Wang became a household name for anti-communist civil disobedience, while his misogyny was a prominent theme in his self-published Chinese-language media. As the author who documented both sides of Wang's ministry, I also received the same treatment as Lily Hsu did. See Li Ma, *Religious Entrepreneurship in China's Urban House Churches: The Rise and Fall of Early Rain Reformed Presbyterian Church* (New York: Routledge, 2019); Li Ma, *Babel Church: The Subversion of Christianity in An Age of Mass Media, Globalization and #MeToo* (Eugene: Cascade Books, 2021).

20. Gerda Wielander, *Christian Values in Communist China* (London: Routledge, 2015). Chloe Starr, *Chinese Theology: Text and Context* (New Haven: Yale University Press, 2018). Alexander Chow, *Chinese Public Theology: Generational Shifts and Confucian Imagination in Chinese Christianity* (Oxford: Oxford University Press, 2018). About abuse-related controversies, also see Li Ma, *Religious Entrepreneurism in China's Urban House Churches: The Rise and Fall of Early Rain Reformed Presbyterian Church* (London: Routledge, 2019).

21. Janet Moore Lindman, "Beyond the Meeting House: Women and Protestant Spirituality in Early America," in Catherine A. Brekus, ed., *The Religious History of American Women: Reimagining the Past* (Chapel Hill: University of North Carolina Press, 2007), 143.

22. Li Ma, *Christianity, Femininity and Social Change in Contemporary China* (New York: Palgrave MacMillan, 2020), 3.

23. There was one piece about China's Bible Women, but it was also about a much earlier historical phase. Alexander Chow, "The Remarkable Story of China's 'Bible Women'," *Christianity Today*, March of 2018. https://www.christianitytoday.com/history/2018/march/christian-china-bible-women.html Popular media outlets such as *Christianity Today* opted out of interviews with female scholars only to make room for male scholars.

24. When American female scholars publish new books on Chinese Christianity, they also tend to mention Christian men (male church leaders and scholars) only. See Chloe Starr, *Chinese Theology: Text and Context*.

25. Dale Spender, *Women of Ideas: And What Men Have Done to Them* (New York: HarperCollins, 1991). Reprint version.

26. Catherine A. Brekus, "Introduction," in Catherine A. Brekus, ed., *The Religious History of American Women: Reimagining the Past* (Chapel Hill: University of North Carolina Press, 2007), 34.

27. Ibid., 13.

28. My research has always been on Chinese Protestantism. Sometimes I use Chinese Christianity in a broad sense when it comes to China's political climate, but most empirical research is on Protestantism, the fastest-growing part of Chinese Christianity.

29. Examples include works by male scholars such as Fenggang Yang, Ying Fuk Tsang, Carsten Vala, and so on.

30. The prediction by Fenggang Yang about China set to be the "Most Christian Nation" has been covered by multiple western media such as *The Telegraph*, *CBN News*, *Christian Post*. For one example see Anugrah Kumar, "China to Have World's Largest Christian Population by 2025, Religion Expert Says," *The Christian Post*, April 27, 2014. https://www.christianpost.com/news/china-to-have-worlds-largest-christian-population-by-2025-religion-expert-says.html

31. See Carsten Vala, "Book Review: Religious Entrepreneurism in China's Urban House Churches by Li Ma," *Review of Religion and Chinese Society* 7 (1) 2020: 149–52. In this review, Vala considers the inclusion of sexual abuse allegations into a scholarly work as "partisan" while faulting the author (myself) for neglecting "to firmly situate her work in the scholarship on church-state relations in authoritarian China." It would be helpful to also know that Fenggang Yang is the editor-in-chief of this journal.

32. Elisabeth Fiorenza, *In Memory of Her: A Feminist Theological Reconstruction of Christian Origins*, 2 Revised Edition, (London: Hymns Ancient & Modern Ltd., 1996), xlvii.

33. Denis R. Janz, *World Christianity and Marxism* (New York: Oxford University Press, 1998), 4.

34. Fiorenza, *In Memory of Her*, xlvii–xlix

35. Ibid., 13. Hayden White and Claude Lévi-Strauss both agree that history is never just "history of" but always also "history for," emphasizing its general narrative discourse. See Hayden White, *Metahistory: The Historical Imagination in Nineteenth-Century Europe* (Baltimore: Johns Hopkins University Press, 1973), 11.

36. Ibid., 18.

37. Lutz, *Pioneer Chinese Christian Women*, 13.

38. Marilyn J. Westerkamp, "Puritan Women, Spiritual Power, and the Question of Sexuality," in Catherine A. Brekus, ed., *The Religious History of American Women: Reimagining the Past* (Chapel Hill: University of North Carolina Press, 2007), 67–68.

39. Lin was imprisoned in 1960 and later executed in 1968 for her outspoken voice during the Hundred Flowers Movement of 1957 against Mao Zedong's policies. In 2003, independent filmmaker Hu Jie produced a documentary *In Search of the Soul of Lin Zhao*, which popularized her story. This documentary also mentioned her Christian upbringing and conversion during imprisonment. It popularized the image

of Lin Zhao as a Christian martyr like Watchman Nee, who was imprisoned during the same time. Lin's anti-communist martyrdom was again picked up by historian Xi Lian in his 2018 book titled *Blood Letters: The Untold Story of Lin Zhao: A Martyr in Mao's China* (New York: Basic Books, 2018).

40. Meanwhile, this is not to deny that women who achieved power through the reputations of their husbands can make excellent scholarly projects. See Kate Bowler, *The Preacher's Wife: The Precarious Power of Evangelical Women Celebrities* (New Jersey: Princeton University Press, 2019).

41. I appreciate these monographs for shedding light on the historical context, but there is more work to be done in order to reshape dominant historical narratives.

42. Hershatter, *Women and China's Revolutions*, xvii.

43. I prefer not to use the word "post-communism" because China's Communist Party remained a ruling party and there has been campaigns to revive the communist ideology.

44. Kwok, *Postcolonial Imagination and Feminist Theology*, 30.

45. Ibid., 37.

46. Ibid., 287.

47. Li Ma, Christianity, Femininity and Social Change in Contemporary China (London: Palgrave Mamillan, 2020).

Part I

THE ERA OF REVOLUTIONS

MISSIONARIES, PHYSICIANS, REFORMER-EDUCATORS

As the last imperial dynasty of China was declining in power following the Opium Wars (1839–1842, 1856–1860), missionary activities through "unequal treaties" increased. Reform-minded local gentry class mingled with liberal Protestant missionaries and embraced ideas of social progress related to Christianity. In the 1890s, Western-style medicine and education became the premier areas of progressive experiment. After the Boxer Rebellion (1899–1901), the Qing government initiated reforms including the abolition of the Imperial Exam (1905), clearing the way for easier upward mobility through alternative ways of education. This created the precondition for exponential growth in missionary education programs that nurtured and trained up China's next generation leadership.

Endowed with privilege, however, these missionary-educated Chinese politicians and businessmen did not live up to the hope of China's "first Christian Republic" (1912). Soon, political corruption, rising social inequality, and domination of Protestant mission led to increasing populist resentments and culminated in the Anti-Christian Movement (1922–1927). Meanwhile, Soviet communism, another strand of progressive influence to Chinese under the Republican regime, gained inroad among Chinese intellectuals and college students who became dissatisfied with the presence of Western Christianity. Japanese invasion (1937–1945), prolonged warfare, and the Republican government's incompetence and reliance on America further pushed most Chinese reformers to embrace Chinese communism which eventually gained victory (1949). Decades of Protestant missionary expansion came to a halt. Shortly after the founding of China's communist regime, and in the midst of the US-Korean War (1950–1953), the country's Christian colleges became first casualties to Soviet nationalization and strong anti-foreignism.

Chapter 1

Foreign Devils and Heathen Sisters

In 1879, 25-year-old American medical missionary Katharine Bushnell expanded her medical ministry in the treaty port city of Jiujiang.[1] It was one year after she first arrived in China, where "the largest missionary enterprise ever mounted by the Christian world" was taking place.[2] One day, a local gentry-turned-pastor Mr. Shi led his seven-year-old young daughter Shi Meiyu to see this American doctor, who by that time had won wide respect from local Chinese. He pleaded Bushnell to help train this young girl so that one day she could live an independent life in the service of others, just as these American woman missionaries were. The father of Shi Meiyu, after having lost his family estate and property during the Taiping Rebellion (1850–1864), made a living by teaching the Chinese language to missionaries. Later, Mr. Shi became the first Methodist pastor in Central China.[3] His request to Katherine Bushnell and other women missionaries such as Gertrude Howe came as a surprise, given the previous hostility these foreigners had experienced.

When the collective memory of the Taiping Rebellion was still fresh and haunting to local Chinese, a new wave of Western missionaries fluxed in with more determination to Christianize China. Their uninvited presence continued to create fear and aversion. First, most of them found the physical appearance of the Westerner, with long noses and deep-set blue eyes, disturbing. Thus, the term "foreign devil" became commonly used: "The Chinese were frightened of them, thinking the missionaries were devils, and their grey and blue eyes were due to their lack of nourishment, which they made up by eating the eyes of Chinese children."[4] Rumors like these were invented to fan up hostility against mission workers. Second, to the Chinese, the motives of foreign diplomats, traders, and missionaries appeared to be similarly intrusive and self-serving. Most local Chinese people did not differentiate between these subgroups of foreigners. Lastly, for Chinese civilians living under imperial control, association with Western missionaries had repeatedly proved to be a social and political hazard. As historian Gail Hershatter writes, "Chinese who converted were expected to rework family and community relationships in ways that could cause considerable friction and property disputes, particularly if missionaries intervened to support Chinese Christian converts. Foreign consuls and troops were sometimes brought in to support missionary activities and property claims, further inflaming local tensions."[5]

Yet, Western missionaries continued to be captured by the imagination of "a Christian China." Realizing that their efforts in the first half of the century yielded only a meager number of converts, missionaries legitimatized unequal treaties as God's providential way to conquer China. Some historians remark that "[i]ndeed between 1840 and 1900 every Western invasion of China was almost unanimously conceived of by these American missionaries as an act of providence."[6] Others also reckon that "[t]he basic fact about the missionaries in China, which no amount of love and service on their part could alter or make up for, was that for a whole century only Western imperial power held the door of China open for them."[7] Understandably, there was much trepidation and distrust toward foreigners among indigenous Chinese.

Like many others, Katherine Bushnell also desired to "bring the advantages of Christianity to women in foreign lands."[8] She first arrived in Jiujiang, a port city which opened up to foreign trade and mission work after the Treaty of Tianjin (1858). Soon, the region rose economically as a center for rice and opium trade. The city of Jiujiang also became the headquarters of the Methodist Episcopal Church in Central China. When Bushnell arrived, a mission school set up by the Women's Foreign Missionary Society was already established. She learned of indigenous hostility when hearing how the school had once been attacked by local residents.[9] In the latter half of the nineteenth century, after the Second Opium War (1856–1860), an imperial China reluctantly allowed Western missionaries to enter through its treaty ports. They came across the globe from a modernizing part of the world with technological conveniences and reformist aspirations. Crossing from that world into China felt like time travel to a primitive medieval era that was "mired in the timeless dirt, death, and degradation of the ages."[10] Westerners possessed apparent material superiority over those whom they saw as "heathen." Believing that "Christianity leads to flourishing," foreign missionaries attributed the backward living conditions and social ills to the lack of Christianity, their perceived source of modern sciences and democratic virtues. Their evangelistic fervor was compounded by this conviction. At a time when most foreigners chose to live with some commercial conveniences in China's port cities, missionaries had been the first group to venture into the country's impoverished inland areas. They had been instrumental to merchants and diplomats by writing English-Chinese language books and cultural guides, in addition to serving as translators. Back in their home countries in Europe and North America, missionaries' outlook and reports on people in other parts of the world profoundly shaped ongoing perceptions of Westerners.

In response to civilian antagonism in China, Western medical ministry was considered by missionaries as an effective "wedge" that reached out to needy Chinese who mainly relied upon traditional medicine or witchcraft for illnesses. Moreover, the presence of woman missionaries was seen as less intimidating.[11] Therefore, the mission board recruited young and capable women such as Katharine Bushnell to answer the call. By 1905, one-third of China's 300 medical missionaries were women.[12] This was also partly due to the fact that most Chinese women were reluctant to be treated by male physicians.[13] In their own country, American women still had a marginalized role in churches that endorsed Victorian domesticity. However, when they ventured to other lands as missionaries, education and medicine opened up fulfilling career opportunities for American women. Single women missionaries became more appreciated because missionary wives, desiring to be role models of Victorian virtues, were mostly preoccupied with child rearing and serving their husbands.[14] Some mission boards soon found that sending single women missionaries enabled them to expand in what used to be hostile local environments.[15] Over a period of time, mission boards were gladly surprised that "the entrance of single woman missionaries appointed by woman's boards elevated the elimination of foot-binding and other gender-based Chinese customs to a high missional priority."[16]

Back home in the mission-sending countries, when missionaries went back on furlough while doing fundraising, the image of missionary women added a purifying and benevolent nuance to Western expansionism.[17] In a public address entitled "Woman's Work for Woman," A. P. Happer addressed the 1877 missionary conference that "the condition of women in heathen lands presents the most pressing and urgent calls to Christian women to use their most strenuous efforts to communicate to them the knowledge of the blessed Gospel of our Lord."[18] This change of public image was beneficial for women missionaries themselves, allowing them to practice social activism. By the late 1870s, women missionaries had outnumbered men.[19] Soon afterward, the Western missionary community saw the "feminization of the mission force" in China.[20] In 1890, among nearly 1,300 missionaries who were active in China, 707 were women with 316 of them unmarried.[21] Timothy Richard, secretary of the influential society for the Diffusion of Christian and General Knowledge among the Chinese, published numerous articles and books about reform, praising the contributions of Western women in China.[22]

Armed with traditional Christian doctrines and modern science, American women missionaries' initial encounter with a late imperial Chinese society must have been full of culture shocks. American missionary and social activist Adele Fielde wrote in 1887 about the general status of Chinese women: "[She] does not walk in the street with her husband; she does not eat with him, but takes what is left after the men of the family have finished their meal; she has no legal right to anything whatever, apart from her male relatives."[23] They saw how Chinese women were secluded and homebound with distorted, bound feet. Most of these women were illiterate, complying with early arranged marriages. Young girls from poor peasant families were often sold as commodities or concubines for rich landlords. Even worse was frequent female infanticide. In comparison, women in the West seemed to be enjoying much more freedom and equality, which they deemed redemptive benefits of Christianity. Due to these contrasts, it was hard for Western female missionaries not to sympathize and thus confront some oppressive practices in China. They set out to help heathen Chinese sisters the best they could. As Western women "carved out new opportunities for themselves,"[24] a "missionary-imperial feminism" came into being. As historian Kristin Du Mez puts it, "This emancipatory narrative was central to the missionary impulse, and to the women's missionary movement."[25] This women savior complex sometimes even played out "at the expense of their 'heathen sisters'."[26]

Before Katherine Bushnell met the young Shi Meiyu, the American doctor had successfully treated the family member of a high-ranking official before that family had exhausted all medical options. This work helped her gain a widely positive reputation.[27] Indigenous hostility was reversed because of an official endorsement of Bushnell's medical service. It was also because of this incident that Mr. Shi began to dream of a worthy life for his young daughter to become just like Dr. Bushnell.[28] Already reformist in spirit, he lamented many ill social practices that oppressed women. From Katharine Bushnell's success and how well-received these medical services were to both Chinese officials and commoners, Mr. Shi saw a different future was possible for his young daughter. The first thing Rev. Shi and his wife resolved to do was to leave the seven-year-old girl's feet unbound. As a friend of Shi Meiyu later recalled to a Western Christian audience, "With a faith that was strong and clear, Meiyu's parents brought her up with natural feet, thus giving her the distinction of being the first native girl, not a slave, in Central and West China, to have her feet left as God had made them."[29] Though a progressive woman herself, Mrs. Shi did not unbind her own feet "in the hopes that people would understand that she had left her daughter's feet unbound out of principle, not ignorance."[30]

Shi Meiyu's mother belonged to the first "Bible women" trained by Western missionaries in Jiujiang. With support from her husband, Mrs. Shi was able to move around freely with other Bible women who were widowed. They visited the needy in nearby villages, retold Bible stories, and sometimes preached to a group of curious villagers. For their time and travel, missionaries often paid them a small salary and considered them helpful coworkers. Some literate Bible women also helped missionaries translate documents and accompanied them on trips that needed communication aides. Later, Mrs. Shi was trusted by Gertrude Howe to help run a missionary school.

When missionaries were first allowed to preach in China's interior regions in the 1860s, Chinese women joined the church at a slow rate. However, the latter half of the nineteenth century saw "the proliferation of women's mission societies," involving both Western women and Chinese women.[31] By 1921, the total population of indigenous female Christians in China increased to 128,704, about 37 percent of the Christian population.[32] During this era, social realities such as foot-binding, concubinage, and female illiteracy in China were the first roadblocks that Chinese women pioneers needed to push through, both for themselves and for all of society. Historian Paul A. Cohen states that the missionary enterprise brought about the emancipation of Chinese women in these areas.[33] Take foot-binding, for instance. Some Chinese evangelists and pastors had already written against the practice as early as the 1870s. Most of the adult women who first unbound their feet were either preachers' wives, Bible women, or teachers at girls' schools.[34] Adele Fielde challenged foot-binding:

> The evils that accrue from this custom are very great. It makes cripples of nearly half the population, and adds immensely to the misery of the poverty-stricken multitudes. It disables women from supporting themselves and from caring for their children, and is one of the causes of the great prevalence of infanticide. . . . It incapacitates women for traveling, and keeps her and her thoughts in the narrowest of spheres.[35]

In 1895, a more organized anti-foot-binding movement was launched when British activist Alicia Little founded the Natural Foot Society in Shanghai. Soon afterward, branch societies were organized in many cities.[36] More Christian schools made unbinding a definite requirement for admission. One woman said, "I feel as if I had added two pounds to my Christian weight since I unbound my feet."[37] Around 1900, however, the anti-foot-binding effort was temporarily halted when the Boxers singled out Christians for persecution. As Kwok writes, "The large feet of Christian girls made it more difficult for them to hide. Most of them had to rebind for a time to avoid the hunt."[38] In 1902, in response to mounting social pressure both from the Chinese literati and the foreign community, the Empress Dowager issued an edict banning foot-binding.[39]

The next area of dramatic change was girls' education, both in content and methodology. Since the 1890s, more and more families among the Chinese gentry began to embrace Western-style education for their daughters. Shi Meiyu's parents requested help from an American woman missionary, Gertrude Howe. Mrs. Shi became an administrator for Howe's mission day school and developed a close friendship with Howe. Mr. Shi was clear about wanting a Western type of education that would eventually train Shi Meiyu to become a medical doctor. Back then, it was an unusual idea even to American missionaries. As Shi Meiyu herself recalled, Howe was initially "startled" by the unusual request of this Chinese father.[40] Gertrude Howe knew very well that the time for girls' education had not come. She foresaw the resistance even from within the missionary community. Later, against the overwhelming objection from her missionary community, Howe decided to tutor Shi Meiyu, together with Kang Cheng (Howe's adopted daughter), in English and Western science.[41] Within a few years, Shi Meiyu became a young medical translator and assistant for American doctors.[42] Both Shi's parents and the few American women missionaries invested much in her, hoping that she could represent "a new Chinese Christian womanhood"[43] for the future. This was an epoch-making move, because within a decade, private tutoring and small-scale girls' schools would blossom into a major education sector, which then expanded to a powerful network of Christian colleges.

As historian Gail Hershatter comments, it was a general trend that "missionaries began to hold classes for girls and women six decades before the Qing dynasty started to experiment with girls' schools."[44] Initially, before both private and public girls' schools became the norm, the curriculum still centered on women's role in the household.[45] Missionaries hoped that if they gained the wives and mothers of this generation, then they would have secured the next. In some places, evangelism was prioritized over women's rights. For example, if parents withdrew their preadolescent daughters from a missionary girls' school in order to proceed with arranged marriages, missionaries did not object if the groom was a Christian.[46] Within a decade, girls' education became an added value to their future career or marriage prospects. Historian Ryan Dunch writes that in 1913, Christian brides in Fuzhou publicly displayed their diplomas as the dowry procession into their new marriage homes.[47] Some women missionaries, however, did challenge the perpetuation of gender roles through girls' education. One case did occur in 1902, when American Presbyterian missionary Helen Nevius adapted the Confucian classic *Four Books for Women* by first deleting certain "pagan" practices such as chastity suicide and ancestor worship, and paternalistic rituals that demanded women to obey first her father, then her husband, and lastly even her son.[48] Against the wider trend, the education Shi Meiyu received was also tailored toward more independence and careerism outside of marriage. The singlehood of Western missionaries such as Bushnell and Howe also inspired an entire generation of Chinese women. Some young women who graduated from mission schools were able to break free from marriage norms; they found work as aides to missionaries and remained single.

Amid the frail Qing dynasty that Katharine Bushnell and Gertrude Howe entered around the turn of a new century, a critical reformist spirit was gaining momentum among the Chinese people. The indigenous souls were about to enter into a stormy history of change and even revolutions. The issue of equality for women was often central to reformists' proposals, yet it was tokenized as history would later prove. For example, Liang Qichao (1873–1929), China's own premier reformer of that time, charged that female illiteracy caused women to be dependent on men and affected the quality of motherhood, thereby weakening the Chinese people.[49] But Liang's advocacy had flaws. He failed to acknowledge the fact that even ancient China had produced elite women who were educated and productive as artists and poets. He even criticized these educated women in ancient history for wasting their talents on trivial things such as depicting scenery. Liang also erased women's past contribution to household economy and blamed women's lack of independence as a reason they remained subordinate to men. Liang's teacher Kang Youwei was even more utopian on the issue of women while recognizing their participation in farm labor and their literary talent. As Kang wrote, "Women are not different from men; . . . Nowadays the women of Europe and America are generally free in studying, talking, entertaining, traveling about, and sightseeing, choosing their husbands or getting divorces. . . . As for all the nations of Asia and Africa, they all bind and restrict their women."[50] Both Liang and Kang were active coordinators of the late Qing reform in 1888. Their writings on the women's issue was part of their political agenda. Although more and more reform-minded rich and the literati classes in China began to advocate for more female education, many shared the nationalistic rhetoric and overgeneralization of Liang Qichao. As historian Gail Hershatter comments, "Liang had put into circulation a powerful, if incomplete, notion of how gender arrangements worked in China . . . ensured that the figure of Woman emerged into public conversion as deficient, in need of uplift, and potentially a danger to the survival of China—not as laborer whose contributions were essential to families, communities, and the nation."[51]

Both historians Jessie Lutz and Dana Robert confirm that in late Qing it was the Chinese (some who were pastors) who initially pushed for education for girls.[52] Many started with their own daughters. The entry of Western women missionaries who founded mission schools helped further such aspirations. In the 1890s, most schools for girls in China had been missionary institutions. A decade later, the imperial Chinese government began to open schools for girls.[53] Although only a few Chinese women enjoyed the privilege of formal higher education overseas, they left indelible marks in history.

During this time, Chinese reformers were open and tolerant toward areas Western missionaries critiqued about Chinese traditions enslaving women and men. But a historical reversal awaits them when within two decades, for continued missionary domination in the education sector would lead to a stronger hostility against Christian education among both Chinese intellectuals and the uneducated masses.

In 1892, both Shi Meiyu and Kang Cheng traveled to American and entered the medical school of the University of Michigan. Two years later, Shi Meiyu wrote to her mother, asking that Mrs. Shi also unbind her feet. As historian Connie Shemo writes, "In asking her mother to unbind her feet, Shi was erasing from her family the last vestiges of a custom that marked China as barbaric in the eyes of most Westerners."[54] While in America, however, the young Shi Meiyu took great pride in her Chinese lineage. In 1896, at her graduation ceremony at the University of Michigan, Shi and Kang presented themselves wearing traditional Chinese attire.[55] Both of them also spoke and showed determination to practice medicine in China.[56] This event not only won them wide admiration in America, but also the approval of Chinese reformers back home, including Liang Qichao, who later praised Kang and Shi for showing a sense of national pride and dignity.[57] Shi's academic excellence from an American medical school and her dedicated wish to serve the health of Chinese women together stirred up hopes for reform-minded intellectuals in late imperial China.

In 1896, Shi Meiyu and Kang Cheng returned to Jiujiang, where they cofounded the Women and Children's Hospital. In a one-room facility, they treated more than 2,000 outpatients during the first 10 months. They insisted on gathering an all-Chinese team, despite skepticism from the American missionary community, who generally believed that only Westerners were able to run a modern health care system.[58] Shi Meiyu and Kang Cheng had been acutely aware of this prejudice while going through medical school in America. It made them more determined to prove that Chinese women could also excel in medical work, if given the opportunity.[59] Later, at her own practice, Shi Meiyu even refused to hire foreign nurses. In her mind, only an all-Chinese-run hospital can "show the people of other nations that the only reason why Chinese women have for centuries lived such narrow lives is that they have not had opportunity to develop native powers."[60] Biographer and historian Connie Shemo confirms in her writing that racism by American missionaries has unfortunately tarnished their mission integrity toward indigenous coworkers. In the case of Shi Meiyu, for example, residential intermingling between American missionaries and Chinese staff were discouraged.[61] Persisting racial hierarchy also became manifest in the area of unequal compensation for work.[62] The rationale behind these practices was to protect missionaries' privilege. As Kwok Pui-lan explains, "To protect their identity and to minimize the danger of native women's usurping their superior position, it was advantageous not to stress commonality of gender, but to exaggerate racial and class distinctions."[63] So despite many letters and reports Shi wrote to the Women's Foreign Mission Society about financial needs, staff's salaries and conditions in the hospital facility did not improve for a long time.[64]

Indigenous hopes for these young Chinese women doctors, nevertheless, presented a great contrast with prejudice from the missionary community. A peasant patient once told the two women doctors that "We were afraid of the foreigners, but you can understand us."[65] Local communities celebrated their service and granted Shi the elite status of a "great scholar."[66] The Jiujiang government also showed great respect for Shi Meiyu by prohibiting traffic on the street near her home when she was sick and resting.[67] Even peddlers nearby lowered their voices to show respect. Indeed, conservative reformers such as Zhang Zhidong praised Shi Meiyu for her service.[68]

In a few years, when the newly built Elizabeth Skelton Danforth Hospital in Jiujiang was opening, it got disrupted by the Boxer Rebellion (1899–1901).[69] The rebels targeted Christian ministries and missionaries with violence.[70] Rev. Shi, the father of Shi Meiyu, was brutally killed by a mob.[71] Shi Meiyu and her coworkers fled to Japan. After the unrest ended, with the support of American medical doctor Isaac Newton Danforth, a new hospital was built with 15 rooms, allowing Shi Meiyu and her nurses to treat 5,000 outpatients each month.[72] Shi also began translating textbooks and training manuals. When the concept of surgery was unknown in China, Shi trained her nurses on surgical operations and gave them a great degree of autonomy.[73] Within China, the school also frequently received visits from "officials and their retinue."[74] To the public, Shi always shared credits by praising the Chinese nurses as "beautiful, devoted" and "self-denying."[75] Shi also raised their visibility to American audiences: "Like the white Easter lily growing out of the black dirt of marshy soil, . . . so these women taken from the dark heathen surroundings when given the Gospel message of love have blossomed out into a service of love and holiness unto the Lord."[76] By praising her Chinese staff, Shi Meiyu wanted "her mission hospital to both help Chinese women overcome their own self-doubts, and to dispel the image held by many foreigners of the helplessness of Chinese women."[77]

On a different front, Shi Meiyu's mentor Katherine Bushnell also began to face the dark realities spawned by the American missionary enterprise. Her personal trajectory soon took a dramatic turn which differentiated her from most other women missionaries, who conformed to Western missionary expansionism. Later while serving in Singapore and Hong Kong, Bushnell investigated an appalling system of public prostitution. She concluded that it was entirely "the product of Western civilization," since such systemic abuse of women were "utterly unknown in China except in the treaty ports."[78] She even attributed it to "the culpability of *Christian* men" who profited from maintaining these public prostitution systems.[79] In her report written with another American woman missionary Elizabeth Andrew, Bushnell pointed out that "it was the influence of Western Christian 'civilization' that exploited Chinese practices and fashioned the system of sexual slavery that had taken hold wherever the two cultures intermingled."[80] Furthermore, she found it hard not to blame a gender-biased Chinese translation of the Bible for bringing such crimes to fruition. Bushnell's daring challenge turned a new page of ministry for her as she "accused biblical translators and interpreters of collaborating in man's rebellion by portraying women's subordination as the will of God."[81] Her encounter with China triggered a difficult but revolutionary journey toward reestablishing "women's God-given authority."[82] For Katharine Bushnell and a few others like her, witnessing the appalling distortion of the missionary expansion project whereby indigenous women were mistreated "at the hands of Christian men" awakened her to a dark reality about imperialism and domination in the name of Christian global mission.

In 1906, American missionary Jennie Hughes came to Jiujiang and joined Shi Meiyu's ministry. The two women would enjoy each other's company as ministry partners for a few decades.[83] From the beginning, Hughes departed from the more comfortable missionary compound and moved into Shi's little native house.[84] This was an unusual move because at the time "missionaries had segregated themselves socially from their Chinese equivalents, and that this was a structural result of mission socialization."[85] Historian and biographer Connie Shemo suggests an intimate relationship began to form between Shi and Hughes.[86] She writes that "physical affection between women in general seems to have been acceptable in missionary society, and women missionaries who lived and worked as a family unit were a normal feature."[87] This relationship between Shi and Hughes did not involve racial domination. For Shi Meiyu, the cherished relationship with Hughes was "a microcosm of her hopes for Chinese Christians and American missionaries mutually cooperating without hierarchy."[88] Later Shi Meiyu also wrote in praise of Jennie Hughes that "her close contact with the Chinese, living in heartfelt sympathy with them, has made her a refuge where these weary souls have poured their hearts out, knowing that they would find in her a friend in need."[89]

Nevertheless, the tensions between Shi Meiyu and her American mission board continued to the late 1910s. Shi Meiyu applied for a Rockefeller Foundation scholarship and studied at Johns Hopkins University from 1918 to 1919. While in America, she also spoke regularly to raise funds for the hospital. With excellent public speaking skills, Shi had fundraising capacities not possessed by most American missionary women.[90] Numerous American missionary publications wrote about Shi and her ministry in China.[91] But according to Connie Shemo, in the 1910s, structural obstacles to incorporating Chinese women in leadership roles actually increased.[92] While fundraising in America, she felt the tension and dilemma between two opposing narratives: "Stressing that her work was controlled by Chinese women, even while largely funded by American contributions, allowed her to expand American images of Chinese women. Yet to raise funds in the United States, she also drew heavily on images of sick and vulnerable Chinese women."[93] Instead of leaning on the stereotypical image of Chinese women as victims of these powers, Shi advocated for their roles as "active healers."[94] By insisting on all-Chinese medical work, Shi intentionally challenged missionary dominance by "white" women.[95]

In 1919, the May Fourth Movement in China further fueled anti-foreign sentiments. Since then, "the issue of who was in charge of Christianity was an explosive one, tied in directly with the emotionally charged causes of national unity and anti-imperialism."[96] Meanwhile, with the founding of the Nurses Association of China and the rising trend of scientific medicine into the 1920s, Shi's nursing school was facing a demand to upgrade its education standards. With the help of Jennie Hughes, Shi enrolled some graduate nurses in Knowles Bible school, which offered science courses.[97] However, some battles with entrenched ideologies in the mission field continued for Shi Meiyu. It was a time when Chinese Christians and American missionaries alike confronted the "largely unacknowledged ideologies of racial hierarchy that underlay so much of missionary policy."[98] In 1920, the rift between Shi and Women's Foreign Mission Society took place amid the larger controversy of the fundamentalist-modernist controversy in America that impacted China mission.[99] Historian Dana Robert also reckons that many ministries led by missionary women became "the casualties of doctrinal struggles" during this controversy.[100]

Shi Meiyu's evangelistic fervor had already shown in her earlier medical work. She was known to have prayed for every patient first before performing an operation. Even a few years prior to the founding of Bethel, in1918, Shi Meiyu once publicly lamented at the conference that less than 2 percent of patients in her hospital had accepted Christ.[101] In her late forties, Shi Meiyu felt increasingly strong about indigenous evangelism. Before Shi left to study at John Hopkins University, she had cofounded China Inland Evangelistic Society with six other prominent Chinese church leaders. Through this platform, Shi Meiyu traveled across China to lead evangelistic meetings. A Chinese pastor recalled that Shi publicly announced that she would soon quit her medical career and focus on evangelism. In a letter Shi wrote to a friend, she revealed this conviction: "As disease came through sin, ignorance, poverty and superstition, so the Gospel message of Health, Liberty, and the Abounding Life through Jesus Christ must be preached. . . . Then indeed our

bodies are made holy, fit temples for His continued dwelling."[102] In 1920, Shi
and Hughes began Bethel ministry in Shanghai in order to promote Chinese
leadership in the church and interdenominational work.[103] Shi Meiyu's disillusionment with a joint effort in Western medical missionary work represented a broader climate. As historian Robert Bickers writes, although by
1921, Protestant mission societies had founded over 250 hospitals and 9
medical colleges in China, and these medical work was never well funded,
"'hospital' was in many ways an aspirational description for many of the
institutions concerned."[104]

Despite its progressive programs such as orphanages and schools, Bethel's
evangelistic work mainly included famous Chinese preachers of the day,
such as Ji Zhiwen (Andrew Gih).[105] Their fundamentalist theology consisted
of a simple message of sin and salvation.[106] She often referred to the "three-
fold cord of the Gospel" as consisting of "medical work side by side with
the evangelistic and the educational."[107] Unlike her role model Katherine
Bushnell who later turned toward seeking a more open "feminist corrective"
to traditional Christianity,[108] Shi Meiyu's theology became more confined
by doctrines. Indigenous evangelist John Sung (Song Shangjie), who was to
become arguably Southeast Asia's most influential Chinese revivalist in the
1930s, once wrote in his diary that a Western friend had told him not to join
the Bethel church in Shanghai. This comment triggered Sung's interest in
visiting anyway, and he was invited to preach once. That was the beginning
of John Sung's participation in Bethel ministry. From 1919 to 1927, Sung
studied in the United States and obtained a PhD from Ohio State University.
After a brief time of study in Union Theological Seminary, he experienced
mental health problems and even spent months in a sanatorium. After returning to China, John Sung became an independent evangelist and rejoined the
Bethel team in 1931.[109] But Sung's abrasive preaching style and theological
extremism led to his leaving in 1934.

During this time, Shi Meiyu continued to engage with social reforms.
In 1923, Shi became the leader of the Woman's Christian Temperance
Movement, opposing the use of opium, alcohol and cigarette smoking as major
ills affecting the health of the nation.[110] Meanwhile, she always wanted these
programs to be conducive to Christian evangelism. By 1924, representatives
of Bethel ministry traveled to more than 130 cities in China, reaching over
5,000 people with their messages. Their zeal was also motivated by a strong
sense of nationalism for a New China.[111] But among liberal-minded reformers
in China, Shi Meiyu's later dedication to Christian fundamentalism undermined the public recognition of her later work.[112] In 1927, in response to the
Anti-Christian Movement, the Republican government implemented policies
to secularize curriculum at Christian schools and colleges. Shi Meiyu objected
and insisted on allowing students of the nursing school take mandatory Bible

classes.[113] Her action later earned approval from Madame Chiang Kai-shek, who issued a formal document of appraisal.[114] In 1937, when the Japanese invaded Shanghai, Shi was forced to flee. Bethel ministry later relocated to Hong Kong, limiting its work to caring for war orphans. At the age of sixty-four, Shi Meiyu went to California and stayed with her lifelong companion Jennifer Hughes near the Hughes's family. There she passed away in 1954.

Women pioneers like Shi Meiyu witnessed drastic social change as China passed from a declining empire to a fragile republic, from foreign invasion to civil war. They were among the first Chinese women to study abroad. Ideals and images of modern womanhood were envisioned by indigenous reformers and rekindled by women missionaries as well as Chinese women's own exposure to modernity through overseas experiences. Meanwhile, despite being beneficiaries of Western women missionaries, these Chinese women leaders were not blind to the racial domination from the same group of white women. They were acutely aware that even the concept of "global sisterhood" helped sanctify imperialism and missionary domination.[115] For example, as an iconic figure, Shi Meiyu has been quoted in missionary literature as being a living testament to the effectiveness of Christian missions.[116] But even Shi had to advocate for her supervisory roles to no avail. How to live with the power structures that were endemic to the Western missionary enterprise had been a lifelong struggle for Shi Meiyu.

Behind white missionary women's own complicity were dynamics of gender, and socioeconomic status intersecting with racism. Even women missionaries did not escape the paternalistic tendency to infantize indigenous converts. As feminist theologian Margaret D. Kamitsuka writes, "The danger that whatever white theology turns its attention to will be absorbed into its institutionally dominant discourse, domesticated and neutralized."[117] Embedded in a history of colonial missionary racism, such practices caused distortion of feminist efforts to advance the dignity of indigenous women. In this sense, Shi Meiyu pioneered in institutionally challenging not just sexism, but also racism through the expression of Western missionary domination.[118] To mitigate the abuse of missionary power, Shi and other Chinese women pioneers unabashedly advocated and established all-Chinese institutions. Their medical and educational institutions paved the way for greater representation of Chinese women in these professions. Shi Meiyu's struggle for shared authority and partnership envisions a cross-cultural relationship with continuing commitment and common struggle to create more egalitarian faith communities. To her, partnership was not a substitute for liberation from oppression. It concerned how Christian believers relate to each other in a way that overcame roles of domination. Fortunately, in her relationship with Jennifer Hughes, Shi Meiyu experienced genuine sisterhood in Christ and discipleship of equals.

NOTES

1. Katharine C. Bushnell, *Dr. Katharine C. Bushnell: A Brief Sketch of Her Life Work* (Hertford: Rose & Sons, 1932).

2. Pro Mundi Vita, "China and the Churches in the Making of One World," in Lutheran World Federation, Pro Mundi Vita, ed., *Christianity and the New China* (South Pasadena: William Carey Library, 1976), 7.

3. Ibid., 29.

4. Sun Shuyun, *The Long March: The True History of Communist China's Founding Myth* (New York: Anchor Books, 2006), 159.

5. Hershatter, *Women and China's Revolutions*, 49.

6. Stuart C. Miller, "Ends and Means: Missionary Justification of Force in Nineteenth Century China," in John King Fairbank, ed., *The Missionary Enterprise in China and America* (Cambridge: Harvard University Press, 1974), 254.

7. Vita, "China and the Churches," 12.

8. Kristin Du Mez, *A New Gospel for Women: Katharine Bushnell and the Challenge of Christian Feminism* (New York: Oxford University Press, 2015), 27.

9. Connie Anne Shemo, *The Chinese Medical Ministries of Kang Cheng and Shi Meiyu, 1872-1937* (Bethlehem: Lehigh Univerisity Press, 2011), 22.

10. Jane Hunter, *The Gospel of Gentility: American Women Missionaries in Turn-of-the-Century China* (New Haven: Yale University Press, 1984), 1.

11. Annie Ryder Gracey, *Medical Work of the Woman's Foreign Missionary Society*, Methodist Episcopal Church (Dansville: A. O. Bunnell, 1881), 176.

12. Bays, *A New History*, 69.

13. Irwin T. Hyatt, *Our Ordered Lives Confess: Three Nineteenth-Century American Missionaries in East Shantung* (Cambridge: Harvard University Press, 1976), 84. John R. Stanley, "Establishing a Female Medical Elite: The Early History of the Nursing Profession in China," in Jessie Gregory Lutz, ed., *Pioneer Chinese Christian Women: Gender, Christianity, and Social Mobility* (Bethlehem: Lehigh University Press, 2010), 275.

14. Dana L. Robert, "The 'Christian Home' as a Cornerstone of Anglo-American Missionary Thought and Practice," in Dana L. Robert, ed., *Converting Colonialism: Visions and Realities in Mission History, 1706–1914* (Grand Rapids: Eerdmans, 2008), 134–65.

15. Dana L. Robert, *American Women in Mission: A Social History of Their Thought and Practices* (Macon: Mercer University Press, 1996), 162.

16. Ibid., 175.

17. Antoinette Burton, *Burdens of History: British Feminists, Indian Women, and Imperial Culture, 1865–1915* (Chapel Hill: University of North Carolina Press, 1994), 17.

18. A. P. Happer, "Woman's Work for Woman," in Records of the General Conference of the Protestant Missionaries of China Held at Shanghai, May 10–24, 1877, 147. Quoted in Jinhua Jia, Xiaofei Kang and Ping Yao, *Gendering Chinese Religion: Subject, Identity and Body* (New York: State University of New York Press, 2014), 177.

19. Ryan Dunch, "Christianizing Confucian Didacticism: Protestant Publications for Women, 1832–1911," *Nan Nu* 11 (1) (June 2009): 65–101, 78.

20. Hunter, *Gospel of Gentility*, Preface, xiii.

21. Hyatt, *Our Ordered Lives Confess*, 68.

22. Timothy Richard, "Western Women are Beneficial to China," trans., Cai Erkang, WGGB n.s. 8/129 (October 1899), 1–2. Quoted in Kwok, *Chinese Women and Christianity*, 106.

23. Adele M. Fielde (Adele Marion), *Pagoda Shadows: Studies from Life in China* (London: T. Ogilvie Smith, 1887), 1.

24. Ibid.

25. Mez, *A New Gospel for Women*, 31.

26. Ibid. Shemo, *The Chinese Medical Ministries*, 5, 23; Robert, *American Women in Mission*, 162.

27. Quoted in Shemo, *The Chinese Medical Ministries*, 34.

28. "Shi Meiyu (1873–1954): Christians Who Changed the World," BREAKPOINT
http://www.breakpoint.org/2013/04/shi-meiyu-1873-1954/

29. A recollection by Shi Meiyu's lifelong friend Kang Cheng (Ida Kahn), quoted in Emily T. Sheets, "Doctor Mary Stone," Women's Foreign Missionary Society, Methodist Episcopal Church Publication Office, Boston, Mass. 1918. Digical archive: https://archive.org/stream/ldpd_10998228_000/ldpd_10998228_000_djvu.txt

30. Margaret E. Burton, *Notable Women of Modern China* (New York: Cosimo Classics, 2005), 154. Quoted in Shemo, *The Chinese Medical Ministries*, 47.

31. Kwok, *Chinese Women and Christianity*, 87.

32. Luella Miner, "The Place of Woman in the Protestant Missionary Movement in China," *Year Book* 9 (1918): 341.

33. Paul A. Cohen, "Christian Missions and Their Impact to 1900," in John King Fairbank, ed., *The Cambridge History of China, vol. 10, Late Ch'ing 1800–1911* (Cambridge: Cambridge University Press, 1978), 582–83.

34. Kwok, *Chinese Women and Christianity*, 112.

35. Fielde, *Pagoda Shadows*, 31.

36. Alicia Little, *In the Land of the Blue Gown* (London: T. Fisher Unwin, 1902), 305–70.

37. Quoted in E. G. Wycloff, "Reform in Footbinding," *Life and Light* 34 (1904): 576.

38. Kwok, *Chinese Women and Christianity*, 114.

39. Ibid., 115.

40. Mary Stone, "Miss Gertrude Howe," quoted in Shemo, *The Chinese Medical Ministries*, 29. Even girls born into gentry class families hardly received education at that time. See Dorothy Ko, *Teachers of the Inner Chambers: Women and Culture in Seventeenth Century China* (Stanford: Stanford University Press, 1994). Susan Mann, *Precious Records: Women in China's Long Eighteenth Century* (Stanford: Stanford University Press, 1997). Education ministry to Chinese young girls were a groundbreaking and even scandalizing attempt at the time within the Western missionary community. Most believed that Chinese girls should be taught only skills of everyday chores as wives and mothers.

41. Single American female missionaries' ministry methods often incurred criticisms and opposition from within the male-dominated missionary community. Later, Gertrude Howe and missionary wives disagreed about who should be in control of the mission schools. see Robert, *American Women in Mission*, 185–87.

42. "The Middle Kingdom's Miracle Maidens, Dr. Mary Stone and Dr. Ida Kahn," ChinaMissions, http://www.chinamissions.com/stonekahn.html

43. Connie Shemo, "Able to Do Things of Which They Have Never Dreamed: Shi Meiyu's Vision of Nursing in Early Twentieth Century China," *DYNAMIS, Acta Hispanica ad Medicinae Scientiarumque Historiam Illustrandam* 19 (1999): 329–51.

44. Ibid., 46.

45. Hyatt, *Our Ordered Lives Confess*, 82–83.

46. Lutz, *Pioneer Chinese Christian Women*, 401–2. Carol C. Chin, "Beneficent Imperialists: American Women Missionaries in China at the Turn of the Twentieth Century," *Diplomatic History* 27 (3) (June 2003): 327–52, 336.

47. Ryan Dunch, "'Mothers to Our Country': Conversion, Education, and Ideology among Chinese Protestant Women, 1870–1930," in Jessie Gregory Lutz, ed., *Pioneer Chinese Christian Women: Gender, Christianity, and Social Mobility* (Bethlehem: Lehigh University Press, 2010), 333.

48. Quoted in Dunch, "Christianizing Confucian Didacticism."

49. Liang Qichao, "On Establishing Girls' Schools" and "Concise Rules for Founding an Anti-Footbinding Society," in Liang Qichao, *Collected Works of Liang Qichao* (Shanghai: Zhonghua Shuju, 1936), vol. 2, 19–20, 20–30.

50. Kang Youwei, *Book of the Great Community* (Da Tong Shu), (London: Allen & Unwin, 1958) 193. Adapted and cited by Jonathan Spence, *The Gate of Heavenly Peace* (New York: Penguin Books, 1981), 72.

51. Hershatter, *Women and China's Revolutions*, 64.

52. Lutz, *Pioneer Chinese Christian Women*, 22. Robert, *American Women in Mission*, 173–89.

53. Shemo, *The Chinese Medical Ministries*, 76.

54. Ibid., 47. Mrs. Shi not only agreed but gave a public testimonial about it at the 1894 Central China Conference, an annual meeting for all missionaries serving in the area, but Rev. Shi also spoke in support of her decision. See Burton, *Notable Women*, 154. Quoted in Shemo, *The Chinese Medical Ministries*, 47. Also see Robert, *American Women in Mission*, 176.

55. They were known as Mary Stone and Ida Kahn among their fellow American students.

56. Amy Whitesall, "The New Women of China," *Global Michigan*, January 7, 2011. https://global.umich.edu/newsroom/the-new-women-of-china/

57. Liang, "Chi Chiang-his K'ang nu-shi," 119–20. Or Liang Qichao, "An Essay on Miss Kang of Jiangxi" (in Chinese), *Yinping Shih ho-chi*, I: I 119–20 (Shanghai: Chung-hau shu-chu, 1932). Quoted in Shemo, *The Chinese Medical Ministries*, 11. This essay of Liang Qichao became a basic document for the later biography of Shi by Chinese writers. In China, many Chinese nationalist reformers attributed the declining power of the Chinese nation to acute problems, such as women's lack of education, practices such as foot-binding, and the government's neglect of public health.

See Ono Kazuko, *Chinese Women in a Century of Revolution* (Stanford: Stanford University Press, 1996). Ruth Rogaski, *Hygienic Modernity: Meanings of Health and Disease in Treaty Port China* (Berkeley: University of California Press, 2004).

58. There was also a common narrative which these American women missionaries used when raising funds—Western female missionary doctors were needed to reach out to Chinese women, who were victims of heathen medical practices. See Hunter, *Gospel of Gentility*, 15.

59. Even the advice from Gertrude Howe that they should begin working in a foreign mission hospital did not change their minds. Shi Meiyu also contended with the missionary community's hesitation to place her in supervisory roles.

60. Burton, *Notable Women*, 212–13.

61. Exclusionary residential arrangements not only segregated but alienated indigenous leaders from their mentors, who tended to dwell in nicer compounds. Shemo, *The Chinese Medical Ministries*, 2. As Shi Meiyu recalled, "After we returned to China Miss (Gertrude) Howe left the beautiful home of the missionaries and came to live in a little Chinese home that she built for us out of her own money." Later, people who admired Shi Meiyu and visited her also found that her living condition too humble to match up with her rising fame. See Stone, "Miss Gertrude Howe," 6. Quoted in Shemo, *The Chinese Medical Ministries*, 48.

62. For many years, Shi Meiyu had to pay back the loans from a mission board. Afterward, she received a salary of $450 gold a year, compared to $600–$650 gold a year among American missionaries. See Shemo, *The Chinese Medical Ministries*, 48. The unequal pay experienced by Chinese coworkers of a foreign missionary enterprise has continued until today. For example, in the early 2000s, I observed how Campus Crusade for Christ, an American organization, recruited Chinese local workers in Shanghai. Not only did these college-educated evangelists receive half of that of their American supervisors dispatched by the organization, but these Chinese locals need to constantly fundraise in order to cover their living expenses.

63. Kwok, Pui-lan, *Post-colonial Imagination and Feminist Theology* (Louisville, KY: Westminster John Knox Press, 2005), 18.

64. In one particularly assertive fundraising letter, Shi described how the crammed hospital had been compromised in the quality of its hygiene. In it, she urged that "we are looking forward all the time for signs or signals from the women of America to build our new hospital, but not a letter comes to bring us this kind of message." Burton, *Notable Women*, 171.

65. Gertrude Howe, "Danforth Memorial Hospital," *WWFE* 23(2) (June 1902): 59. Quoted in Kwok, *Chinese Women and Christianity*, 118.

66. Burton, *Notable Women*, 170.

67. Ibid.

68. He even proposed to Gertrude Howe that Shi and Kang set up a medical department in his school. The offer was turned down because Shi wanted to stay in Jiujiang. See Burton, *Notable Women*, 130–31.

69. The uprising happened between 1899 and 1901 when villagers in northern China resisted against Christian missionaries who ignoredabused their extraterritorial

rights. Boxer righters who practiced a set of martial arts believed that they were invulnerable to foreign weapons.

70. Months of violence and murder ensued in Shandong and regions in the North China Plain, leading to the massacre of a few hundred foreign missionaries and thousands of Chinese believers. See Nat Brandt, *Massacre in Shansi* (Syracuse: Syracuse University, 1994), xiii.

71. Li Yading, "Shi Meiyu (Mary Stone)," Biographical Dictionary of Chinese Christianity, online resource. http://bdcconline.net/zh-hans/stories/shi-meiyu

72. It also became a nursing school where many Chinese women received training from Shi. She trained nurses both in basic medical knowledge and Bible lessons. Her wish was to "train . . . evangelistic workers and teachers for the great needy field that is white unto harvest." See Shi Meiyu, "Introduction to Jennie Hughes," Shi Meiyu, *Chinese Heart-Throbs* (New York: Fleming Revell, 1920), 9.

73. Apart from obstetrics, Shi herself also treated tumors and cleft lip by surgeries. Because Shi was the only physician in the hospital, she relied on the nurses and trained them with a set of more sophisticated skills than were available to most nurses in the United States at the time.

74. Women's Foreign Mission Society minutes, 1903–1904, 176–77. Quoted in Shemo, *The Chinese Medical Ministries*, 76.

75. Ibid., 86.

76. Meiyu, "Introduction in Jennie Hughes," 10–11.

77. Shemo, "Able to Do Things of Which They Have Never Dreamed," 329–51.

78. Elizabeth Andrew and Katharine Bushnell, *Heathen Slaves and Christian Rulers* (1907; Project Gutenberg, 2004). Quoted in Mez, *A New Gospel for Women*, 79.

79. Ibid., 79.

80. Ibid., 83.

81. Ibid., 2. Bushnell, *Dr. Katharine C. Bushnell*, 20.

82. Ibid.

83. Historian Jane Hunter refers to the relationship of these two women as "the most notable special friendship on the mission field." In her personal life, Shi turned down many marriage proposals from Western-educated Chinese men, because she was so dedicated to her medical work.

84. Sheets, "Doctor Mary Stone."

85. Robert Bickers, *Britain in China: Community, Culture and Colonialism, 1900–1949* (Manchester: Manchester University Press, 2017), 94.

86. It was said that visitors to Shi Meiyu's humble home observed that Shi and Hughes had been sharing the same bed.

87. Shemo, *The Chinese Medical Ministries*, 75.

88. Ibid., 76.

89. Meiyu, "Introduction in Jennie Hughes," 11.

90. Hunter, *Gospel of Gentility*, 196–204. It was noted that "notwithstanding her prominence, she is simple and unassuming" when speaking in public. See T. Sheets, "Doctor Mary Stone."

91. Missionary biographical files in the United Methodist Archives. Patricia Hill, *The World Their Household: The American Women's Foreign Mission Movement*

and Cultural Transformation, 1870–1920 (Ann Arbor: University of Michigan, 1985), 3.

92. Shemo, *The Chinese Medical Ministries*, 143.

93. Ibid., 73.

94. Ibid., 6.

95. Ibid.

96. Daniel Bays, "Rise of an Indigenous Christianity," in Daniel Bays, ed., *Christianity in China: From the Eighteenth Century to the Present* (Stanford: Stanford University Press, 1999), 265–68.

97. This collaborative program benefited many Chinese women who later excelled in more advanced medical professions. She also promoted a few of them for Rockefeller Foundation scholarships to study overseas.

98. Shemo, *The Chinese Medical Ministries*, 8.

99. Ibid., 210. But on the local scene, it was mainly the mission board's dissatisfaction with Shi and Hughes's involvement with Knowles Bible school which triggered the severing of ties. Jennie Hughes had a dispute with the mission board, because Shi and Hughes demanded the Chinese take over the leadership of the Christian church in China. From Archives and Special Collections on Women in Medicine, The Medical College of Pennsylvania. But the Women's Foreign Mission Society continued its discriminatory policies against Chinese Christians. Quoted in Shemo, "Able to Do Things of Which They Have Never Dreamed," 329–51.

100. Dana L. Robert (ed.), *Gospel Bearers, Gender Barriers: Missionary Women in the Twentieth Century* (Marykoll: Orbis Books, 2002), 4.

101. Shemo, *The Chinese Medical Ministries*, 77, note 28.

102. Quoted in Shemo, *The Chinese Medical Ministries*, 214.

103. Ibid., 211.

104. Robert Bickers, *Out of China: How the Chinese Ended Western Domination* (Cambridge: Harvard Univeristy Press, 2017), 258. He quoted from Milton T. Stauffer (ed.), *The Christian Occupation of China: A General Survey of the Numerical Strength and Geographical Distribution of the Christian Forces in China, 1918–1921* (Shanghai: China Continuation Committee, 1922), 419, 425, 429; and Mary Brown Bullock, *An American Transplant: The Foundation and Peking Union Medical College* (Berkeley: University of California Press, 1980).

105. Ji Zhiwen founded the Evangelize China Fellowship (ECF) in 1947. After the communist victory, he moved to Hong Kong. In the 1950s, Ji began an evangelistic tour around Southeast Asia. One of the seminaries he founded in Indonesia later graduated famous evangelists such as Tang Chongrong (Stephen Tong) whose influenced spread in mainland China since the 1990s. See MacInnis, Donald E., "Gih, Andrew" in Anderson, Gerald H. ed., *Biographical Dictionary of Christian Missions* (Grand Rapids: Eerdmans Publishing, 1997), 241.

106. "In memory of Dr. Mary Stone," Newsletter of Bethel Mission of China, Inc., 1955

http://www.chinamissions.com/14-in-memory-of-mary-stone.html

107. Kiangsi Conference Minutes, 1917, p. 4, UMCA. Quoted in Shemo, "Able to Do Things of Which They Have Never Dreamed," 329–51.

108. Mez, *A New Gospel for Women*, 1.

109. Bays, *A New History*, 138.

110. Kwok, *Chinese Women and Christianity*, 121–22.

111. As historian and biographer Connie Shemo analyzes, "Shi and the leadership at Bethel combined a version of Christian fundamentalism with Chinese nationalism to promote a vision of a Christian church that welcomed friendship with and funds from foreign Christians, while rejecting foreign control. While Shi's hospital in Bethel specialized in obstetric work, she no longer embraced the ideology of 'woman's work for woman.' Rather, Bethel put forward a model of committed Christians, male and female, Chinese and foreign, united by a common conversion experience and a commitment to an 'old-fashioned Gospel'." See Shemo, *The Chinese Medical Ministries*, 201.

112. Ibid., 77.

113. The Anti-Christian Movement (1922–1927) targeted missionary control and demanded educational autonomy. One of the criticisms was Christianity's oppression of women. See Alice H. Gregg, *China and Educational Autonomy* (New York: Syracuse University Press, 1946), 101–42.

114. Connie Shemo, "Shi Meiyu's 'Army of Women' in Medicine," *Salt and Light: Lives of Faith that Shaped Modern China,* Carol Lee Hamrin, ed. with Stacey Bieler (Eugene: Wipf and Stock Publishers, Pickwick Publications, 2008).

115. Shemo, *The Chinese Medical Ministries*, 262.

116. Ibid., 202.

117. Margaret D. Kamitsuka, *Feminist Theology and the Challenge of Difference* (New York: Oxford University Press), 11.

118. Historians like Denis R. Janz comments that "the spirit of the crusade, the ideology of conquest, and the attitude of paternalism infused all their efforts." See Janz, *World Christianity and Marxism*, 126. Eric O. Hanson also reckons that "the missionaries . . . demonstrated the nineteenth-century Westerner's great capacity for racism, nationalism, power hungriness, and institutional pride." See Eric O. Hanson, *Catholic Politics in China and Korea* (Maryknoll: Orbis Books, 1980), 28.

Chapter 2

A Confucian Christian Feminist

During the Christmas of 1911, just months before the collapse of the Qing dynasty, an eighteen-year-old young woman Zeng Baosun (or Tseng Pao Swen) was baptized in an Anglican church in Hangzhou. Her conversion to Christianity marked a paradigm shift for China's privileged gentry class, the guardians of Confucianism. During the late Qing dynasty, the clan of Confucian scholar Zeng Guofan (or Marquis Tseng Kuo-fan) from Hunan Province enjoyed great prominence. The Zeng family was known as "a stronghold of Confucian values."[1] Zeng Guofan was also known as a statesman and military general who organized a provincial force to assist the Great Qing's suppression of the Taiping Rebellion.[2] But within two decades of his death, students of Chinese history would be surprised that a great number of descendants from this prestigious Confucian family would have converted to Protestant Christianity.[3] The first convert among them all was Zeng Baosun, the great granddaughter of Zeng Guofan. Her life raises important questions: To what extent can a Christian woman like Zeng Baosun, who continued to embrace Confucianism be viewed as a feminist? Isn't Confucian feminism an oxymoron?

As a system of ideas, Confucianism occupies a unique place in Chinese civilization. It has time and again been used and abused by those seeking to legitimize statecraft throughout history. The term "Confucianism" as we know it was actually an invention by Jesuit missionaries rather than a literal translation of the indigenous expression. Central to this term is the concept of *Ru*, which dates back to pre-Qin texts and means learnedness, meekness, and humility. Additionally, it includes the moral code of *Ren*, a virtue-based personhood. Traditionally, it begins with filial piety and deference, and then extends to selfless neighborly care for all. Applying these moral principles to both public service and domestic home making, Confucianism has practically influenced all aspects of social life in East Asian countries.

Initially trained as a Confucian scholar, Zeng Baosun's father worked for the government, until he later became interested in some translated Western literature through the ministry of Timothy Richard. He then studied chemistry and electrical science. By the late 1890s, the progressive-minded Mr. Zeng decided that his first daughter would grow up with natural feet, and he did not arrange an early marriage for her. The young girl grew up reading Confucian classics at home, taught by her grandmother, the Elderly Yifang. The Zeng family boasted a private library of thousands of books. Female figures like Zeng's grandmother modeled a benevolent womanhood in the Confucian tradition. Throughout her life, Zeng Baosun also lived by and defended these traditional values. As her biographer Thomas L. Kennedy puts it, "Zeng's ancestry and upbringing endowed her with a feeling of pride in Chinese culture and a sense of mission to preserve and advance it."[4] Zeng's father was well aware of the social crisis in Chinese society. The reality of foreign influence was compounded by the public memory that ever since China's lost a war with Japan in 1895, foreign powers have threatened to "chop up China like a melon." Yet, his liberal training taught him that China needed to open up and face the West sooner or later.

One needs to realize how unusual this stance was in a cultural climate when Confucianism was considered obsolete and targeted for a range of social problems by Chinese reformers. For example, scholars often blamed Confucianism for women's oppression. "Victimized, illiterate, rural Chinese women systematically oppressed by the patriarchal family, which was in part supported by the feudal ideology of Confucianism, became the symbol of what was wrong with Old China."[5] When orthodox Confucianism waned in the late Qing dynasty run by the Manchus, who were seen as usurpers of state power, Chinese intellectuals grew increasingly alienated from their traditional culture. It gave way to the emergence of a nationalist consciousness. Since 1902, three years before Qing's demolition of the imperial exam system, leaders like Liang Qichao had been advocating the need for a "new people." His understanding was that China's ideologies and morale were not only weak but also wrong. A leading Confucian-Mercian scholar, Liang reconstructed his master's ideals to envision a revolutionary Chinese Republic. Considering Western influence necessary to dismantle the rule of Qing, his view of post-Boxers' missionaries and their progressive projects was largely positive. As a result, the rift between Confucian conservatives and the cultural alliance between reformist Chinese and Western Christian presence expanded. As historian Joseph R. Levenson wrote, "If Confucian officials disparaged Western values in the non-material sphere, Christian educators returned the compliment. Not only science, they insisted, but western political and ethical values must come into China and displace their Chinese counterparts."[6]

Within this social context, Zeng Baosun was a living testimony to the enduring legitimacy of the Confucian tradition while embracing Western values. Although progressive-minded Chinese women during this time felt the pressure to take on the cultural dimension of their gender identity, Zeng Baosun did not yield to the predominant trend. Her convictions, nevertheless, benefited from a lifelong privilege as a member of the cultural ruling class. In 1909, at the age of sixteen, Zeng Baosun entered an Anglican high school in Hangzhou near the east coast of China. There she made more progress in English. Through a discipline incident at the school, Zeng developed a close connection with the principal Louise Barnes, whose prayers greatly moved her.[7] Another missionary-teacher Miss Stuart, who had been orphaned and experienced paralysis at the hand of the Boxers, also impressed Zeng with her forgiveness and zeal to serve the Chinese.[8] Zeng's increased interest in Christianity found further affirmation in several revival meetings by Chinese evangelists, who preached a message that Christianity would change China. During this time, she carefully read the *Gospel of Mark* and the book of *Job*.

One day, Zeng Baosun took a walk around the West Lake at Hangzhou and reflected on the meaning of life. She came to the realization that Christianity offered a power to change people. And if people could be changed, then China could too. In her own words, Zeng reflected: "The Christian spirit is so wonderful, it can make ordinary people extraordinary. . . . I felt that China needed the spirit of Christian 'practice,' and I decided to become a Christian."[9] Soon afterward, Zeng Baosun wrote a letter home, expressing her wish to convert to Christianity. Although her grandmother was displeased, Zeng's father did not object.[10] He even wrote a letter in reply, introducing the stories of Xu Guangqi, a Chinese politician-convert from the Ming dynasty, and the Jesuit missionary Matteo Ricci. He also encouraged Zeng Baosun to first read some secular books before making the decision. Zeng followed her father's advice and read through some translated works, including *Evolution and Ethics* by Thomas Henry Huxley, *The Study of Sociology* by Herbert Spencer, and *The Origin of Species* by Charles Darwin. Afterward, Zeng was still determined that Christianity was an ideal for herself and for China.

In 1912, accompanied by her teacher British missionary Louise Barnes, Zeng transferred to a high school in London. Later, while studying at the University of London, Zeng Baosun confided to her cousin Zeng Yuenong that she would not marry but dedicate herself to China and the world. "If I marry," Zeng said, "I would at most raise up ten children. But if I devote myself to education, I can raise up thousands of children."[11] Zeng Baosun's choice of singleness was due to a passion of nationalistic obligation. As Zeng's biographer Thomas L. Kennedy summarizes it, "Christianity and overseas study would never have been compatible with an arranged marriage."[12] Historian Jane Hunter affirms this global commonality among many other Christian women.[13] Unbound by domestic duties and equipped with professional skills, they also grew into a clearer gender consciousness. It was also during this time that Zeng Baosun affirmed the necessity of having Chinese-run educational institutions.[14] A few years later (1916), Zeng became the university's first Chinese graduate, earning a bachelor of science. Before returning to China, she spent another year of teacher's training at Oxford and Cambridge.

During and after World War I, the delicate relationship between Chinese nationalist reformers and Westerners took an unfortunate turn. Basically, the effort to establish the cultural equivalence of China with Western civilization ended in failure, making culture an ineffective unit of comparison. Among the general public, there was a growing acceptance of the existence and authority of a Chinese nation on par with the West. In this sense, Chinese nationalism emerged as a denial of culturalism. After all, Confucianism as an ideological system had exerted law and order when the ruling class needed it. Their sacred text itself has abundant examples of classism and sexism. For example, Confucius was known to have famously stated that "women and petty men (*xiaoren*) are especially hard to handle."[15] Not only is the master's general disparagement of women hard to dismiss, nowhere in *The Analects* is it suggested that the Confucian ideal for self-cultivation and moral perfection was applicable to women. Confucianism remained China's cultural root. Whenever a regime encountered a legitimacy crisis, it tended to gravitate toward Confucian traditionalism. Thus, when the corrupt Republican government failed to deliver a sense of nationalistic dignity, it still resorted to a mixture of quasi-Confucian and Christian values (see Chapter 3, "China's First 'Christian Republic'").

Also during this time, the maturing of Chinese women's gender consciousness was demonstrated by the emergence of women's journals. By 1911, there were at least seventeen of them, introducing feminist ideas to a broader audience.[16] As Kwok Pui-lan comments, "Nationalistic in tone, these feminist publications advocated a drastic change of society and promoted an image of women beyond the domestic confines."[17] Interestingly, these indigenous women's desired ideal of womanhood was already becoming more radical than the Victorian concepts of gender embraced by their contemporary women missionaries from the West.[18] As Kwok explains, "Victorian concepts of womanhood introduced by the women missionaries might not be adequate for China, which was dominated by foreign powers and was on the point of a revolution."[19] It was on the brink of this impending social change when Zeng Baosun returned to China.

With a passion to advocate for women's education, Zeng Baosun founded the Yifang Girls' Collegiate School in Hunan Province in 1917.[20] This school brought her contrasting progressive and traditional ideals together. As Zeng wrote, "What I have encountered in life, early education in the family school, elementary education in missionary schools and higher education in England, all came at a time when education for women was in its infancy."[21] On the one hand, Zeng wanted it to be "a modern girls' school for China," which she insisted be "run entirely by Chinese."[22] Zeng stipulated this staffing principle because she was well aware of the changing power dynamics between foreign missionaries and indigenous Chinese Christians.[23] On the other hand, Zeng named it Yifang to commemorate her grandmother, a role model demonstrating the "compatibility of traditional Confucian values with the emergence of strong, independent womanhood."[24] While serving as the founding principal of Yifang School, Zeng Baosun was also invited to act in an administrative role at other institutions in Hunan, including the First Hunan Women's Normal Teachers' School. She was also active on the provincial and national political committees.

Yifang School was different from other mission schools because students were given the right of self-government in community affairs. Its religious atmosphere also balanced self-spontaneity with biblical piety. Chapel was not compulsory, but Bible lessons were. As the principal Zeng Baosun started each day with a devotional from the Bible for the whole student body. As her cousin Zeng Yuenong who taught at Yifang School recalled, students were taught by Zeng Baosun that "all individuals are equal in front of God."[25] Biblical themes such as self-sacrifice, justice, and stewardship were also emphasized. Students from Yifang School were known for being outspoken and independent women. For example, when the Students Union of China requested that Yifang students make donations for building the Sun Yat-sen memorial in Guangzhou, these young women replied: "The Father of the Nation himself definitely would not endorse this huge waste of money on such an unconstructive project."[26]

In 1919, responding to the unrest and the bourgeoning May Fourth Movement after the Paris Peace Conference, Yifang School founded its own Student-Faculty Association. Zeng Baosun considered it "a training ground for democracy" because "the students greatly outnumbered the faculty in the Association and the real authority in the school lay with them."[27] Zeng praised young women at Yifang School for a large donation during the Hunan drought, because the fund was "second only to the relief funds disbursed by the provincial government."[28] She further commented that their "Christian spirit of saving lives and benefiting society was amply demonstrated."[29] Meanwhile, the school was likened to a congenial family, where no record of student demerits were kept.[30] Zeng Baosun also integrated what she experienced in residential colleges that she had attended in England. She hoped that the school would provide a kind of pastoral mentorship as well as a pleasant living environment to nurture young women's sense of self-worth and refinement.

The morals of this school epitomized the integration of Zeng Baosun's values, including nationalism, Confucian harmony and Christian activism. As Zeng wrote, "I saw no conflict between Confucianism and Christianity and that Christianity could awaken China from its lethargy."[31] Her approach aiming for synthesis left a deep influence on later China's prominent theologian T. C. Chao (or Zhao Zichen, 1888–1979), who advocated for the indigenization of Christian theology by not forsaking interfaith dialogues. However, the daily curriculum at Yifang School fell short of that promise. Even Zeng Baosun herself later admitted that since the school had a lower standard for Chinese literature and history,[32] it had been rightly faulted for alienating students from their own Chinese culture.[33] In the long run, the elitist approach of Zeng Baosun inevitably led to unintended consequences, such as opportunism and cultural inbreeding. For example, Yifang School had a close connection with Yale-in-China, an American missionary-funded education program located in Changsha of Hunan Province. The project was initiated after the martyrdom of Yale graduate Horace Pitkin in the Boxers' Rebellion of 1900. His death motivated a surge in missional zeal among young American college students, leading to the founding of Yale China Mission soon afterward.[34] For the next two decades, Yale-in-China produced young business and political elites during China's first republic. In 1920, an American visitor wrote that Yifang School gathered top-class young women in Hunan, and many of them later became excellent wives for the young male graduates of Yale-in-China.[35] Zeng Baosun granted awards to students in both institutions. In 1922, when Yale-in-China's Hunan campus decided to recruit women students, Zeng also recommended some alumni from Yifang School. These two education projects certainly produced young people with excellent training and credentials in all walks of life. But the downside was that its homogenizing effect helped to cement upper-middle-class privileges within the Christian education setting. According to historian Charlotte Furth, while the new intellectual class helped usher in an urbane and Western-oriented modern culture, "it was also threatened by a new estrangement from the rest of the Chinese society" because of its elitist Western education and its distance from the center of political power.[36]

Her reputation and singleness made Zeng Baosun a frequent international delegate at key Christian conferences. She was an elected member of the National Christian Council of China from 1923 till 1928, delegate to the International Missionary Council Conference at Jerusalem 1928 and delegate to the Institute of Pacific Relations Third Biennial Conference in Kyoto in

1929. In all these roles, Zeng Baosun stood out because of her credentials and public image representing a respect for China's past. She was sometimes elevated by Chinese male intellectual leaders to preside meetings and to act as a spokesperson. On a personal level, these public appearances did not diminish Zeng Baosun's personal piety as a Christian woman. For example, while attending conferences in Jerusalem, Zeng Baosun experienced a moving spiritual experience while worshipping in the Garden of Gethsemane on Good Friday.

In the public sphere, Zeng Baosun had no tolerance for radicalism. When educated Chinese criticized Confucianism and China's own tradition in a wholesale fashion for the oppression of women, Zeng Baosun found it necessary to offer a counterargument. In 1931, during the fourth Biennial Conference of the Institute of Pacific Relations in Shanghai, Zeng gave a keynote speech titled "The Chinese Woman, Past and Present." In this important public address, Zeng proved herself to be a thoughtful and lucid thinker. She summarized Chinese women's past liberation from social oppression and their quest for a positive identity.[37] Looking back on history, Zeng argued that women in China had not always lacked social status. In fact, in ancient China under the Song dynasty, they were notable contributors to Chinese households and civilization. Limiting women's role within the home was a much later cultural and social construction by men. She also blamed the introduction of Indian religion for subjugating women to patriarchal bondages.[38] Over time, women themselves began to internalize these norms. As Zeng wrote, "A woman under such hypnotic suggestion really does feel that only by striving after such an ideal can she find her true self."[39] Looking ahead, Zeng envisioned women in China to be "free in mind and behavior, eager to learn and to serve, seeking to work out the destiny of her people, and striving to set right the social and economic wrongs of her nation."[40]

Following late Qing reformers, Zeng's public speech and writings continued to engage with the conceptualization of "womanhood." In Chinese, its equivalent word is *nvxing*. Before the 1910s, this term only referred to the biological female sex. "A sense of universal womanhood [of this word] did not appear in the Chinese language until the early twentieth century during the May Fourth Movement."[41] This term symbolizes two breaks from tradition: first, woman's role was no longer conceived within the bound of familial relationality; second, it became a discursive equivalent of the Western use of "woman" which is kinship-neutral. It is particularly fascinating that Zeng Baosun traced a modern interpretation of womanhood back to Chinese tradition. She was inviting the Chinese to treasure their past in a climate where a radicalizing trend advocated for the abolition of the central familial values.

Zeng Baosun's resistance to radicalism had another incidental cause. Apart from Yale-in-China, another adjacent institution to Yifang School was Wang Fuzi Temple Association, an organizational base for the newly organized Chinese Communist Party, including the young Mao Zedong. A quirk of history is that Mao Zedong and Zeng Baosun both born in 1893, once hailed from the same rural Hunan region. Since 1918, Mao acted as one of the leading political figures using adjacent mission institutions to channel funds for communist mobilization.[42] Zeng Baosun was aware of these activities and called out the Wang Fuzi Temple Association for being "a communist base from which they spread lies and attempted to subvert the lawful government."[43] Around 1927, radicalism escalated in Hunan as Chiang Kai-shek started the North Expedition. Hostility from radical groups came from the *Hunan Daily News*, lambasting Yifang School: "Yifang being privately operated and Christian in outlook, was slandered more than the others; there was even a special edition dedicated to over-throwing Yifang."[44] The name of Zeng Baosun was also singled out and attacked as "a local tyrant, an evil gentry, a landlord, a feudal remnant, and a running dog of imperialism."[45] The radical group even occupied the clan shrine of Zeng's family for some time. The attacks became more frequent and violent to the extent that Zeng thought, "Yifang might be better off without me."[46] Operation of the school was suspended during this tumult. When Zeng Baosun, her cousin Zeng Yuenong, and Louise Barnes were being evacuated to safer regions, Barnes passed away due to a sudden heart attack. After this incident, military forces occupied Yifang School for more than a month. Some students secretly went into the campus and recovered the school's roster and other documents, hoping that these would be useful in the future when Yifang School resumed classes. To Zeng Baosun, these experiences with the revolutionary communists "drove her to an irrevers-ible stand."[47] It largely shaped Zeng Baosun's negative attitude toward Chinese communists from early on. In the 1930s, in response to Chiang Kai-shek's regime intolerance against the communists, she endorsed the former uncritically.

From 1922 to 1927, during the Anti-Christian Movement, mission schools in China were criticized for their use of English as a teaching medium, compulsory chapel services, and religious education. As elitist training sites, these institutions were also blamed for having alienated the students from the Chinese masses. At the Jerusalem symposium, Zeng Baosun offered a balanced view: "Early girls' schools were founded by Christian missionar-ies, on whom so much blame has been heaped in recent years that we are apt to forget this great service they have rendered to the women of China. Mission schools were certainly open to criticism in many important respects, but their attitude towards women has been consistently liberating."[48] Raising up women for a strong China had been the enduring pursuit of Zeng Baosun, because it was out of "a resolute spirit of nationalism born of the struggle against communist rebels and Japanese invaders" that she became increasingly confirmed in this aspiration.[49]

In fact, Protestant missions in China or in larger East Asia have always been entangled with the problem of patriotic nationalism from the very beginning. With the anomaly of Korea where patriotic identities were successfully fused with Protestantism, all other countries saw resistance and even violence against foreign missions.[50] Contrary to missionaries' intention to "gain respect" by nurturing an elite class of Christian leaders, their strategies somehow helped intensify Chinese nationalism, as historian and China missions expert John Fairbank once claimed.[51] Missiologist Scott Sunquist also pointed out that American Protestantism during this time was "a catalyst" to resistance and independence.[52]

Despite the antagonism of conservative-leaning scholars against communist radicals, there was a shared sentiment of nationalistic pride. Zeng Boasun always cherished a national pride and patriotic sentiment. Her Confucianism and Christianity further cemented this nationalistic tendency, especially in the 1930s. In October 1931, a month after Japan invaded the northeastern part of China, Zeng Baosun attended conferences organized by the Institute of Pacific Relations in Shanghai, Nanjing, and Hangzhou. When Zeng found that there were Chinese delegates who tried to appease Japan, she quit the meeting in protest. In 1936, Zeng Baosun published an article in the *Chinese Recorder*, which started with questions like "Shall Christians become spectators when your own country was being invaded?"[53] She advocated for pacifism and attributed the pro-war attitudes to popular ignorance about other cultures, a profit-driven war industry, and media propagation. In 1938, Zeng gave a speech at England's famous Eton College entitled "China Must Win the Anti-Japanese War."

During the prime years of her influence, Zeng Baosun was also a prolific writer. She wrote many volumes of "social problem fiction," a women's literary genre first pioneered by a famous Chinese writer Xie Wanying during the May Fourth Movement in 1919 (Chapter 7). This genre integrated literary creation with social justice and feminism in an intensifying political environment. In 1933, Zeng Baosun published a collection of short novels titled *Wayward* through the YWCA. The five short stories all centered around Chinese women in the context of social problems. For example, the story titled *Pearl Necklace* is about interracial romance. *Covenant Forever* is about Chinese women's self-independence. *Two Lotuses* is a tragic tale about a young woman from a previously prominent family who had to marry a military general as a concubine, after her family status declined. *Light Blue Envelope* depicts how an educated woman reacts to her husband's extramarital affair. *Photo of the Orange Orchid* tells the story of a husband's reminiscence of his deceased wife amid frictions with his current wife. This collection demonstrated Zeng Baosun's insightful social analysis with regard to the role of Chinese women in marriage and society, despite the fact that she remained unmarried herself.

Once in a while, Zeng also spoke at evangelistic meetings within China that reached more people than her international public speaking engagements. During the summer of 1935, she made an itinerant speaking tour to twelve Chinese cities, lasting for about six months. Her messages about the Christian faith reached tens of thousands of young people. Other speakers who took part in this tour included two Christian professors teaching in Shanghai and Fujian. These speakers noted a rising passion among students from non-Christian institutions. In her speeches, Zeng Baosun also reflected on problems within the Chinese church. As well, she brought the messages and reflections of the Chinese church to a global audience. Zeng Baosun spoke at the World Peace Conference in India, addressing more than 20,000 people, in 1949.

From the 1930s to 1940s, China saw more and more female political figures in the public sphere. In newly created institutions, forums and journals, women had a visible presence. By then, more of them unbound their feet, attended schools, learned English and some even went abroad for higher academic degrees. Issues they addressed ranged from women's education, social norms around dating and marriage, childbirth and health to workplace equality and foreign relations. Elite educated women like Zeng Baosun modeled for many young women what was considered appropriate speech, conduct, and career. She also demonstrated her political leadership. In 1947, Zeng ran for election in her hometown against someone who was previously vetted by the Nationalist Party. She won and became a delegate on the First National Assembly in Nanjing in 1948. Only thirty-eight women sat in the assembly, out of the more than one thousand delegates chosen to represent the provinces and cities of China. At the assembly, contrary to people's expectations, Zeng Baosun objected to the proposal of reserving only 10 percent of the seats for women. She insisted that women should be given equal opportunities through fair and open elections, and this proposal was adopted by the committee.

Zeng Baosun established a prominent intellectual stature among educated Chinese. Her stature in indigenous Christian scholarship is later attested even by many male Chinese scholars. In 1933, eleven Chinese Christian intellectuals, including T. C. Chao and Liu Tingfang, gathered at Yenching University. These male scholars all voted for Zeng Baosun to become the president of the committee overseeing a publication project. Zeng also changed the social norm of marginalizing Chinese women and the "Chinese woman" question in public life. As Gail Hershatter describes, it had long been considered appropriate among Chinese intellectuals that "Men inaugurated these discussions, but educated women also joined the debates."[54] Not many Chinese intellectuals envisioned women as politically active citizens in their own right, though. By holding to the idea central that "the status of women would help to determine the fate of China," they nonetheless tokenized women. Zeng Baosun's public accomplishments effectively challenged this perception.

When the Chinese Communist Party came to power in 1949, Zeng Baosun moved to Hong Kong and then to Taiwan two years later. Her main responsibility there was to preserve and curate the historical archives of the Zeng Guofan family. That role made her the primary historian of her clan. While in Taiwan, Zeng Baosun had good relationship with Madame Chiang Kai-shek and other officials of the Republican government. She also served as a member of the national women's commission. In 1953, Zeng Baosun represented the Republic of China at the UN Commission on the Status of Women. In 1971, seventy-eight-year-old Zeng Baosun donated the collection of original documents of the Zeng Guofan clan to the National Palace Museum, thereby enriching Taiwan's intellectual history.

Zeng Baosun's life has been a rich experiment in integrating the traditional with the modern, East with West. Her life story poses a counterargument to many modernist critiques against Confucianism as inherently incompatible with feminism. For example, in a book *About Chinese Women* by French feminist Julia Kristeva, she has a chapter titled "Confucius—An Eater of Women."[55] Another female scholar Margery Wolf also considers this ideology of Old China synonymous with patriarchy and misogyny.[56] Their common tendency is to reduce Confucianism to a system of hierarchical kinship while overlooking its other ethical components. In fact, it has been largely due to feminists' caricature of a narrowly understood Confucianism that the latter has been perceived as a lesser system of belief than Western ideals.[57] Doing so also risks the oversimplification of the lived experiences of Chinese women. To Zeng Baosun, however, Confucianism was an organic belief system lived out by her matriarchal clan. Zeng had been inspired by a model of lived matriarchy, or the rule of women, in her own Confucian family. There was a felt warmth akin to the feminist ethic of care through a closely knit social relationships and daily rituals. Although her grandmother's realm of power was mainly in managing the household, Zeng Baosun, who remained single all her life, later practiced a matriarchal presence in the broader social and political circle. In this way, a confluence between Confucianism, feminism, and progressive Christianity was viable as played out in her own life.

By selecting the fitting title *Confucian Feminist* for Zeng Baosun's memoir, her biographer Thomas Kennedy commented that "throughout her life, she followed the Confucian way."[58] She valued Confucianism because it enabled a loving relationship within her extended family. Zeng Baosun also firmly believed in the power of education to strengthen women, as shown by "[h]er lifelong intellectual reliance on the classic literature from which the teachings of Confucianism are derived, and her determination, when faced with choices, to do what was right rather than what was profitable."[59] At the same time, however, because Zeng Baosun came from an elite upper class background, as her biographer rightfully points out, Zeng Baosun was largely oblivious to "the widespread landlord abuse upon which communist revolution fed."[60] It was also due to her Confucian conservatism that "she had no patience with those who would destroy the traditional social order through which the culture was expressed, be they communists or warlords."[61]

The example of Zeng Baosun's singlehood also inspired more young women not to marry and thereby serve the wider society. By the 1930s, the singlehood of professional women has become a social trend in China's urbanizing regions. Present-day Chinese novelist Chen Danyan created a nurse character who remained single living in Shanghai set during that period: "In this snobbish but free city, she had good education and spoke English. She became a single professional woman of self-reliance, not humiliation in marriage. That was not easy but common among female physicians and nurses."[62] As the novel depicts, most highly educated women who preferred celibacy came from Christian family background.

For Shi Meiyu and Zeng Baosun, unfortunately, within a decade or so after they established trailblazing institutions, following the climax of China's Anti-Christian Movement in 1927, this growth trend waned. Responding to the Anti-Christian Movement (1922–1927), many Christian leaders tried to develop an apologetic that emphasized the humanity of Jesus. It was also during the Anti-Christian movement that Christian women pioneers of this late Qing to early Republic period developed a theological capacity to publicly reason their faith with opponents. For example, Zeng Baosun wrote, "As a perfect human being, Jesus sacrificed himself on behalf of human beings, thus elevating human personality nearer to God."[63] She came very close to writing a new creedal formula by saying: "Chinese women can only find full life in the message of Christ, who was born of a woman, revealed His messiahship to a woman, and showed His glorified body after His resurrection to a woman."[64] Like many of her contemporary Christian intellectuals, Zeng's humanistic understanding of Christology, nonetheless, did not often win the debate.

Meanwhile, the Protestant establishment in China continued to diversify and even created the preconditions for a radicalized communist revolution. At this early phase of China's urbanization and industrialization, society became stratified into a hierarchy composed of elite intellectuals, middle-class bourgeoisie, an expanding working class, and a majority peasantry. Among the third group, revolutionary and radical ideas also gained traction. A cognitive gap enlarged as "the demands being made by students and urban intellectuals of the May Fourth era were realistic for students and urban intellectuals, but they were hopelessly irrelevant to the lives of rural or working-class women."[65] To a certain extent, what the May Fourth Movement in 1919 meant for China can be compared to what the French Revolution did in Europe. An old social order was brought down; in its place emerged an irreligious "new" order. In twenty years, independent "womanhood," which used to be a sign of "modernization," became a symbol of bourgeoisie affiliations challenged by radical communists. Activists with a heightened feminist consciousness criticized Christianity for being not merely conservative and patriarchal, but also complicit with Western imperialism. Christian reformers such as Timothy Richard had propagated the idea that Western Christianity contributed historically to the emancipation of women. But into the twentieth century, many Chinese intellectuals, with a more sophisticated knowledge of the West, were able to discern that Christianity was only one of many institutions contributing to the crises in Western society. Not only was the credibility of a Christian Europe compromised during the World War II, its influence in the West was also declining due to ongoing power abuses in the Western church and broader trends osecularization. Moreover, in the 1920s, socialist literature introduced a more radical strategy for women's liberation. By rejecting old gender stereotypes and biases, the women's movement morphed to embrace new forms of gender identity tokenized by new political ideologies.

With rising nationalistic sentiments and the radicalization of student movements since 1925, some Chinese women pioneers' gender consciousness soon merged with an ever-stronger anti-Western, political consciousness. Their Christian outlook gradually metamorphosed into a Marxist worldview, stressing women's economic and political subjugation. They even considered liberal Christian feminists' efforts too "bourgeoisie." These emphases did not need to be mutually exclusive, but radicalization made them so.[66] The Christian community in China, both missionaries and Chinese, became increasingly divided about the emerging communist movements.[67] For example, leaders who grew up in upper-middle-class background like Zeng Baosun tended to favor more gradual reforms rather than abrupt and radical approaches suggested by the growing ideology of Chinese Communism. The fledgling microaggressions Zeng experienced in her local Hunan hometown with a strong elitist missionary presence reflects an escalating conflict for Christianity, communism, and the role of women.

NOTES

1. Thomas L. Kennedy, "Preface," in Zeng Baosun, ed., *Confucian Feminist: Memoirs of Zeng Baosun, 1893–1978*, translated and adapted by Thomas L. Kennedy (Philadelphia: American Philosophical Society, 2002), xii. Zeng Guofan was said to

have descended from Zeng Zi (or Tseng Tsi), a disciple of Confucius in sixth century BC.

2. Zeng Guofan (1811–1872) played a significant role in late nineteen-century Chinese politics, military campaigns and Chinese literature.

3. Le Zhang, "From Confucians to Christians: The Christian Members of Zeng Guofan Clan and Their Religious Views," *Beijing Social Sciences*, 6 (2017): 76–86.

4. Thomas L. Kennedy, "Epilogue," in Zeng Baosun, ed., *Confucian Feminist: Memoirs of Zeng Baosun, 1893–1978*, translated and adapted by Thomas L. Kennedy (Philadelphia: American Philosophical Society, 2002), 160.

5. Li-Hsiang Lisa Rosenlee, *Confucian and Women: A Philosophical Interpretation* (New York: State University of New York Press, 2006), 1.

6. Joseph R. Levenson, *Confucian China and Its Modern Fate: A Trilogy* (Berkeley: University of California Press, 1968), 79.

7. Jane Hunter summarizes this experience of Zeng Baosun as a "complex interaction of mission school experience and nationalist consciousness." But Zeng was able to let "the force of national loyalty and Christian faith push her in a surprisingly consistent direction." See Jane Hunter, *The Gospel of Gentility*, 247–48. The incident happened when Zeng raised concerns about the school's practices through a newspaper. Louise Barnes invited Zeng to talk about her opinions, eventually convincing Zeng of her own faults. But Barnes's gentle and humble attitude warmed Zeng and led to a trusted relationship between the two. Later when Zeng Baosun studied in England, Barnes gave up her post-retirement pension so that she could accompany Zeng to finish her degree. The self-giving mentorship by Louise Barnes to Zeng Baosun was similar to the influence of Gertrude Howe on Shi Meiyu.

8. *Biographical Dictionary of Chinese Christianity*, online resource: http://bdc conline.net/en/stories/zeng-baosun

9. Zeng Baosun, *Confucian Feminist: Memoirs of Zeng Baosun, 1893–1978*, translated and adapted by Thomas L. Kennedy (Philadelphia: American Philosophical Society, 2002), 35. Quoted in Kwok, *Chinese Women and Christianity*, 169. Thomas L. Kennedy, "Preface," in

10. His progressive mindset was in sharp contrast with most traditional patriarchs. Jane Hunter writes, "Even after the Boxer uprising, traditional Chinese from the major cities of the hinterland continued to look down upon Christianity." See Hunter, *The Gospel of Gentility*, 232.

11. Dao Wang, *Their Lives Bloomed like Flowers in March: Women in Republican China* (Hangzhou: Zhejiang University Press, 2013), 287–89.

12. Kennedy, "Preface," xiii.

13. Hunter, *The Gospel of Gentility*, 249–50.

14. Entry about Zeng Baosun, in *Biographical Dictionary of Chinese Christianity*.

15. Arthur Waley, *The Analects of Confucius* (New York: Vintage Books, 1989), 17:23.

16. Charlotte L. Beahan, "Feminism and Nationalism in the Chinese Women's Press, 1902–1922," *Modern China* 1 (1975): 380.

17. Kwok, *Chinese Women and Christianity*, 108.

18. Ibid., 108–9. Elisabeth Croll, *Feminism and Socialism in China* (London: Routledge and Kegan Paul, 1978), 64–65.

19. Kwok, *Chinese Women and Christianity*, 133.

20. Zeng Baosun took the name of this school "Yifang" from her grandmother's courtesy title.

21. Zeng Baosun, *Confucian Feminist: Memoirs of Zeng Baosun, 1893–1978*, translated and adapted by Thomas L. Kennedy (Philadelphia: American Philosophical Society, 2002), 157.

22. Ibid., 56.

23. Bond, Jennifer, "'The One for the Many': Zeng Baosun, Louise Barnes and the Yifang School for Girls at Changsha, 1893–1927," *Studies in Church History* 55 (2019): 441–62. doi:10.1017/stc.2018.9.

24. Kennedy, "Epilogue," 159. In the Chinese language, Yifang literally means "arts and fragrance," indicating cultured living. Zeng's grandmother enjoyed a courtesy name as Elderly Yifang.

25. Wang, *Their Lives Bloomed like Flowers in March*.

26. Biography of Zeng Baosun, https://mr12345.com/article/26111

27. Zeng, *Confucian Feminist: Memoirs*, 80–81.

28. Ibid., 79.

29. Ibid.

30. Ibid.

31. Ibid., 30.

32. Zeng, *Confucian Feminist: Memoirs*, 26–27.

33. Hunter, *The Gospel of Gentility*, 239.

34. Nancy E. Chapman and Jessica C. Plumb, *The Yale-China Association: A Centennial History* (Hong Kong: Chinese University of Hong Kong Press, 2011). Bays, *A New History*, 94.

35. "Biography of Zeng Baosun," online resource, https://mr12345.com/article /26111

36. Charlotte Furth, "Intellectual Change from the Reform Movement to the May Fourth Movement, 1895–1920," in John Fairbank, ed., *The Cambridge History of China*, vol. 12 (Cambridge: Cambridge University Press, 1983), 322–23. See Y. C. Wang, *Chinese Intellectuals and the West, 1872–1949* (Chapel Hill: The University of North Carolina Press, 1966). Also see Jerome Chen, *China and the West: Society and Culture, 1815–1937* (New York: Routledge, 2018).

37. Zeng Baosun, "The Chinese Women Past and Present," in Sophia H. Chen, ed., *Symposium on Chinese Culture* (Shanghai: China Institute of Pacific Relations, 1931), 281–92.

38. Ibid., 283.

39. Ibid., 286.

40. Ibid., 288.

41. Rosenlee, *Confucian and Women*, 45. Also see Ching-ki Stephen Chan, "The Language of Despair: Ideological Representations of the 'New Woman' (*xin nvxing*) by May Fourth Writers," *Modern Chinese Literature* 4 (1988): 1–2, 19–39.

42. For example, in 1918, Yale-in-China's Hunan campus, the predecessor of Francis Wei's Hua Chung College, appointed a young man Mao Zedong as the editor of its Chinese journal, *The New Hunan*. The mission rented space for Mao to run a bookshop. Using this base, Mao opened more stores, each of which sold communist

literature and funneled profits to the growing communist movement in the 1920s. see Jonathan D. Spence, *To Chang China: Western Advisers in China* (Westminster: Penguin Books, 2002), 174.

43. Zeng, *Confucian Feminist: Memoirs*, 89.

44. Ibid.

45. Ibid., 90.

46. Ibid.

47. Kennedy, "Epilogue," 160.

48. Zeng Baosun, "The Chinese Woman, Past and Present," Sohpia H. Chen Zen (ed.), Symposium on Chinese Culture (St. Paul: Paragon House, 1969 [1931]), 286.

49. Kennedy, "Preface," xiv.

50. Danielle Kane and Jung Mee Park, "The Puzzle of Korean Christianity: Geopolitical Networks and Religious Conversion in Early Twentieth-Century East Asia," *American Journal of Sociology* 115(2) (2009): 365–404. Li Ma and Jin Li, "Diverging Paths of Protestantism and Asian Nationalism: A Comparison of Two Social Movements in Korea and China in 1919," *International Bulletin of Mission Research*, 42(4) (2018): 316–25.

51. John King Fairbank (ed.), *The Missionary Enterprise in China and America* (Cambridge: Harvard University Press, 1974), 3.

52. Scott W. Sunquist, *Explorations in Asian Christianity: History, Theology and Mission* (Westmont: InterVarsity Academic Press, 2017), 65.

53. Zeng Baosun, "Religious Situation among Chinese Youth," *Chinese Recorder* 67 (April 1936): 199–204.

54. Hershatter, *Women in China's Revolutions*, 57–58.

55. Julia Kristeva, *About Chinese Women*. Trans. Anita Barrows (New York: Urizen Books, 1977), 66–99.

56. Margery Wolf, *Women in Chinese Society* (Stanford: Stanford University Press, 1975), 253.

57. Chenyang Li, *The Sage and the Second Sex: Confucianism, Ethics, and Gender* (Chicago: Open Court, 2000) 1.

58. Kennedy, "Epilogue," 158.

59. Ibid.

60. Ibid., 159.

61. Ibid., 160.

62. Chen Danyan, *Shanghai Hongyan Yishi* (Beijing: Zuojia Press, 2000), 15.

63. Zeng Baosun, "My Christian Faith," in Wu Yaozong, ed., *Christianity and a New China* (Shanghai: Youth Literature Bookhouse, 1940), 241.

64. Zeng Baosun, "Christianity and Women as Seen at the Jerusalem Meeting," *Christian Recorder* 59 (July 1928): 443. Quoted in Daniel Bays, *Christianity in China: From the Eighteenth Century to the Present* (Stanford: Stanford University Press, 1999), 455.

65. Margery Wolf, *Revolution Postponed: Women in Contemporary China* (Stanford: Stanford University Press, 1985), 13.

66. Judith Stacey, *Patriarchy and Social Revolution in China* (Berkeley and Los Angeles: University of California Press, 1983).

67. Luella Miner, "Christian women's education," *China Mission Yearbook* 1 (1914): 79–85.

Chapter 3

China's First "Christian Republic"

When Yuan Shikai, the first president of the new Chinese Republic, set aside a National Prayer Day in 1913, many Americans considered it as the fulfillment of their missionary purpose—the beginning of a Christian China. According to a media outlet in America, the *Christian Herald*, the day of prayer echoed none other than the victories of Constantine and Charlemagne "in subjecting pagan nations to the yoke of Christ."[1] Some even called it China's first "Christian Republic."[2] But according to historian Daniel Bays, "A British old China hand remarked on how this incident above all showed 'the easy gullibility of pious America.' "[3] To be fair, this impulse to hastily celebrate the Christianization of China had some shreds of reality to ground it. The 1910s marked over a century since the first Protestant missionary arrived in China, and the missionaries' wish for Christianity to gain respect and desirability seemed to have been realized. From early days, the strategy was as follows: "If missions were to survive, such thinking went, and to have any chance of proselytizing, they would have to be seen to be genuinely aiding China in practical terms."[4] What followed was a massive wave of education projects and institution-building. As historian Jonathan Spence notes, "Through their texts, their presses, their schools, and their hospitals, the efforts of foreign Christians affected Chinese thought and practice . . . they protested foot-binding, commiserated over opium addiction, offered religion and education as sources of solace and change, and a new perspective on social hierarchies and sexual subordination."[5] A wide spectrum of social forces to promote Christianity have changed China dramatically.

Among the missionary institutions established to promote gender equality for Chinese women, the Young Women's Christian Association (YWCA) was most worth mentioning. Founded in the 1910s as the largest women's association advancing social reform and gender equality in areas of literacy, vocational training, PE, hygiene, and nutrition, YWCA attracted both Christians and non-Christians.[6] In 1913, Ding Shujing joined the Beijing branch of the YWCA and participated in its religious activities and Bible studies.[7] Her activism and leadership soon won wide recognition within this organization.

Ding Shujing did not grow up in a Christian home. Her family, in fact, practiced Buddhism, which had adapted so well that many Chinese considered it their own religion. At age six, in the middle of the night, Ding observed her mother's devout pleading in front of a statue of the Buddha. That scene sowed in her the seed of mystic curiosity and a sense of awe toward the transcendent.[8] It would continue to shape her appreciation for indigenous religions of the Chinese. For instance, three decades later, as incumbent YWCA national general secretary, Ding Shujing would require that "Western secretaries sent to China have a deep-rooted Christian faith but also appreciate the truth in other religions."[9] In Ding's teenage years, her parents converted to Christianity and send her to mission schools. In 1907, with financial support from her local church, Ding Shujing attended North China Union College, the first Christian college for women in China. This institution had been founded two years prior and faced tremendous challenges, such as lack of funding, faculty, and students. After Ding's graduation in 1911, the Qing dynasty came to an end.

During her early involvement, Ding Shujing synthesized biblical themes with Confucian teachings. For example, the idea of Jesus Christ bringing reconciliation in Ephesians 2:14 was interpreted in line with the Confucian pursuit of harmony according to the Way. Ding concluded that "Only when we have the love of Jesus Christ can we realize the dream of Confucius."[10] She emphasized relational harmony, collegiality, and unity as common ground for Chinese Christians who also respect the Confucian tradition. Ding Shujing also regarded Jesus as a man who lived to the fullest: "The life of Jesus is an exemplar . . . He has genuine love for humankind. With steadfast and relentless power, he fulfills the task of saving human beings and the world."[11] She also added that Jesus showed great filial piety toward his mother and respect for his women friends, restoring women to their rightful position.[12] Over the next few years, Ding's collegiality and practical skills in organizing events so impressed many senior foreign staff that in 1922 they recommended her for a scholarship training program by the YWCA National Training School in New York.

Meanwhile, the radical nature of emerging Chinese nationalism showed its first signs in 1915 when the journal *New Youth* (*xin qingnian*) declared its rejection of all things "servile, conservative, retiring, isolationist, formalistic, and imaginary," and proposed that as a guiding principle young people embrace everything that was "independent, progressive, assertive, cosmopolitan, utilitarian, and scientific."[13] In the following years, "Scores of magazines and journals were established—by one calculation just over 600 new titles appeared in a very short period of time. All seemed to have the word 'New' in their title."[14] The May Fourth Movement in 1919 cemented a collective Chinese desire for education as an effective approach of self-strengthening: "Democratizing and expanding education lay at the heart of the New Culture Movement, and May Fourth thinking. . . . Literacy was the key to reforming the citizen, and the nation, enabling men and women to better their personal lot, as well as China's cultural and political standing."[15] In the background was also a widespread dissatisfaction with China's traditional Confucian values that had underpinned feudalist patriarchy. For example, the May Fourth Movement was first kindled as "a call for family revolution—an end to coerced arranged marriages and an increased say for young people in determining their own lives."[16] Furthermore,

Many writers and activists concluded that a political revolution alone could not change China. They believed that a cultural revolution was needed, and that what they called New Culture should begin in the most fundamental of social units: the family. In the family, they said, people learned habits of subservience. This prevented them from becoming autonomous individuals and free citizens, which, in turn, weakened the Chinese polity. Furthermore, many argued, the emancipation of women was key to overthrowing the Chinese family system. . . . The benighted, ignorant, confined, and victimized figure of Woman, who could only be liberated by new ways of thinking and new political action, became a standard image in fictional writings, polemics, and news reports.[17]

At the same time, more and more educated Chinese were more critical in weighing the value of Western ideals represented by the dominant education institutions set up by missionaries. The common Chinese also felt betrayed by Western acquiescence in Japan's invasive urges toward China. As Daniel Bays comments, "The bloody debacle of internecine warfare in Europe was costly to the image and credibility of Christianity insofar as the prospect of becoming as progressive or as 'civilized' as the West was a frequent apologetic for Christianity."[18] Other colonial behaviors also caused irritation. After decades of the unequal treaties with Asia, missionaries still occupied a privileged position. Some revered foreign missionaries not because of their ecclesiastical authority but their extraterritorial legal status which largely conditioned their monopolizing projects of Christian schools, hospitals, and other structures of the "Sino-Foreign Protestant Establishment."[19] As Bays comments, this dominant foreign presence was "a historical anomaly" even for global mission history, and was "entirely inappropriate in an age of nationalism and national sensitivities."[20] Consequently, grassroots Chinese resistance to the diplomatic failures of their governments and to foreign domination grew from popular uprisings to radicalized student movements and later revolutionary impulses. Waves of social movements after the May Fourth Movement by college students in 1919 revived the later Anti-Christian Movement that brought attacks on missionary institutions like the Young Men's Christian Association (YMCA) and Christian colleges. Within two years the Chinese Communist Party was founded. It not only fused patriotism with a Chinese identity that had little to do with Christianity but also served as a harbinger of a hostile intellectual trend among the educated secular elite.[21]

In 1920, when two well-known American crusaders, John R. Mott and Sherwood Eddy, preached to young students in China, promoting Western civilization and Christianity, they presumed that the Chinese would be ready to embrace both the ideas of progress and Christianity.[22] These teachings did capture many young Chinese Christian intellectuals who were generally enamored by a progressive view of history, confidence in Christian civilization, intense patriotism, and high hope for China's national rejuvenation.[23] Many favored Christianity as the best remedy for saving the Chinese national identity and civilization from extinction.[24] However, a few years later, with the oversized expansion of educational missions, sometimes with malpractice by and favoritism of foreign missionaries, local resistance resurged. Too closely tied to the privileges of external powers, missionaries continued to rely on economic enticement and political privileges. This overdependence contributed to the compromised integrity of their mission projects.[25] Ironically, although many leaders of the Republic China government and military were known as baptized Christians with a liberal and reformist accent, they comprised a corrupt and incompetent government. As historian Jeffrey Trexler comments, the beneficiaries of Protestant mission through elitist educational projects "either became unscrupulous businessmen or self-serving politicians."[26] It was a system of crony capitalism assisted by Christian favoritism. What epitomized this best may be the Song family whose three Wesleyan College-educated daughters all married into influential business or political clans. Chiang Kai-shek, known formerly as the "Red General," when marrying Soong Mei-ling, sister-in-law of Sun Yat-sen, in 1930 publicly announced his conversion to the Methodism of the Soong family. Daniel Bays describes these well-connected elite families as "prominent" in the Sino-Foreign Protestant Establishment.[27] Later Chiang Kai-shek often called on the goodwill, funds, and connections of Western missionaries.

With increasing official corruption under China's Republican government and social inequality, more and more Chinese looked for other options of governance. After the Bolshevik Revolution in 1917, Soviet Communism promoted its ideology into a messianic quasi-world religion, seeking to compete with the expansionism of Enlightened Christianity from the West. As early as 1920, Soviet leaders strategically canceled the unequal treaties with China in order to win her over as a communist ally. This important step freed the Soviet Union from Chinese charges of imperialism and won the goodwill of the Chinese, especially secular intellectuals. In contrast, some Western missionaries proposed only treaty revision but never overthrew them.[28] Russian Communists found fertile soil among Chinese intelligentsia for the spread of their ideas. In a revived market of ideas since the 1920s, progressive Protestant theology competed with libertarian values, humanism, Soviet Communism, and Confucian conservatism in China. Secular Chinese intellectuals criticized Christianity because they contrasted Buddha's entry to China riding an elephant with Jesus' ambassadors arriving with gunboats.[29] In addition, Christianity was called out for tarnishing its integrity through unequal treaties by the West. The ongoing competition between these two world religions would soon reshape a new world order of international communism contending with the West. For the future of China, communism seemed to embody a new form of progressivism that did not offend the patriotic pride of the Chinese. It thus began to gain popularity.[30] Although some viewed Christianity with favor, they still thought that it did not offer a total program for China's national rejuvenation. As David Paton, a missionary of the same period, wrote, "although large numbers of intellectuals were educated in mission schools, they sided with the Communist Party rather than the church."[31]

By then, apart from Christian colleges, two clusters of missionary institutions dominated China's public life: YMCA and YWCA. When the earliest communist leaders started mobilizing students and workers, they viewed YMCA and the YWCA as a popular but competing influence.[32] From the late 1920s to 1930s, they used the tactic of joining these organizations themselves to learn mobilization strategies as well as to recruit activists.[33] Benefiting from extraterritorial rights guaranteed by unequal treaties, China's foreign-founded Christian colleges became freer hubs where all streams of intellectual thoughts were circulated and discussed. The intellectual freedom on these college campuses soon spawned an unintended consequence—the rising of communist influence among young progress-minded college students.

Embedded within such popular anti-Western resistance was the Anti-Christian Movement (1921–1927),[34] a campaign which was preceded and triggered by the mission-based publication of *The Christian Occupation of China* (1922), a large-scale survey of China's Protestant Christian churches and ministries.[35] Although Chinese translators gave it a less aggressive title (*zhong hua gui zhu*, meaning China Belongs to the Lord), many Chinese intellectuals whose nationalist pride was bursting found the tone of this document highly offensive. Although affirming the necessity for turning church leadership over to the Chinese, the book's militant title invited hostile responses from the Chinese public. Historian Daniel Bays describes the release of this massive 500-page document with such a provocative English title as "a public relations disaster."[36] How this triggered the largest and most sustained Anti-Christian Movement in China, of course, had other contextual factors. Scholars who explore the historical context of this time list "the growth of national feeling, the spread of the spirit of new learning, the support which Christianity gave to the warring countries, the attitude of indifference of the Peace Conference to the problems of the Far East and of China, the lack of recognition given to China by the League of Nations, the example of Soviet Russia and of Turkey, and last but not least the influence of Chinese returned students from Russia and France" as causes that have "added to the rising tide of hostility to the Christian cause."[37] Liberal Chinese intellectuals published lambasting articles criticizing educated Christian leaders' siding with Western powers. In response, prominent Christian intellectuals such as T. C. Chao wrote mostly from a self-critical stance that Western church institutions have indeed corrupted their testimony in China. The fact is, these Western-trained Chinese intellectuals who converted to Christianity were "as patriotic as any other Chinese," yet "it was easy for critics of Christianity to tar them with the brush of disloyalty and untrustworthiness because they were part of a 'foreign religion'. "[38] As historian Robert Bickers comments, although various Protestant mission societies embraced the theory of making indigenous churches self-supporting and self-governing, "in practice missionary culture had often become bound into the wider world of colonialism internationally, and in China had relied on extraterritorial privilege and the infrastructure of foreign power."[39] Bicker further argues:

> Did they really sacrifice themselves for their beliefs? Undoubtedly, missionaries would reply, who had their martyrologies to hand listing their dead at the hands of Boxers, bandits, and Communists, but they were on far shakier ground when it came to charges of complicity in empire, and of cultural imperialism. Their own language hardly helped. Calling their 1922 survey of the missionary presence *The Christian Occupation of China* had been problematic even then, but the language of the Church militant was taken literally by its new enemies.[40]

In 1923, a "Claim Back Education Rights" campaign by the Republican government triggered a nationwide popular movement against Christian colleges. Educational sovereignty became the rallying point of secular intellectuals against the massive Christian presence in higher education. Leading secular scholars such as Hu Shih, Ding Wenjiang, and Tao Menghe argued that education should not serve as an instrument for religion.[41] Cai Yuanpei, the renowned chancellor of Beijing University, called for separation of education and religion and argued that good morals could be cultivated through aesthetic education instead.[42] These views profoundly shaped the ethos of young students. Progressive public opinions were shifting. For example, *Young China* magazine, founded by the anti-imperialist Young China Association, published three issues about similar discussions against Christian education.[43] Christian colleges were considered "philosophical, curricular, and administrative transplants" from America.[44] As a result, in 1925, the Republican government's Ministry of Education banned proselyting even on private college campuses founded by foreigners.[45] Religion and theology moved to the periphery.[46]

Another group of Chinese intellectuals attacked Christianity with an awareness of growing secularism in the West. They affirmed that China could learn from the West without accepting Christianity. The intellectual battlefield was surrendered to Marxism partly because of the overwhelmingly intense patriotic sentiments on all sides. During this time, many notable Chinese intellectuals had traveled the road from liberal Protestantism to communism. For example, the founding father of Chinese Communist Party and its first Chairman-elect, Chen Duxiu, had early exposure to Christianity and was an admirer of Jesus. Penning an article entitled "Christianity and the Chinese People" in 1920, Chen admitted being attracted to "the personality of Jesus."[47] He praised Christianity for being an "extremely effective religion" and observed that "Confucianism has not seemed to be able to combat it." He wanted to boost the image of Christianity among Chinese intellectuals. But soon after his short foray, Chen grew disappointed with Christianity because he was not satisfied with its promise of national salvation for China. A year later, Chen cofounded the Chinese Communist Party and was elected the first chairman of its central committee. As Daniel Bays writes, Chen Duxiu's spiritual pilgrimage was "emblematic of the rapid change of sympathies toward Christianity of a large portion of the intellectual elite of China."[48]

Not much has been written concerning the reasons Chinese leaders who were initially attracted to Christianity later chose to abandon it or even to attack it. As historian Robert Bickers argues, "Missionaries were blamed for creating Chinese nationalism through their educational efforts. Evangelical Protestants from the United States were the main target of this abuse, and inevitably anti-American bias played a role."[49] Apart from missionary domination in the education sector, the close ties between Western missionaries with the corrupt and the wealthy under the Republican regime, and the reproduction of social inequality through these missionary education projects might be reasonable clues. For example, the China-West Girls School (*zhongxi nvshu*) founded by American Methodist missionaries in Shanghai (1902) was considered an upper-class institution where the three Soong Sisters attended.[50] Students all came from wealthy families, who desired to raise their daughters to become socialites and cultural celebrities. The desired trajectory for these young women was that one day they could marry into wealthy and political influential families. Thus, the school designed a curriculum that taught young girls how to prepare Western-style salad and organize parties. They also watch many documentaries about how different world brands were manufactured and priced. The purpose was for these young women to have the know-how in brand name shopping and account-keeping in future marriages. "They naturally became constellations of stars pursued by major newspapers and magazines in Shanghai. Different business brands also hired these young girls for boosting their reputation."[51] For example, a famous restaurant Apricot Blossoms posted an advertisement, saying "Famous Cantonese Cuisine Favored by China-West Students and Cultural Elites."[52] Chinese reformers still viewed women as a productive project for China's national well-being. For example, even the most celebrated liberal scholar and philosopher Hu Shih was known to have delivered a public speech at China-West Girls School, famously saying to young women that "without big boobs, one cannot nurture healthy children."[53] His remark to encourage a healthy and desensitized view of the female body, paradoxically, still implied maternal productivity as a main role for women in China. Some graduates also criticized the school's curriculum for its America-centered worldview as "instilling so-called Western civilization."[54] Even when it came to religious courses, many students took them as potential opportunities for overseas study in the future.

In 1925, Ding Shujing's deeper involvement with YWCA coincided with a society-wide crisis. The May Thirtieth Movement (*wusa yundong*) triggered by the British Shanghai Municipal Police's opening fire on Chinese protesters pushed anti-foreign sentiments and Anti-Christian activism to its peak, sparking nationwide demonstrations and riots. It aroused public opinion against beneficiaries of the unequal treaty system, including the YWCA. According to American YWCA Secretary Helen Thoburn, the aftermath of May 30 showed "how ignorant Western missionaries were to the depth of anti-imperialist feeling of the Chinese that the Incident painfully exposed."[55] By then, American women staff made up "by far the largest national group among the YWCA Secretaries in China."[56] The shock of this movement brought urgency to refashioning YWCA's organizational identity. In other countries, its branches were founded at the invitation of existing mission boards. Often, it was the wives of missionaries who had identified a need for a special ministry program to women in that region. Then the nationals and foreigners would start a YWCA board together. But in China, early founders and leaders were all American women. When they began to promote "Chinese womanhood," American women staff did not have clear culturally sensitive mandates. The outburst of anti-foreign sentiment in 1925 challenged them to examine the extraterritorial privileges enjoyed by all foreigners in China. They needed to come up with a collaborative strategy along with Chinese women leaders to redefine the institutional identity of YWCA in China. As some women missionaries recall, "The shooting of May 30th crystallized public opinion. . . . The terrific question put to every group was: Are you Chinese or foreign? The YWCA has answered, 'We are Chinese.'"[57]

In the same year, when the national YWCA gathering announced policies to promote indigenous leadership in China, Ding Shujing referred to this transition as "the self-awakening" of Chinese women. Many Western staff, however, expressed hesitation about a potential phase of chaos under indigenous leadership. During waves of what later historians called the Anti-Christian Movement, more Chinese Christian leaders advocated for indigenous leadership. Ding Shujing also endorsed that these changes would demonstrate to the non-Christians that "Christian work in China is not imperialistic and capitalistic, but works for the coming of the Kingdom of God, which is goodwill and brotherhood among all men."[58] It was during this historical conjuncture that in 1926, Ding Shujing was promoted to become the first Chinese woman to head the YWCA as its general secretary. When she agreed to act as the associate general secretary three years prior, Ding had said: "I as a Chinese woman must do it."[59] As Kwok Pui-lan also points out, "when the leadership of . . . YWCA was passed onto Chinese hands, Chinese women leaders began to see that Christian reformist activities in Europe and America had their limitations."[60] As a result, American secretaries reformulated documents affirming that "justice to China demands readjustment of treaty relations between China and other nations."[61] As YWCA American secretary Eleanor MacNeil asserted, "A white man has no special rights just because his skin is white. Has a Christian any rights at all except to love and suffer?"[62] In a time of anti-foreignism, Ding Shujing's inclusive attitude toward Westerners was also a further step toward collaborative maturity.

Under Ding Shujing's leadership, and in response to rising criticisms, the YWCA also strategically expanded its coalition with Chinese women from working classes and peasantry demographics.[63] As historian Karen Garner noted, because a real understanding of China's nationalist aspirations had developed among American YWCA Secretaries in the post-May 30 period, "American Secretaries did not resist the Chinese Secretaries' call for a shift in programming focus from training 'middle-class' educated Chinese women for leading social positions to serving the interests of the majority of Chinese womanhood, the working poor."[64]

Years after cotton and silk workshops modernized into factories, by 1915, over 620,000 women joined the labor force across China.[65] Many of these factories were dominated by foreign capital. Most women workers migrated to cities from the countryside for economic opportunities. By the 1930s, more and more rural women were recruited from their villages. Among them were very young girls picking silk from cocoons in hot water in silk filatures of Shanghai. They were taken away by labor contractors who signed an agreement with their parents. The deplorable work and living conditions of women laborers, sometimes known as "slave workers (*bao shen gong*)," attracted the advocacy of many missionaries and Chinese reformers. Waves of workers' strikes inevitably happened in the 1920s: "Women silk workers were more militant than cotton mill hands, even though the industry was dominated by Chinese capital and so nationalist protests against imperialism were not a factor. The main grievances in the silk filatures were economic. Strikes tended to erupt in summer, when the heat in the filatures became unbearable."[66]

In Shanghai, YWCA also organized women factory workers and supported the emerging revolutionary forces.[67] But after 1926, violent military campaigns of the Northern Expedition further divided the Western Christian community in China. YWCA and many Christian organizations continued to face attacks that came from students under Marxist influence.[68] Thus, ongoing changes such as student unrests, the labor movement, and Marxist criticism "helped Christian women leaders to see the bourgeois nature of the Christian women's movement and the need to integrate their efforts with those of the poorer and working classes."[69] In 1927, although faced with Chiang Kai-shek's purge of radicals in Shanghai, Ding Shujing was willing to include radical groups because of her enthusiasm for women's movement and public service. In a public speech, Ding advocated that women should be treated as full participants in the body of Christ, since Jesus respected women and granted them leadership in ministry.[70] Within a year, the YWCA opened six schools for basic literacy in industrial zones among women workers. Five of these were night schools. After a few years, these programs reached out to rural women too. Although Ding Shujing may never have wanted the YWCA to become an incubator for the communists, it effectively nurtured the latter's mobilization as an unintended consequence. After 1937, "an overwhelming majority" of women activists in the labor movement and the Chinese Communist Party attributed their "initial political awakening" to the night schools offered by YWCA.[71]

In north China, Yale graduate Yan Yangchu (James Yen) became an important reformer leading a movement for rural reconstruction. After having become a Christian by attending missionary schools in the 1910s, he became involved in YMCA activities. He and many other U.S.-trained Chinese intellectuals were embedded in "an intertwined network of philanthropic, educational and development activities and interests: Rockefeller, the publishing magnate Henry Luce, . . . and the YMCA."[72] After the anti-missionary incidents of 1926 and 1927, these Chinese leaders continued to profess the Christian faith but also "rejected any notion that foreign Christian or mission institutions had a leading role to play."[73]

By 1928, Ding Shujing addressed the second YWCA national convention, stressing the necessity of participating in national reconstruction, not simply charity work.[74] In the same year, when YWCA in South China organized a campaign against keeping domestic maids, Ding Shujing advocated that this "inhumane" practice "degrades women and adversely affects the image of the nation and the spirit of the Chinese people."[75] YWCA set up a study committee and collaborated with other organizations to push for its abolition. Newspapers in Beijing gave wide coverage of this campaign, which earned positive social appraisal for YWCA.[76] Ding Shujing once wrote an article which best summarized her view of social transformation during this period: "The foundation of a national construction depends on people's personality; healthy personalities can build a healthy nation. . . . If we build our nation on this foundation, it will be strong and firm."[77] YWCA's engagement with the urban poor was in line with the nationwide liberal activism to address social inequality. As historians note, "By the early 1930s the Chinese countryside might seem to be bursting with different species of experimental initiatives and model districts, schools and agricultural stations. The rural or agrarian question seemed never to have been so prominent, nor to have exercised so many different strands of thought."[78]

For the ruling Nationalist Party led by Chiang Kai-shek, there was little substantive interest in rural reforms, even after it issued a new Land Rent Law in 1930 as a response to Mao Zedong's Hunan Peasants Report in 1927. Protestant mission, in colluding with Christian politicians, contributed to the worsening of classism in China. While acknowledging the need for change to better the life of millions of rural poor, the elite class of China was unwilling to "go to the People," leaving the opportunity to the communist mobilizers. In urban China, programs like YMCA and YWCA trained worker-students to combat systemic injustices through strikes.[79] But their approach "did not call into question the legitimacy of the entire system."[80] As a result, Christian reformers achieved little during the Nanjing Decade (1927–1937), because they were "stymied by the old rural elite and its prerogatives in the country-side and by the urban business and industrial power structures in cities like Shanghai," according to Daniel Bays.[81] The Christian reformism of National Christian Council or other parts of the Sino-Foreign Protestant Establishment could not go so far as to address structural injustice faced by peasants and workers.[82]

Even the New Life Movement promoted by the Republican government in 1934, with its strange mixture of traditional Confucian values, exhortations to patriotism, and a ban on uncivic behavior, only invited derision from Chinese intellectuals. Considered "[r]igidly authoritarian and first loyal to Chiang above all, it was of no use in promoting needed social and economic reforms, and faded from the scene in the late 1930s, with its Christian

supporters losing face among liberals and progressives."[83] When it comes
to the movement's agenda on women, historian Gail Hershatter comments
that "[t]he educated and employed New Woman was less controversial than
she had been a decade earlier. But her mischievous younger sister—the irresponsible, seductive, and duplicitous Modern Girl—emerged as a new figure
of unease on the urban cultural landscape."[84] In the 1930s, the New Woman
has acquired some definitive characteristics: "Eager to acquire knowledge
and attain economic independence, trained in a profession, not subservient
to men, frugal, modest in dress and self-presentation, politically informed,
attuned to contemporary social problems."[85] She continues:

> The New Woman was supposed to do and have it all. After education in a
> new-style school, she would pursue a career in business, education, medicine,
> journalism, or the arts, at least until she married a modern, forward-looking New
> Man. In the workplace, she would avoid any hint of scandal—no gossip about
> seduction or extramarital affairs. After marriage . . . she would run a scientifi-
> cally managed home, . . . As a politically aware consumer, she would honor
> the frequent boycotts of Japan and buy products produced in China. In all these
> respects, the New Woman was a worthy descendant of the virtuous woman
> of the late Qing. Both types of Woman were expected to work hard, sacrifice
> themselves, and show sexual restraint. Both were seen by the elites of their day
> as key to the well-being of the larger polity—the threatened empire during the
> Qing, and imperiled nation during the Republic.[86]

YWCA projects catered to this cultural image of new womanhood. But history did not afford them time to fully enact these ideals for Chinese women.
This is because at the same time, missionary projects in China began to face
a funding problem as America entered the Great Depression. Also, extraterritoriality created large loopholes that allow foreigners to set up a network of
property and finance companies that answered to neither Chinese nor foreign
laws. For example, the enterprises created by Frank Jay Raven, a municipal
councilor from 1931 to 1934, had been insolvent for years. Its collapse in
1935 undercut the financial stability of many U.S. missionary organizations
in China.[87] In the late 1930s when Japanese aggression grew, many rural
initiatives had to cease.

Among the wider missionary community, the gap between fundamentalist and liberal-modernist understandings of the role of Protestant mission in
China enlarged. Take Pearl Buck, for example. As a daughter of missionaries
that had grown up in China, upon returning in 1914 after college education
in America, Buck and her husband saw education as a way of renewing
China. Both taught at the private, missionary-founded University of Nanking
for more than a decade from 1920 to 1933. Having witnessed the war-torn

China with streets swarming with protesters against foreign aggression, Pearl Buck's view of mission took a dramatic turn. In 1930, she gave a public address titled "Is There a Case for the Foreign Missionary?" to a group of 2,000 mission-minded Presbyterian women in a New York City hotel. Buck argued that China did not need an institutional church dominated by missionaries who had little knowledge about the Chinese ethos and social context. In her novel *The Good Earth* (1931), the Pulitzer Prize winner strived to humanize Chinese peasants while still presenting a shocking encounter with rural China from a Westerner's perspective. Four years later, when the earlier New York City speech of Pearl Buck was published in *Harper's Magazine*, it created a controversy within the Presbyterian China mission board, leading to Buck's resignation.[88] It also ignited a storm of agitated debates between critics and defenders of global mission in all quarters of American Protestantism. Historians note it as "a sign of the times" for both China missions and American involvement in overseas expansion after the Great Depression. After the early 1930s, the YMCA, YWCA and other well-established mission institutions in China faced a massive financial crunch. A large part of these programs declined, and missionaries headed home. Somehow the narrative of Christianity bringing liberating benefits for Chinese women lost its appeal as the modernist-fundamentalist controversy continued to create polarizing theological trends. The middle ground of collaborative efforts across different theological camps has vanished. It was during this leadership vacuum in the 1930s that male independent leaders such as John Sung, Wang Mingdao and Watchman Nee grew their indigenous influence for another decade.[89]

Even in the midst of radical politics and intense antagonism against foreigners, Ding Shujing did not give in to the prevailing ideological division. Her earlier views had already reflected an inclusive transnationalism. Before she became general secretary, when foreigner staff members were asked to leave the YWCA in 1924 in order to hand over leadership to indigenous women, Ding's response was that staffing policies should not be based on race, but upon more general qualifications.[90] In December 1927, the Chinese National YWCA initiated the planning of "a pageant of international goodwill" for world peace. It materialized two years later, advocating "ideals of brotherhood and justice [that] ruled the actions of nations rather than the conquest and greed that ruled the 'old' era."[91] In 1928, Helen Thoburn wrote in praise of Ding's internationalism: "There is a present day fashion here of exalting Chinese leadership (a necessary transition stage). Our Chinese general secretary goes well beyond this stage and says: 'Chinese instead of foreign?—there is something better than that. In this our international undertaking we want the *best* person for each place.' "[92] In 1931, Ding Shujing also wrote words of appreciation for American YWCA staff: "Such a joint staff in the Association is the means by which we can accomplish world fellowship."[93] Even after the Japanese invasion, in 1935, when Ding Shujing attended a national YWCA assembly in Japan, she openly discussed current affairs with Japanese women delegates. Ding felt the same eagerness among Japanese women to know what was really happening and to see the war end. But she also realized that Japanese media were trying to cover things up.

Ten years after she assumed top leadership of YWCA, in 1936, 46-year-old Ding Shujing visited America, where she contracted a dental infection. The treatment led to septicemia, which claimed her life. By then, she had mentored a few younger women leaders who would resume leadership of the YWCA in China for the following decades. Ding's contemporary and YWCA staff Sarah Lyon remembers her as "no selfish nationalist, but a true patriot who loved her own country and was one of its best interpreters."[94] As YWCA staff Elizabeth A. Littell-Lamb writes, "The YWCA's survival in both the Japanese-occupied cities and in unoccupied China . . . testified to Ding's success."[95] Currently, the YWCA has survived China's most turbulent political turmoil and remains its oldest women's organization.

With rising nationalistic sentiments and the radicalization of student movements since 1925, some Chinese women pioneers' gender consciousness soon merged with an ever-stronger anti-Western, political consciousness. Their worldview gradually metamorphosed into a Marxist one that stressed women's economic and political subjugation. Some even considered liberal Christian feminists' efforts through medicine and literacy too "bourgeois." As historian Judith Stacy comments, "These emphases did not need to be mutually exclusive, but radicalization made them so."[96] Polarization happened when the popular sentiment has been radicalized. As Philip West summarizes, "Questions had to be refined: which pattern of change, reform or revolution; which model, socialist Russia or capitalist America; which ideology Marxism or Christian liberalism; whom to serve, the government in power or revolutionary movements."[97] With continuing geopolitical warfare, the belief in using education to bring national salvation weakened substantially. Meanwhile, the secular Chinese intelligentsia, viewing themselves as bearing the true spirit of Enlightenment, advocated the idea of separation of church and state to downplay the influence of Christianity in Chinese society. Ironically, the same kind of patriotism that motivated Chinese Christians such as Ding Shujing who strove to promote Christianity for national salvation eventually became the biggest hurdle to the spread of Christianity. Agitating patriots wanted a quick solution, and they now desired a Soviet-type revolution. As cited, these radical ideas made large inroads into student circles in mission schools and Christian colleges by the early 1930s.

NOTES

1. Latourette, Kenneth Scott, *A History of Christian Mission in China* (Piscataway: Gorgias Press, 2009), 611–12.

2. Goossaert Vincent and David A. Palmer, *The Religious Question in Modern China* (Chicago: Chicago University Press, 2011), 69.

3. Bays, *A New History*, 92.

4. Bickers, *Out of China*, 93. Also see James C. Thompson Jr, *While China Faced West: American Reformers in Nationalist China, 1928–1937* (Cambridge: Harvard University Press, 1969).

5. Spence, *The Search for Modern China*, 208.

6. Alison R. Drucker, "The Role of YWCA in the Development of the Chinese Women's Movement, 1890–1927," *Social Service Review* 53 (3) (September 1979): 421–40.

7. Knowk, *Chinese Women and Christianity*, 136.

8. Elizabeth A. Littell-Lamb, "Ding Shujing: The YWCA Pathway for China's 'New Women'," in *Salt and Light: Lives of Faith That Shaped Modern China*, edited by Carol Hamrin and Stacey Bieler (Eugene: Pickwick Publications, 2009), 80.

9. Ibid.

10. Ibid., 80–81.

11. Ding Shujing, "Fullness of Life," *Young Women* (The YWCA Magazine) 7 (4) (1928) 4: 3–7. Quoted in Kwok, *Chinese Women and Christianity*, 172.

12. Ding Shujing, "The Position of Women in the Church," *Young Women* 7(2) (March, 1928): 22.

13. Chen Du Xiu, "Call to Youth," trans. in Ssu-yu Teng and John K. Fairbank, *China's Response to the West: A Documentary Survey, 1839–1923* (New York: Atheneum, 1970), 240–46.

14. Bickers, *Out of China*, 33.

15. Ibid., 95, 96.

16. Hershatter, *Women and China's Revolutions*, 93.

17. Ibid., 94, 95.

18. Bays, *A New History*, 106–7.

19. Ibid., 108.

20. Ibid.

21. In fact, Chinese nationalism also went through a process of metamorphosis: conceived in military defeat around 1905, born through the May Fourth Movement in 1919, and matured into a more radical Anti-Christian form by the May Thirtieth Incident in 1925. Tse-tung Chow, *The May Fourth Movement: Intellectual Revolution in Modern China* (Cambridge: Harvard University Press, 1960), 21–43.

22. Xi Lian, *The Conversion of Missionaries: Liberalism in American Protestant Missions in China, 1907–1932* (University Park: Penn State University Press, 1997), 153.

23. Albert Wu, "Forever a Patriot," *Journal of the American Academy of Religion*, 85 (1) (March 2017): 130.

24. John. K. Fairbank, *China: A New History* (Cambridge: Harvard University Press, 1992), 224.

25. Timothy Brook, "Toward Independence: Christianity in China under the Japanese Occupation, 1937–1945," in Daniel Bays, ed., *Christianity in China: From the Eighteenth Century to the Present* (Stanford: Stanford University Press, 1996), 317.

26. Jeffrey Trexler, *Education with the Soul of a Church: The Yale Foreign Missionary Society and the Democratic Ideal*, PhD Dissertation, Duke University, 1991, 211.

27. Bays, *A New History*, 125.

28. Paul A. Varg, "A Survey of Changing Mission Goals and Methods," in Jessie G. Lutz, ed., *Christian Missions in China: Evangelists of What?* (Boston: D. C. Heath, 1965), 9–10.

29. Meng Lin Jiang, *Tidings from the West* (Taiwan: China Daily, 1957), 3–4. Quoted in Peter Tze Ming Ng, *Chinese Christianity: An Interplay between Global and Local Perspectives* (Leiden: Brill Academic, 2012), 153.

30. Jessie Gregory Lutz, *China and the Christian Colleges, 1850–1950* (Ithaca: Cornell University Press, 1971), 238–39, 254.

31. David Paton, *Christian Mission and the Judgment of God* (Cambridge: Eerdmans, 1953), 15.

32. Feiya Tao and Philip Yuen-Sang Leung (eds.), *Re-Interpreting East Asian Christianity* (Hong Kong: Chinese University of Hong Kong, 2003), 116, 122.

33. One founding member of Chinese Communist Party Yun Daiying was active in the YMCA before 1920. Han Lingxuan, "Early Yun Daiying and Christianity," *Modern History Research*, 44 (2) (1988): 249–61. Tan Xiaofang and Yu Zixia, "Yun Daiying and YMCA," *Huazhong Normal University Journal* 6 (2009): 122–29.

34. Lewis Hodous, "The Anti-Christian Movement in China," *The Journal of Religion*, 10 (4) (October 1930): 487–494. Tatsuro Yamamoto and Sumiko Yamamoto, "The Anti-Christian Movement in China, 1922–1927," *The Far Eastern Quarterly*, 12 (2) (1953): 133–47. Paul A. Cohen, "The Anti-Christian Tradition in China," *Journal of Asian Studies*, 20 (2) (February 1961): 169–80.

35. Thomson, *While China Faced West*, 50–51.

36. Bays, *A New History*, 109.

37. Hodous, "The Anti-Christian Movement in China," 487.

38. Bays, *A New History*, 113.

39. Bickers, *Out of China*, 277.

40. Ibid., 277.

41. Peng Deng, *Private Education in Modern China* (Westport, CT: Praeger Publishers, 1997), 67–68, 74.

42. Ibid.

43. Ibid.

44. Philip West, "Reframing the Yenching Story," *Journal of American-East Asian Relations* 14 (2007): 174.

45. Ibid., 67.

46. Peter Tze Ming Ng, "The Changing Phases of Religious Education-Core or Periphery?" in Peter Tze Ming Ng ed., *Changing Paradigms of Christian Higher Education, 1888–1950* (Lewiston: Edwin Mellen, 2002), 103–4.

47. Chen Duxiu, "Jesus the Incarnation of Universal Love," in Jessie G. Lutz, ed., *Christian Mission in China: Evangelists of What?* (Boston: D. C. Heath, 1965), 47–50.

48. Bays, *A New History*, 93.

49. Bickers, *Britain in China*, 94.

50. Soong Ai-ling, Soong Mei-ling (Madame Chiang Kai-shek) and Soong Ching-ling (wife of Sun Yat-sen) all played major roles in influencing their husbands, who shaped the course of Chinese history. Their father Charlie Soong was an American-educated Methodist minister who later made a fortune in banking and printing. Soong was also a long-term patron of Sun Yat-sen.

51. Cai Degui, *World Citizen Yan Yaqing: A Biography* (Guangzhou: Huacheng Publishing, 2013), 37.

52. Ibid.

53. *Republic Daily* (*minguo ribao*), August 10, 1927. Quoted in Degui, *World Citizen Yan Yaqing*, 47.

54. Ibid., 49.

55. Karen Garner, "Redefining Institutional Identity: The YWCA Challenge to Extraterritoriality in China, 1925–30," *Women's History Review* 10(3): 409–40, 413.

56. Ibid.

57. Mary Dingman, *The Sleeping Giant Wakes and Stretches* (New York: The Woman's Press, publication of the American National YWCA [September 1925]), 633. Quoted in Garner, "Redefining Institutional Identity," 416.

58. Ding Shujing, "Chinese Women Leaders Conception of the Missionary," *Chinese Recorder* 57 (1926): 122.

59. Letter from Ding Shujing to Mrs. Waldegrave, July 2, 1923. Quoted in Littell-Lamb, "Ding Shujing," 79.

60. Kwok, *Chinese Women and Christianity*, 133.

61. "Statement Regarding the China Situation Issued by the Committee of Reference and Council, Foreign Mission Conference of North America," July 16, 1925, Subject Files up to and including 1950, Reel 52, National Archive of the YWCA of the United States. Quoted in Garner, "Redefining Institutional Identity," 418.

62. Eleanor MacNeil, "The Devolution of an Imperialist," *The Green Year*, publication of the Chinese National YWCA (July 1, 1925), 18.

63. YWCA of China, *Introduction to the Young Women's Christian Association of China, 1933–1947* (Shanghai: The National Committee of the YWCA of China, n.d.), 1. Quoted in Kwok, *Chinese Women and Christianity*, 131.

64. Garner, "Redefining Institutional Identity."

65. Sally Borthwick, "Changing Concepts of Women from the Late Qing to the May Fourth Period," in David Pong and Edmund S. K. Fung, ed., *Ideal and Reality: Social and Political Change in Modern China, 1860–1949* (Lanham: University Press of America, 1985), 83.

66. Hershatter, *Women and China's Revolutions*, 113.

67. Emil Honig, "Christianity, Feminism, and Communism," in Daniel H. Bays, ed., *Christianity in China from the Eighteenth Century to the Present* (Stanford: Stanford University Press, 1996), 243–62.

68. Shirley S. Garrett, *Social Reformers in Urban China: The Chinese Y. M. C. A., 1859–1926* (Cambridge: Harvard University Press, 1970), 179.

69. Kwok, *Chinese Women and Christianity*, 136.

70. Shujing, "The Position of Women in the Church," 21–25.

71. Emily Honig, *Sisters and Strangers: Women in the Shanghai Cotton Mills, 1919–1949* (Stanford: Stanford University Press, 1986), 217. Honig also writes that "Although the number of women trained in the YWCA factory classes were small, a disproportionate number of those women went on to join the Chinese Communist Party in the mid-1930s, and to fight for revolutionary changes in China's social, economic, political, and international relations." See Maul M. Russell, *Oral History, Midwest China Oral History and Archives Project* (St. Paul, Minnesota, 1976), 15–16. Quoted in Garner, "Redefining Institutional Identity," 428. Also see Li Wang, "China's YWCA: An Alternative Approach for Gender Equality," *Guangming Daily*, November 9, 2008.

72. Bickers, *Out of China*, 97.

73. Ibid.

74. Ding Shujing, "Beijing YWCA," *Nianjian* 5 (1918): 201–4; "Mission of the Chinese YWCA Today," *Nvqingnian* 7(7) (November 1928): 3–10. Quoted in Kwok, *Chinese Women and Christianity*, 136.

75. Ding Shujing, "The Movement to Abolish Domestic Maids," *Nvqingnian* 7(2) (March 1928): 54.

76. Li Wang, "China YWCA: An Alternative Approach for Gender Equality," *Guangming Daily*, November 9, 2008. http://epaper.gmw.cn/gmrb/html/2008-11/09 /nw.D110000gmrb_20081109_3-07.htm?div=-1

77. Shujing, "Fullness of Life."

78. Bickers, *Out of China*, 98. Also see Charles Hayford, *To the People: James Yen and Village China* (New York: Columbia University Press, 1990), 111–15.

79. Honig, *Sisters and Strangers*, 217–24.

80. Bays, *A New History*, 127.

81. Ibid.

82. Ibid.

83. Ibid., 128.

84. Hershatter, *Women and China's Revolutions*, 130.

85. Ibid., 143.

86. Ibid., 143.

87. Bickers, *Out of China*, 184.

88. Pearl S. Buck, "Is There a Case for Foreign Missions?" *Harper's* 166 (January 1933): 143–55.

89. Bays, *A New History*, 124.

90. *Carol Hamrin and Stacey Bieler* (eds.), *Salt and Light: Lives of Faith That Shaped Modern China*, Volume 1 (Eugene: Pickwick Publications, 2009), 93.

91. Within the Four Seas: A Pageant of World Unity, Synopsis and Selections, Supplement to the Green Year (December 1929), 15–17. Quoted in Garner, "Redefining Institutional Identity," 430.

92. Helen Thoburn, *Between Acts in China* (New York: The Woman's Press), XXII (March 1928), 158.

93. Ting Shu Ching, Character Growing for Nation Building, The Woman's Press, XXV (June 1931), 353. Quoted in Garner, "Redefining Institutional Identity," 430.

94. Sarah Lyon, "A Talk at Memorial Service for Miss Ting," in "Some Appreciations." Quoted in Littell-Lamb, "Ding Shujing," 97.

95. Littell-Lamb, "Ding Shujing," 97.

96. Stacey, *Patriarchy and Social Revolution in China*, 75.

97. Philip West, *Yenching University and Sino-Western Relations, 1916–1952* (Cambridge: Harvard University Press, 1976), 146.

Chapter 4

Life and Death of Christian Colleges

When American journalist Edgar Snow arrived in Yan'an in 1936, the region had been turned into a Red Capital after Chinese communists made the historic Long March to relocate their headquarters there.[1] By then, key communist leaders and propagandists had learned successful mobilization techniques from organizations, such as the YMCA and YWCA.[2] Many idealistic young students affiliated with these Christian organizations also joined forces with revolutionaries in Yan'an. Edgar Snow wrote for the *New York Sun* and London's *Daily Herald* about life in Yan'an. His *Red Star Over China* became a popular primer of Chinese communism, positively shaping the Westerners' impression of the Red Army and Mao Zedong. By presenting a puritanical Yan'an compared with the corrupt Nationalist regime, Snow praised the ethos of Chinese communists as being in line with progressive reformism. The apparent solidarity in Yan'an under the Chinese Communists set in a sharp contrast with prolonged warlord turmoil in other places governed by Chiang Kai-shek's Nationalist ruling class.[3] A former missionary wrote about his assessment of Yan'an: "This is the kind of China which I have always hoped to see."[4] Others were encouraged to witness the vibrant diversity and cosmopolitan character of this remote and impoverished communist headquarters:

> A *New York Times* correspondent . . . reported meeting a man who had fought on the republican side in the Spanish Civil War; a pastor and former YMCA worker who had graduated from the American-run St. John's College in Shanghai; a missionary-trained doctor from Fuzhou, and many other medical staff who had studied abroad; other Chinese from overseas; and a former seaman who had "sailed all the world's oceans."[5]

59

Many young women were inspired after discovering that these CCP-controlled areas allowed women to have the same right to vote as men. A massive female labor force also participated in production to reach the goal of self-sufficiency. In nonproductive seasons, women had access to literacy classes in "winter schools."[6] The communists also promoted marriage reform in rural areas "with an eye to breaking this connection between landed power and control of women."[7] Mao Zedong himself gave great emphasis to the role of rural women: "Women have expressed their appreciation for the land struggle, because it can help dissolve the restrictions on their personal freedom."[8] In communist-governed rural China, the Marriage Law of 1934 effectively banned polygamy and other "feudalist" practices such as bride price. The new law also stipulated legal ages for marriage be twenty for men and eighteen for women, making the practice of having child brides illegal. It also permitted unilateral freedom to divorce but made an exception for the spouses of Red Army soldiers. Yan'an became a magnetic holy land for communist mobilization, attracting educated and progressive young people to migrate there. Among the newcomers to Yan'an was Ding Ling, a revolutionary feminist writer. She soon became one of the most influential figures in Yan'an cultural circles, serving as director of the Chinese literature and Arts Association. When Ding Ling arrived, Mao wrote a poem praising her decision to leave the bourgeois life in Shanghai and join the revolution: "Yesterday a young lady of literature. Today you have become a general."[9]

Also in 1936, a group of female students from Ginling College (or Jinling Women's College) participated in the Olympics held in Berlin, Germany. Graduating around a thousand students with bachelor's and master's degrees, Ginling College enjoyed a high reputation, both domestic and abroad. Educators at Ginling advocated for the importance of healthy female bodies as a source of self-respect for young women. The school was known for its unique curriculum. For example, among all colleges in China, only Ginling College integrated aesthetics with PE. Thus, PE was the only required course for students during all four years of college.

In the 1930s, the Sino-Foreign Protestant Establishment, a term coined by historian Daniel Bays in referring to a loose network of Protestant mission institutions that dominated the Republican era, had transitioned to indigenous leadership by educated Chinese. A popular saying testifies to the prominent statures of two Chinese Christian intellectuals who played leadership roles in key Christian institutions: *bei zhao nan wei*, which translates into "one has to know T. C. Chao in the north and Wei Zhuomin (or Francis Wei) in the south."[10] Chao was the dean of the Divinity School at Yenching University, "the flagship" of Christian colleges in China and "the voice" for liberal Protestant theology. Wei served as the president of Huazhong (Central China) University. Another equally prominent educator was Wu Yifang, the female president of Ginling College in Nanjing. A popular saying in China at the time went: "Among men, there is Cai Yuanpei, and among women, there is Wu Yifang," Wu earned the reputation that ranked her side by side with Cai Yuanpei, a renowed philosopher and the president of Peking University. Compared to the Republican government's two public funded universities, China boasted thirteen private Christian colleges and universities. Historian Daniel Bays comments on the benefits of these institutions in bettering women's prospect in society: "The impact of the Protestant churches and schools in showing new public roles and careers in broadening the life possibilities for women was enormous."[11]

Although Wu Yifang held a doctorate degree in biology from the University of Michigan, her own path of pursuing education had been full of adversities. She was born as the second youngest of four siblings into a family of influence in Huangzhou of Zhejiang Province. Her grandfather and father all served as local magistrates. When it became a trend among rich families to send their daughters to school in Hangzhou, Wu's older sister and herself insisted on getting an education there. Initially, the parents declined their request, considering it untraditional for girls to appear in public. By then, the family had chosen to bind the girls' feet. But Wu's sister attempted suicide as a protest. After that, the family send these two girls to a school in Hangzhou, where Wu's scholar-official uncle Chen Shutong lived. Wu Yifang was twelve during the year she started formal education. One day, her uncle reminded both Wu and her sister the importance of grasping a foreign language. Later they applied to a girls' school in Shanghai that offered English classes.[12] There Wu and her sister were taught that women can be patriots and serve their country. After some time in Shanghai, they applied into a girls' school in Suzhou that offered modern courses such as history, biology, and physics. When Wu Yifang reached her late teens, a series of misfortunes began to visit her family. In 1909, Wu's father committed suicide after a political scandal and economic loss, and her family circumstances deteriorated. The family moved to live with relatives. In 1911, when the Xinhai Revolution broke out, Wu's older brother who desired to study abroad felt deep despair about his future and also took his own life. Tragically, in a single month, eighteen-year-old Wu Yifang also lost her mother and sister. Eventually, she moved to live with her benevolent uncle Chen. Seeing Wu's growing melancholy, Chen encouraged her to move on with life. Then he told Wu about great people in Chinese history who had also suffered adversity. Wu recalled her uncle's care as deep and fatherly. Since then, Wu became determined to pursue academic study, but she realized the difficulties due to her bound feet. Then she "imposed on herself . . . the painful processes of unbinding and somewhat lengthening her deformed feet."[13] In 1914, after Wu graduated from school, she moved with her uncle's family to Beijing, where she found her first job teaching English at an elementary school. Wu was overwhelmed with joy when she could finally support her grandmother and younger sister.

The idea of attending college seemed like a luxury for Wu Yifang, when she had to work and support the family. But an American teacher at her former school in Hangzhou returned to China to teach at Ginling College. This teacher wrote and invited Wu to consider attending Ginling. Its founding president was an American missionary Mrs. Laurence Thurston sent by the American Presbyterian Mission. With her uncle's support, in 1916, Wu Yifang attended Ginling College with a cohort of six new students. She cherished the opportunity and strived to achieve academically. Her leadership became widely recognized among faculty and fellow students. Due to her excelling organizational skills, she was elected president of the first student self-government association. At this Christian institution of higher education, she also converted to Christianity in 1916 under the influence of a classmate. When Wu was about to graduate in 1919, the May Fourth Movement took place and soon spread to Ginling College. Deeply concerned with the corruption of the Republican government, Wu Yifang organized over fifty student activists to support the cause. They held a cross, marched in the street, gave public speeches and raised funds. Famous female writer Xie Wanying (or Bing Xin) was greatly impressed by Wu's public speaking.[14] The leadership of this group of young women from Ginling College won widespread applause among Chinese intellectuals in Nanjing. When she graduated that summer, Wu was one of the first Chinese women to obtain a bachelor's degree. She was also overheard saying to a group of freshwomen at Ginling that "it is not true that when you have education, you do not need religion."[15]

In 1922, when anti-Christian activism was gaining momentum in Beijing, Wu Yifang taught English at the Government Higher Normal School for Women. When Wu served as a translator for a female U.S. college president, the latter was impressed by her fluent English and calm composure. This president encouraged her to pursue further study in America and strongly recommended her for a Barbour scholarship at the University of Michigan. Wu Yifang was able to study in the same institution that famously trained Chinese physician and evangelist Shi Meiyu in the 1890s. At the University of Michigan, Wu was elected to be the president of the North America Chinese Christian Students Association. Her patriotic feelings for China grew more zealous in a foreign land. When the May Thirtieth Incident happened in 1925, she closely followed the news in American newspapers and hoped for her motherland to be free of humiliation. In 1926, when an Australian prime minister gave a public speech on campus and referred to China as "not qualified to be a modern nation," Wu Yifang published a critical response the next day in the university newspaper.[16] Both American and Chinese students celebrated her courage and passion for national dignity.

As Wu was completing her doctoral dissertation in 1927, she received an invitation from Ginling College to become its president.[17] Before she accepted the position, Wu challenged the school to adjust its rules, such as creating service programs that reflected indigenous practices and ending a culture of elite superiority. After Ginling College declared these new rules, she accepted the job offer. After her final doctoral defense, Wu Yifang visited many colleges in America, trying to prepare herself by observing best practices in these well-established institutions. In the fall, thirty-five-year-old Wu Yifang returned and resumed leadership as the first Chinese woman to head a higher education institution. Chiang Kai-shek and his wife participated in her inauguration ceremony. The school's motto "Enrich life (*housheng*)" was taken from *Shang Shu*, a classical Confucian text. As Wu Yifang put it in daily language, "To enrich life is the purpose of living. We do not just live for ourselves, but also for helping others and blessing the society through our wisdom and ability. Doing so is beneficial to others, and our own lives can be enriched too."[18] The motto was in harmony with Wu's Christian values.

In Wu Yifang's twenty-three year presidency from 1928 to 1951, she accomplished bold reforms in teaching and administration.[19] In the midst of Japanese air raids, she encouraged students to organize a variety of patriotic activities, such as newspapers, fundraisers, plays, and reading clubs. Like many Christian colleges, Ginling also emphasized Christian values such as service and stewardship. During this time dominated by warlords, Wu tactfully fended off threats of occupation by Yan Xishan's army.[20] Under the Republican government's demand for Christian colleges to comply with secular policies, she negotiated hard with the Ministry of Education, securing the registration status of Ginling College as a nationally recognized institution. At the same time, however, she also made religious content optional, such as chapel time and Bible courses. The college also opened up to non-Christian students during recruitment. To align with standards of Western modern higher education, she adapted Ginling's academic disciplines to include core majors such as History, Geography, Chemistry, Biology, Sociology, Music, English, Chinese, and PE. She also recruited famous scholars to be on the faculty. She was the first college president to begin a credit system with stipulations. Each student should choose four credits of natural science, one credit of social science, and then freely choose electives. There was no barrier to switch majors either. In the area of curriculum design, Wu insisted that it should fit students' needs. When a new student wanted to major in oceanology, Wu Yifang pushed through many obstacles to set up this discipline. Later this student became China's first oceanographer.[21] Wu Yifang's efforts ensured Ginling's stable development as a Christian, feminist, and government-associated institution.[22] In 1939, for example, Wu Yifang successfully created the Department of Home Economics. Her hope for women's education through Ginling is that young women would be trained in how to work for and help rural families. Students formed associations to teach in rural schools, to set up service stations, and to experiment ways of enhancing agricultural productivity. When warfare escalated, Wu Yifang herself headed a Wartime Service Society, guiding Ginling students to care for wounded soldiers and civilians. In 1944, over forty graduates from Ginling enlisted in the army.

From 1937 to 1949, China was enmeshed in a perpetual state of war, both externally and internally. During a time of Japanese invasion, Chinese church leadership was on its own after Western missionaries left. The few Western missionaries who remained in Japanese-occupied China were considered enemy nationals, with restricted movements.[23] In 1942, the majority of these missionaries were put into internment campus, mostly in Shandong or in the suburbs of Shanghai, or the Philippines.[24] As a result, when Western missionaries returned to China after the war, the power relationship between local Chinese believers and these missionaries were dramatically changed.[25] This shift also touched on the status of Christian colleges. Chinese leadership in these postwar colleges resisted the demands from returning mission boards for merging or downsizing.[26] When it comes to the theological climate of the Chinese church, indigenous leaders such as Wang Mingdao preached and wrote more millenarian, end-time sermons, calling for repentance rather than tending to the needy.[27] On the one hand, a fairly large portion of the Chinese church tended to retreat into self-absorbed separatism. On the other hand, certain unifying "visions" emerged to invigorate believers by offering a collective identity. For example, the scattering of believers across northwestern China also led to the creation of the "Chinese Back-to-Jerusalem Evangelistic Band," which Watchman Nee briefly participated in.[28]

A composed negotiator even in intense circumstances, Wu Yifang showed great political leadership which qualified her to be on the People's Political Council in 1938, together with Mao Zedong.[29] She was also the executive committee member of Madam Chiang Kai-shek's women's relief project. At this point, Wu was critical of the Chinese Communist Party because she saw it as a nondemocratic political system. She was equally critical of corruption within Chiang Kai-shek's government. When Chiang and his wife invited Wu Yifang to serve as the Minister of Education for the Republican government, she declined. Madame Chiang visited her again with the same job offer and tried to persuade her that this would further put her motto "Enriching Life" into practice. Wu Yifang declined a second time. Her uncle Chen and her younger sister showed strong preference toward the Soviet Union, and they had a large influence on Wu Yifang. Like how Zeng Baosun came to an anti-communist view in the 1920s, Wu's social location largely conditioned her attitude about whether Chinese Christians should support the Nationalist Party or the Chinese Communist Party. Unlike Zeng, Wu was willing to lend some trust to the communists because she came from a lower social class and had been disillusioned with the corruption of China's first Republic. By then, the fate of Chinese Protestantism had been too closely tied up with politics. What was at stake between Chinese Christians' support for either political party would be the life and death of not just Christian colleges, but the legitimacy of Christianity in China for the next three decades.

Japan's invasion in China provided opportunities for Chinese women leaders to step onto a global stage and to advocate for their country. In 1943, Wu Yifang organized a team of six Chinese professors to tour in America, advocating for support for the Chinese people's anti-Japanese efforts. Wu's leadership in this endeavor won positive appraisal by U.S. president Roosevelt who praised her as "a wisdom goddess." In 1945, as a member of the nonpartisan group, Wu Yifang became the only woman leader among the Chinese delegation at the San Francisco Conference. There she advocated for women's rights and ensured their inclusion in the founding document of the United Nations.[30] Wu was also one of only four women delegates to sign the original UN Charter. This public service gained her great fame. Afterward, she received numerous speaking requests from the United States and two honorary degrees from American universities.[31] Wu Yifang proved herself to be a charismatic public speaker with concise language and composed passion. In 1948, Ginling students celebrated the twentieth anniversary of Wu Yifang's presidency. They staged a drama production about the courtship of a Ms. Wu by many suitors, and this Ms. Wu had eyes for only one love, which is the "god of education."[32] Young women in Ginling used this story to salute Wu Yifang's celibacy as a personal sacrifice for the cause of education.

While much progress for women's education and other issues had been made through women leaders like Wu Yifang in the 1940s, the climate at the communist base Yan'an deteriorated. Within a few years, young women activists who had participated in urban student movements before arriving in Yan'an grew increasingly dissatisfied with the gendered labor practices as well as double standards among CCP leaders. On Women's Day of 1942, Ding Ling wrote an article in an official communist party newspaper, questioning the party's policies concerning women, who were demeaned if they focused on household duties, but also ridiculed if they remained unmarried and worked independently. A more scathing criticism from Ding was that many male communist cadres divorced their unwanted first wives by using the party's divorce provisions just because they wanted to find younger women. She also called for an education campaign concerning gender equality. Historian Margery Wolf writes how the communist revolution failed to deliver its promise: "Women are again being encouraged to give up their jobs in favor of their children and to value their roles as socialist mothers and wives."[33] She adds,

> Beyond a doubt, women participated in China's revolution and believed it to be as much their revolution as their male peers. A few of them along the way saw the revolution narrowing to exclude those principles for which they thought they were fighting and protested. . . . [But] the primary function of the women's organizations remained that of mobilizing women for production . . . any woman who seemed to be suggesting revolution rather than reform as a solution to the burdens of women was quickly accused of error, of neglecting the class struggle in favor of a narrow feminist one.[34]

Given Ding Ling's reputation, her writing sounded a sharp note of dissent. It was met with condemnation from the party leadership, including Mao Zedong himself. As another historian writes, "Perhaps the description of Yan'an cadres casting off their wives hit a nerve. Mao had a reputation for womanizing."[35] Weeks after Ding published an editorial on the *Liberation Daily* about problems in Yan'an, Mao Zedong convened a meeting addressing intellectuals, warning them not to attack revolutionary people or parties. Ding Ling was forced to retract her views and gave a public confession. Ding was forced to withdraw from both political and literary activities for the next two years.[36] In February 1943, the party's decision to avoid discussions of women's social and political inequality was made explicit at the meeting of the Central Committee.[37] To the outside world, Ding Ling wrote and admitted that although women in Yan'an were better off than elsewhere in China, they were still in fact subjected to the double standards of men. Such writings led to her being deprived of her positions and exiled to work in the countryside like any other dissident.[38] As historian Kay Ann Johnson comments, "The party had proclaimed lofty theories of gender equality, but failed to deal with the actual conditions and attitudes which held women in an inferior position."[39]

Around the same time, Wu Yifang's relationship with the Chiang Kai-shek government also deteriorated. In 1946, she protested the violence of the Nationalist Party against students and civilians in the Xia Guan incident and resigned from the National Congress. A year later, a similar incident of violence broke out in Nanjing, leaving student demonstrators injured. Wu Yifang challenged Chiang Kai-shek at a luncheon of the People's Council and demanded the deposition of Nanjing's head of police. Her public censure angered Chiang Kai-shek himself. These few historical moments might have been conducive to Wu Yifang's gradual leaning toward the new regime rulers who had not yet shown such public brutality. In April 1949, Nanjing fell into a chaos when Nationalist Party officials fled to Taiwan. Wu Yifang refused to board the plane with them.

Wu Yifang was not alone in her optimism about the communist regime. In fact, many Western theologians and ministers such as Randolph Sailer, William van Etten Casey, David Paton, and C. S. Song as well as indigenous church leaders Kuang-hsun Ting (Ding Guangxun) and Yao-tsung Wu (Wu Yaozong) did not hesitate in positing that a Marxist China could also be Christian.[40] The Lutheran World Federation even called the international mission community to end mission-sending to China after affirming God's redemptive action in installing the new Chinese regime.[41] As historian Daniel Bays comments, "It was difficult for the Christian churches to avoid lining up behind Chiang Kai-shek's government. After all, he was a baptized Christian."[42] The number of Christian leaders who were "disgusted with the proven incompetence and venality of the Guomindang government" was only a handful.[43] But these key leaders later became catalyzing forces in funneling the Chinese church into a path under the new communist regime. Since 1948, left-wing-leaning Christian leaders, such as Wu Yaozong, have criticized the Sino-Foreign Protestant Establishment for its compliance with imperialist forces.[44] Although the ensuing controversy among Chinese Protestant leaders cost Wu his job as editor of *Tianfeng* (Heavenly Wind), a widely circulated Christian publication, he gained the notice of the Chinese Communist Party. As Daniel Bays describes, in 1950, "it was Wu's reputation and connections that opened doors for them [progressive Christians] to see some top leaders, including Zhou Enlai."[45] Gradually, Wu's rhetoric became more and more clear, one of endorsing the new regime as "the only hope for a Christianity which had lost its reforming spirit and had become a slave to capitalism and imperialism."[46] Many Christian leaders cherished this hope that Christianity would have a new future in China.

As an educator, Wu Yifang's optimism was also due to the fact that China already had an effective education system, which she assumed would work for societal improvement. Her criticism against the new communist regime softened. She began to actively engage in political committees such as the Nanjing People's Representatives in order to continue her advocacy for women's higher education. Wu Yifang also watched with great pride as Mao Zedong proclaimed the establishment of the People's Republic of China. Nevertheless, she certainly had her reservations. For example, in 1951, Wu Yifang declined the offer from Republic China government to be its Minster of Education. She saw the temptation of getting too close to the core of communist power. But meanwhile, Wu Yifang agreed to serve as the Minister of Education for Jiangsu Province, where more organic local social relations could keep things in check.

At the founding of the communist regime, Wu Yifang's conflicted feelings were shared by other Christian educators. On the one hand, they had reservations about revolutionary radicalism that was built into atheistic Chinese communism. On the other hand, they longed for an independent new regime that would make the church truly Chinese. By 1949, Chinese Christians have felt the need to disassociate themselves from foreign missionary connections in order to "divest Chinese Christianity of the imperialist stain."[47] Indigenous church leaders such as Watchman Nee and Wang Mingdao expressed such sentiments. The "three-self" principles promised by Chinese communist leaders appealed to them.[48] Therefore, many chose to believe that the new regime would tolerate the coexistence of Christianity and communism. After all, the voice of progressive, communist-sympathizing voice of young students have been heard on Christian college campuses before an impending communist victory. Society at large, both domestic and international, had certain rosy expectations about a new China. Some mused:

> China's was a path of growth that eventually diverged from that of the USSR and from the Western model. Nor was it geared to wasteful over-consumption, it seemed. . . . This Chinese model accorded dignity to farming people, pioneered new forms of gender relations, and new models of practical democracy. So New China was in some eyes a beacon for the world.[49]

In 1949, upon the independence of China under communist rule, prominent theologian and dean of Yenching's Divinity School T. C. Chao wrote a public letter commending the new communist regime to the faculty and student body of Yenching University, saying, "We who remain have reasons to rejoice in the success of the revolutionary forces, though we are by no means Communists ourselves."[50] In keeping with the need to "modernize China," Chao wrote, "the whole structure of Chinese society must be recreated. A revolution is necessary if the task cannot be accomplished by a process of evolution."[51] He concluded by saying that "no thoughtful Christian in China can regard this unexpected speed without a deep sense of gratitude to God."[52]

The progressive policies of the new communist regime included the New Marriage Law in 1950, which enacted a right to divorce, abolished arranged marriages and marriage by purchase, asserted the equal status of men and women in marriage and their equal rights to property. It required men and women to reach a new legal age in order to marry. The law also inserted a compulsory mediation process into divorce situations. Historian Gail Hershatter states that "By issuing this law, the new national leadership signaled its desire to end marriage practices that had been criticized at least since the May Fourth Movement, as well as its intention to insert the state into marriage, formerly the domain of the family, by issuing marriage certificates."[53] Robert Bickers comments that its implementation was accompanied "by mass campaigns as well as violence . . . [and] it had a revolutionary impact, particularly in rural China."[54]

But as historian Lamin O. Sanneh argues, "Mao was too mindful of his nemesis in the Christian-inspired Kuomintang Nationalist movements led by Sun Yat-sen (d. 1925), and later by Chiang Kai-shek (d. 1975), to ignore Christianity as an ideological foe."[55] Even Wu Yaozong himself noticed during his meetings with Mao Zedong who made mocking comments on Wu's Christian God. Meanwhile, apprehensive missionaries continued to trickle out of China. In September 1950, the London Missionary Society decided to withdraw from China completely. Three months later, China Inland Mission evacuated all 1,000 mission workers. Even at this time, Zhou Enlai affirmed the party's policy for allowing Christians to continue their evangelism. But the party also issued warnings that imperialist and counterrevolutionary elements may hide under the cloak of religion. In fact, mixed messaging and conflicting mandates about religious affairs coexisted throughout the history of the People's Republic of China. On September 23, 1950, a document titled *The Christian Manifesto* was published on the front page of the *People's Daily*, China's no. 1 communist newspaper. Wu Yaozong and other church leaders who drafted this document began a campaign to gather signatures. As a politicized test of loyalty, it created polarizing responses from the broader Chinese church. In the following two years, this "Three-Self Manifesto" was signed by over 400,000 Protestants, roughly half of all Chinese Protestants. On January 18, 1951, the new government appropriated all missionary colleges funded by foreign money. In May, Wu Yaozong tried to broaden the support base and recruited twenty Christian leaders, including T. C. Chao to form the "Preparatory Council of the China Christian Resist-AmErica Help-Korea Three-Self Reform Movement," which replaced the functions of the National Christian Council. Later it was renamed as the "Three-Self Patriotic Movement" (TSPM), under the direct supervision of the Religious Affairs Bureau, which was supervised by CCP's United Front Work Department.[56] While the Catholic Church did not make similar moves, its Papal Nuncio was expelled from China in 1952.

Tragically, within just two years of the new regime, China's thirteen Christian colleges became the first casualties of the Communist takeover.[57] After the rapidly escalating U.S.-Korean War which placed U.S./UN forces in bloody combat against the Chinese volunteers from the People's Liberation Army in Korea, the U.S. government froze all Chinese assets in their domestic realm, and the Chinese state retaliated by freezing all U.S. assets in China. With this war and diplomatic impasse came a flush of zealous patriotism and anti-American sentiments within China assisted by a communist propaganda apparatus. Public opinions became radicalized in China, with denunciation meetings extended to all Protestant institutions, including denominations, YMCAs, the Christian Literature Society, and the China Christian Council. Students and young people publicly denounced and humiliated the faculty

of Christian higher education institutions, including T. C. Chao and Lu
Zhiwei, president of Yenching University, as the "running dogs" of American
imperialism. Even Lu's daughter was mobilized to renounce him at a public
denunciation meeting. Francis Wei, just one year after he was a delegate to
the first conference of the TSPM (1951), formulated plans to rid the church of
foreign connections; however, intensified communist campaigns soon forced
Wei to step down from his presidency of Huazhong University (previously
known as Hua Chung College). Later, Wei was marginalized as an instructor
in logic, and he spent the rest of his time writing on the philosophical thought
of Immanuel Kant.

When the communist regime decided to close down all Christian colleges
in 1952, and when Ginling College was asked to surrender its campus to
form Nanjing Normal College, Wu Yifang did not protest and maintained
her leadership position in the wider circle of higher education. On a few
public occasions, Wu even openly criticized the social service programs at
Christian colleges as venues of Western imperialism.[58] Though it remains a
mystery why she expressed support for a course of action that ran against her
ideals, historians have documented the draconian political pressure placed
on Chinese Christian intellectuals. According to Daniel Bays, "The regime
had been relatively successful in discrediting and toppling from power those
Protestant leaders who might be hard to control."[59] By 1955, almost all
prominent church leaders had either been publicly denounced, charged with
imperialist affiliations, or imprisoned. Some left the country and exiled to
Hong Kong or Western parts of the world.

From the late 1930s to 1940s, the hope of gradual reforms dissipated with
subsequent geopolitical conflicts and civil wars. Repeated despair at China's
prolonged indignity and disorder grew into an agitating patriotic impatience
among the urban elites until communism offered a comprehensive but radical solution to uplift China. The rural and urban poor who were mired deeper
in an increasingly stratified China also found communist ideology more
promising than transcendent religious ideas. For the Sino-Foreign Protestant
Establishment which formed in the Republican era, the time had come for
it to face a new political ideology that demanded the status of a civil religion. Both in China and in other parts of the world, observers had yet to
understand what this new regime would bring about. In the 1930s, when the
Chinese Communist Party was just emerging as a worthy alternative to the
Republican regime, many observers failed to notice its oppressive tendency.
Edgar Snow's favorable impression of Yan'an and Ding Ling's experiences
as a revolutionary feminist both reflect the paradoxes offered by this new
path. Though advocating for women's liberation, many revolutionary groups
were essentially guided by an ideology of male dominance.[60] While embracing a more radical Marxist ideology, Chinese women became oblivious to its
new forms of patriarchy. According to the communist regime, the resolution

of the women's question in China is to be "dependent upon the future success of economic modernization."[61]

Chinese women leaders such as Wu Yifang may have found communism and Christianity irreconcilable at the beginning. But they soon began to emphasize the affinity between these two for pragmatic reasons. After all, China's national independence remained their primary devotion. Crossing the fine line between progressive Christianity and revolutionary activism, many Christian women leaders found the Marxist theory a ready-made formula to fulfill their role for a new China. Sometimes their hopes materialized when the regime made legislative changes for the benefits of women. One example was the Marriage Law and Agrarian Reform Law in 1950. As Bickers points out, it was first published in English, and soon women's testimonials appeared in English-language magazines. "This was more than simple propaganda, but it played a central role within the story of New China sanctioned by the state."[62] Like the narrative about peasants' livelihood in Old China, the past for Chinese women was painted "relentlessly bleak."[63] Even the feminist awakening of the 1920s was refashioned as immoral and unprogressive.

It marked an important moment of progress, catalyzing an unprecedented tide of over one million divorce cases.[64] However, while freeing women from some formerly suppressive customs, it also effectively "inserted the state into private and/or community decisions concerning courtship, engagement, marriage, divorce, property arrangements, and even with whom it was appropriate and legitimate to have sexual intercourse."[65] This new institution was also used by communist cadres to bring women into the struggle against the landlords and to encourage them to speak out in public meetings on the land reform issues. In these land reform campaigns, women were also warned explicitly not to let women's "special problems" interfere with the important land reform work.[66]

In her later life, Wu Yifang refused special privileges in daily living offered by the communist regime. Even though the new communist government assigned her a personal assistant and a driver, Wu insisted on using public transportation. These actions of humility won respect from the closest colleagues around her. During the Cultural Revolution when neighbors turned against one another, these two people who used to serve Wu Yifang refused to betray her. In 1982, when she was hospitalized, Wu resigned from the position of vice provincial governor of Jiangsu. Her students recall that Wu had expressed the wish to reopen a women's college. She reasoned that "in co-ed colleges with both men and women, how can we nurture women who can rise to leadership?"[67] In 1985, Wu wrote a formal proposal to Jiangsu provincial government about setting up a Ginling Women's College under Nanjing Normal University. Unfortunately, Wu Yifang never saw this plan come to fruition. She passed away six months later. The Ginling Women's College was founded in 1987, a fitting legacy of Wu Yifang's influence. It is still supported by alumni around the world.

NOTES

1. Edgar Snow, *Red Star over China* (New York: Random House, 1937), 42.

2. One founding member of Chinese Communist Party Yun Daiying was active in the YMCA before 1920 (Han 1988; Tan and Yu 2009). Tan, Xiaofang, and Zixia Yu, "Yun Daiying and YMCA," *Huazhong Normal University Journal* 6 (2009): 122–29. Also see Jun, Xing, *Baptized in the Fire of Revolution: The American Social Gospel and the YMCA in China, 1919–1937* (Bethlehem: Lehigh University Press, 1996), 136.

3. Peter Vladimirov, *The Vladimirov Diaries: Yenan, China, 1942–1945* (New York: Doubeday, 1975), 296. Also see Joseph W. Esherick (ed.), *Lost Chance in China: The World War II Dispatches of John. S. Service* (New York: Rando House, 1974), 178–81.

4. Quoted in Stuart Gelder, *The Chinese Communists* (London: Victor Gollancz, 1946), xxxviii.

5. *The New York Times*, August 20 of 1944, p. 23. Quoted in Bickers, *Out of China*, 236–37.

6. Ono, *Chinese Women in a Century of Revolution*, 168–69.

7. Hershatter, *Women and China's Revolutions*, 168.

8. Mao Zedong, *Report from Xunwu*. Trans. by Roger R. Thompson (Stanford: Stanford University Press, 1990), 216.

9. Quoted in Delia Davin, *Mao: A Very Short Introduction* (New York: Oxford University Press), 86.

10. Quoted in Peter Tze Ming Ng, "Lecture III: On T. C. Chao," *The Four Anglican Theologians I Respected Most* (Kowloon, Hong Kong: All Saints' Church, 2006), 28–39. Also see Li Ma and Jin Li, "The Tragic Irony of a Patriotic Mission: The Indigenous Leadership of Francis Wei and T. C. Chao, Radicalized Patriotism, and the Reversal of Protestant Mission in China," *Religions* 2020, 11 (4): 175. https://www.mdpi.com/2077-1444/11/4/175

11. Bays, *A New History*, 94.

12. Heping Zhou, "Wu Yifang Yearbook," *Journal of Jiangsu Institute of Socialism* (in Chinese), 1 (2013): 3. Wei He, "'The New Women' and Women's Education in Modern China: The Case of Wu Yifang," *Southeastern China of Technology Journal*, 3 (2016): 108.

13. "Biography of Wu Yifang," University of Michigan online archives, https://rackham.umich.edu/project/yi-fang-wu/

14. Bing Xin, "A Great Woman of Her Generation: In Commemoration of Wu Yifang," In Yue Sun et al., ed., *Memory of Wu Yifang* (Nanjing: Jiangsu Education Publishing House, 1987), 140.

15. Ibid., 161.

16. Quoted in Heping Zhou, *Remembering Wu Yifang* (Nanjing: Jiangsu People's Press, 2013), 125.

17. In 1928, Republican government of China claimed back education rights from foreign missionaries.

18. Quoted in "Wu Yifang: A Noble Woman of Her time," China Democratic Society website, September 5, 2019. http://www.mj.org.cn/mjzt/content/2019-09/05/content_334305.htm

19. Helen M. Schneider, "Mobilizing Women: The Women's Advisory Council, Resistance and Reconstruction during China's War with Japan," *European Journal of East Asian Studies* 11 (2) 2012: 217.

20. Mary Jo Waelchi, *Abundant Life: Matilda Thurston, Wu Yifang and Guilin College*, a PhD dissertation at Ohio State University (2002), 121.

21. Huanqi Qian, "Wu Yifang: All for Life-Enriching Education," *Chinese Educators*, June 18, 2019. Online resource. http://www.jyb.cn/rmtzgjsb/201906/t 20190618_242943.html

22. Waelchi, *Abundant Life*, 123.

23. Brook, "Toward Independence," 317–37.

24. Langdon Gilkey, *Shantung Compound* (New York: Harper & Row, 1966).

25. Bays, *A New History*, 143.

26. Liu Jiafeng, "Same Bed, Different Dreams: The American Postwar Plan for China's Christian Colleges, 1943–1946," in Daniel H. Bays and Ellen Widmer, ed., *China's Christian Colleges: Cross-Cultural Connections, 1900–1950* (Stanford: Stanford University Press, 2009), 218–40.

27. Wang Mingdao, *Ling Shi Ji Kan* (*Spiritual Food Quarterly*), (Hong Kong: Olive Press, 1937–1955), 1937 Issue.

28. Bays, *A New History*, 146. Bays states this ministry is different from the purported Back To Jerusalem Movement since 2000.

29. Waelchi, *Abundant Life*, 233.

30. Rebecca Adami, *Women and the Universal Declaration of Human Rights*, Vol. 32 (New York: Routledge, 2019), 35.

31. Judy Yung, *Unbound Feet: A Social History of Chinese Women in San Francisco* (Berkeley: University of California Press, 1995).

32. Kailin Wang, "Different Destinies of Yang Yinyu and Wu Yifang," *Essays* (in Chinese), Issue 6, 2012. Online resource. http://www.linyixianeryuan.com/xingyezix un/34895360.htm

33. Wolf, *Revolution Postponed*, 27.

34. Ibid., 17, 272.

35. Hershatter, *Women and China's Revolutions*, 206.

36. See Spence, *The Gate of Heavenly Peace*. Yi-tsi Mei Feuerwerker, *Ding Ling's Ideology and Narrative in Modern Chinese Literature* (Cambridge: Harvard University Press, 1982).

37. Kay Ann Johnson, *Women, the Family, and Peasant revolution in China*, (Chicago: University of Chicago Press, 1985), 74.

38. Spence, *The Gate of Heavenly Peace*, 289–95. Also see Kumari Jayawardena, *Feminism and Nationalism in the Third World* (1986), 194.

39. Johnson, *Women, the Family, and Peasant revolution in China*, 74.

40. Philip L. Wickeri, *Seeking Common Ground: Protestant Christianity, the Three-Self Movement, and China's United Front* (Maryknoll: Orbis Books, 1988), 7ff.

41. "The Louvain Consultation," 23–25. Quoted in Lamin O. Sanneh, *Disciples of All Nations: Pillars of World Christianity* (New York: Oxford University Press, 2007), 254.

42. Bays, *A New History*, 149.

43. Ibid.

44. Wu Yaozong, "The Present-Day Tragedy of Christianity (1948)," *Documents of the Three-self Movement*, Wallace C. Merwin and Francis P. Jones, comps. (New York: National Council of the Churches of Christ in the United States, 1963), 1–5.

45. Bays, *A New History*, 160.

46. Quoted in Richard C. Bush Jr., *Religion in Communist China* (Nashville: Abingdon Press, 1970), 176.

47. Bickers, *Out of China*, 279.

48. The communists did not invent the philosophy of a "three-self" church. The missiological ideals of self-support, self-governance, and self-propagation were proposed by Rufus Anderson and Henry Venn, heads of the American and British boards of foreign mission as early as in the mid-nineteenth century.

49. Bickers, *Out of China*, 294.

50. Chao, Tzu-. Chen. "Days of Rejoicing in China," in *Collected Works of T. C. Chao* (in Chinese). Volume 5 (Beijing: Religion and Culture Press, 2007), 534–37.

51. Ibid.

52. Ibid.

53. Hershatter, *Women and China's Revolutions*, 222.

54. Bickers, *Out of China*, 303. Neil J. Diamant, *Revolutionizing the Family: Politics, Love and Divorce in Urban and Rural China, 1949–1968* (Berkeley: University of California Press, 2000). Li Fengjin, *How the New Marriage Law Helped Chinese Women Stand Up*, ed. and trans. Susan Glosser (Portland: Opal Mogus Books, 2005).

55. Sanneh, *Disciples of All Nations*, 244.

56. This institutional structure lasted for a decade until Mao's Cultural Revolution abolished all religious institutions in 1966.

57. Deng, *Private Education in Modern China*, 67–68.

58. Helen M. Schneider, "Raising the Standard of Family Life: Ginling Women's College and Christian Social Service in Republican China," in Choi Hyaeweoi and Jolly Margaret, ed., *Divine Domesticities: Christian Paradoxes in Asia and the Pacific* (Canberra: Australian National University Press, 2014), 9.

59. Bays, *A New History*, 165–66.

60. Johnson, *Women, the Family and Peasant Revolution in China*, 43.

61. Phyllis Andors, *The Unfinished Revolution of Chinese Women, 1949–80* (Bloomington: Indiana University Press, 1983), 168.

62. Bickers, *Out of China*, 303–4.

63. Ibid.

64. See Gail Hershatter, *Women in China's Long Twentieth Century* (Berkeley: University of California Press, 2007). Also see Diamant, *Revolutionizing the Family*.

65. Diamant, *Revolutionizing the Family*, xi.

66. Vivienne Shue, *Peasant China in Transition: The Dynamics of Development toward Socialism, 1949–1956* (Berkeley and Los Angeles: University of California Press, 1980).

67. "Wu Yifang: China's First Female College President," History Channel of Sohu.com, November 11, 2009. https://m.sohu.com/n/472950068/

Part II

THE ERA OF MILITANT COMMUNISM

INTELLECTUALS, RESISTERS, ACCOMMODATORS

Communist appropriation of private property took place through land reforms and nationalization of resources in areas from commerce to higher education institutions. The U.S.-Korean War (1950–1953) intensified anti-foreign sentiments and anti-capitalist campaigns. Patriotic church leaders who wanted no foreign control began the Three-self Patriotic Movement (1950). Party control through the three-self system divided the Chinese church, leading to imprisonment of nonconforming leaders. Following the Anti-Rightist Campaign (1957–1959), returnees with Western education experiences became easy targets for demotion and public humiliation. After a brief recuperation from the Great Famine caused by Mao's Great Leap Forward (1958–1961), a new wave of Cultural Revolution again targeted at Christian intellectuals and educated Chinese with Western education background as Maoism became a de facto politicized religion enforced by the state. Many committed suicide during the most intense phase of persecution. By then rural communes and urban work units became the dominant forms of socioeconomic structures, locking individuals into strict grids that were easy to monitor. There was very little space for people to freely assemble or express themselves. Even the family home space became heavily censored and politicized.

There have also been Christians who survived this oppressive regime period by making adaptions in their fields. Some even made significant contributions to society when China made a pragmatic turn toward economic liberalization in the 1980s. Rural communes and collective farming disintegrated. The central planning system gradually gave way to market structures. I term the period from 1979 to 1992 as the phase of Pragmatic Communism when the party embraced partial economic liberalization without clearly redefining private property rights. The urban work unit system was still there, prohibiting large scale of assembly beyond home-gathering groups. State surveillance continued, and the stigma of being Christians was still there.

Chapter 5

Patriotic Intellectuals and the New Regime

Like many Chinese intellectuals studying abroad in the spring of 1949, Zhao Luorui, who was writing her dissertation in the University of Chicago, longed to return and serve a new China that was on the horizon. As the daughter of prominent Chinese theologian T. C. Chao (Zhao Zichen) and a well-known translator of works by T. S. Eliot and Walt Whitman in her own right, Zhao Luorui had enjoyed a respected status among educated Chinese. Meanwhile, civil warfare in Beijing and Tianjing had intensified such that many feared that there might be a disruption in U.S.-China travel. Zhao's father had been urging all his children overseas to return to the motherland.[1] A job has been promised to her at Yenching University. Her husband Chen Mengjia, a reputable poet and archaeologist, had toured around Europe and returned a few months earlier to teach at Qinghua University in Beijing. He also served as a chair-curator for the institution's ancient relics. All these factors led Zhao Luorui to drop her original plan of taking part in the University of Chicago commencement in June. Determined to reunite with her husband and family, Zhao Luorui boarded the last plane to Beijing, at which point the city had already been sieged by the People's Liberation Army. For Zhao Luorui, who deeply believed that "a clean, new government dedicated to social justice was what China needed," this return trip to China was a moment of palpable patriotism and optimism.[2]

Even before Zhao Luorui returned, she had been actively recruiting staff for Yenching University. Wu Ningkun, who was also working on his doctorate at the University of Chicago, was persuaded by Zhao to return and work at Yenching. An enthusiastic patriot, Wu immediately accepted this offer. As Wu recalls, "The lure of a meaningful life in a brave new world outweighed the attraction of a doctorate and an academic future in an alien world."[3] At a farewell party, Wu asked his friend Tsung-Dao Lee whether the latter was also planning to return, and Lee responded: "I don't want to be brainwashed."[4] Wu Ningkun could not wrap his mind around this reply. It took both of them four decades to realize the dark reality of that comment.

Many Chinese intellectuals studying or teaching overseas were faced with a critical decision on whether to return to China. That transitional moment was also a time for Chinese intellectuals inside China to seriously ponder whether to follow the leader of the Nationalist Party Chiang Kai-shek to Taiwan. The experience of Chinese philosopher-diplomat Hu Shih was revealing. Hu was a leading figure in China's New Culture Movement and a pioneer in Chinese liberalism. From 1910 to 1918, Hu studied at Cornell University and Columbia University. In the 1920s, Hu returned to teach in Peking University and led the vernacular Chinese language movement. An ardent defender of liberal democracy, Hu Shih had been an outspoken opponent to communism while a professor at Peking University. At the defeat of Chiang Kai-shek, Hu was determined to move to Taiwan. After settling down, Hu persuaded Chiang Kai-shek to send an airplane to escort more faculty from Peking University to Taiwan. When the plane came back empty, Hu Shih sobbed in tears, knowing that many if not all had vouched their lives to serve the new communist regime. As historian Paul Cohen writes, "An important source of legitimation for China's ruling Communist Party was its part in vanquishing imperialism in the 1940s—and the closure this brought to the country's 'century of humiliation'"[5] And this theme of ending national humiliation fueled patriotism among Chinese intellectuals, who downplayed the hazards of a communist regime. For Chinese Christian intellectuals, the sentiment was the same: "Their apprehension at living under communism was outweighed by their patriotism and desire to make a contribution to the Chinese church."[6] The same historian Daniel Bays continues that given China's past when sectarian religious movements turned into anti-dynastic rebellions, "The new government . . . inherited this default attitude from the imperial past, and added to it another level of animus deriving from its Marxist ideology."[7]

In the fall of 1949, Zhao Luorui began teaching at Yenching University as the chair of the Western Language Department. Zhao also successfully recruited Wu Ningkun to teach in the English department of the same institution. As Wu recalled, by then Zhao was already encouraging him to align instruction with Marxist-Leninist views. Wu later wrote that "in Yenching everybody from the president to teaching staff all held onto an illusion that the school could continue to function as usual. Even until 1951 when Professor Zhao Luorui extended me a job offer, she still believed so."[8] The communist state effectively used the nation-as-mother metaphor to portray the newly independent country as both loving and needy.

When the communists took over in 1949, China was facing a series of socioeconomic problems that included rampant inflation, declining agricultural output, and war-torn transport and communications. Nevertheless, historians consider Mao Zedong's announcement at the inauguration of the communist regime in 1949 that "the Chinese people have stood up!" as the "most ambitious" moment "by human means alone."[9] Because after all, for a century from 1840 to 1940, China and her people had been driven to their knees by the forces of Western imperialism through "unequal treaties," guaranteeing wave after wave of anti-Western discontent among the Chinese.

When the Chinese Communist Party came to power in 1949, the prospect for a Christian China became bleak. By then there were around three million Catholics and one million Protestants in China.[10] But Zhao Luorui's outlook on Chinese politics was much influenced by her father T. C. Chao and other Christian educators of the time. Although the theolo Chao had expressed doubt about the use of violence by communists, it seemed to most leaders that in China's context, nonviolent struggle was not an option toward a radically new China. After the element of violence was teased out, many thinkers like Chao himself began to view the new Chinese regime as a providential platform for global ecumenical solidary. Secular and liberal Christian intellectuals stress the point that it was time for the Christian West to forego its claim to be the arbiter of Christianity, a religion that had been far too closely involved with the bourgeois capitalist system and its imperialist schemes. This shared understanding was the result of having experienced decades of Western missionary domination.

T. C. Chao himself studied at a missionary-founded college in Suzhou since 1905 and converted to Christianity in the early 1910s. Then Chao pursued education in America and returned in 1917 with a graduate degree in sociology, philosophy, and theology from Vanderbilt University. He took a faculty position at his alma mater, Dongwu University. Chao also chose a Western-style education for her daughter. At home, Zhao Luorui learned ancient Chinese classics from her father. In 1926, by the time Zhao Luorui reached her teen years, her father was the dean of Divinity School at Yenching University, "the flagship" of Christian colleges in China.[11] Nevertheless, Zhao Luorui once wrote that "what's memorable about my father is his democratic morale; although none of us were enthusiastic about religion and each chose our own path, he respected us and never imposed his hobbies or religion on us."[12] Zhao also described her father T. C. Chao as "an ardent patriot."[13] Even during the Anti-Christian Movement, Chao's response to secular liberal intellectuals was one of self-criticism. In 1923, T. C. Chao humbly admitted the many "weaknesses" of Chinese Christianity and criticized it as arbitrary in theology, over-ritualized, morally disappointing and collaborative with capitalism, while lacking economic justice and authentic unity, tolerant of deceits, and narrow in mission scope.[14] Chao was also critical of many manipulative behaviors used by some missionaries.

As she grew up, Zhao Luorui was motivated to become a scholar herself.[15] In 1928, after entering Yenching University, she first majored in Chinese but then switched to English literature through the influence of a foreign faculty. Zhao actively participated in extracurricular events in college. For example, she once acted a key role in a Shakespeare play *All's Well That Ends Well* with other members of a student association. A foreign professor was surprised to learn that, by using her father's personal library, Zhao Luorui has already read all the required books included on the course reading list. A few years later, Zhao obtained a graduate degree in British-American Literature from Tsinghua University. In a comparative literature class offered by an American professor, Zhao Luorui first read T. S. Eliot's *The Waste Land* (1935), a milestone in British-American modern poetry. She learned about the literary idioms and structure of this poem in that class. Another Chinese language professor compared Eliot's poem with Chinese poems of the Song dynasty. These all sparked great interest in Zhao Luorui.

In 1936, a year after she began teaching at Yenching University, 24-year-old Zhao Luorui married poet and archeologist Chen Mengjia. Not only had the two families been friends, but Chen Mengjia had once been a student of T. C. Chao (Zhao Zichen) at Yenching University since 1932. By then, Chen had already enjoyed the national fame of a young poet, together with intellectual figures such as Wen Yiduo and Xu Zhimo.[16] In 1936, Chen obtained a master's degree in ancient Chinese language from Yenching's Graduate School. According to a memoir written by Chinese historian and philosopher Qian Mu, Zhao Luorui had many suitors at Yenching University, but she only appreciated Chen Mengjia as a Chinese literary intellectual.[17] She had a love for poetry because her father Zhao Zichen was also a prolific poet.[18] Chen Mengjia wrote in 1933 that they enjoyed reading aloud their co-translated works of William Blake for pure leisure.[19] After they married, Chen first worked as a teaching assistant in Yenching's Chinese language department and later took a faculty position at a university in Changsha.

In a few years, Zhao Luorui finished the Chinese rendition of Eliot's *The Waste Land*. Immediately, she became very well known among Chinese intellectuals. Scholars of literary criticism applauded her translated work: "If Eliot's poem can be seen as a rare medicinal herb in the wasteland of modern poetry, then Zhao Luorui's rendition can be considered as a legendary endeavor in the history of Chinese translation."[20] She became a pioneer by introducing T. S. Eliot's verse to the Chinese audience. Zhao Luorui once wrote that what Eliot described in *The Waste Land* was a timely reflection on what China was going through, searching for hope in the midst of despair.[21] She considered its influence due to an echoing effect from the Western audience with widespread postwar disillusionment. Other poets whose work she translated include Emily Dickinson, H. W. Longfellow, and Walt Whitman.

She also wrote numerous prose and poems while researching the influential Western writers John Keats, Charles Dickens, Bernard Shaw, Thomas Hardy, and others.

In the summer of 1937, Zhao Luorui received a dozen author's copies of her translated *The Waste Land*. Within a few months, however, the Japanese war broke out in a northern part of China. All higher education institutions had to relocate to the south. Zhao Luorui and her husband moved to Kunming, the capital of Yunnan Province. Chen Mengjia taught the Chinese language at Southwestern United University. The school adopted a policy that a married couple could not both be on faculty. Zhao Luorui considered herself "tradition-minded," so she stayed home and took up household chores. She wrote essays about her chaotic life as a housewife, saying "Always a bookworm, and even when cooking, I always had a Dickens on my lap."[22] Two years after the publication of her translated work, Zhao Luorui learned that her Chinese version of Eliot's *The Waste Land* had been widely received by scholars, poets, and translators in China. From 1939 to 1944, she found a teaching job in Yunnan University. She also finished the translation of *Fontamara* by anti-Fascist Italian writer and politician Ignazio Silone.

In 1944, upon the recommendation of American historian John Fairbank at Harvard University, Chen Mengjia was invited by the University of Chicago to teach ancient Chinese paleography and archaeology. Zhao Luorui accompanied him and studied for a doctoral degree in English language and literature. She later recalled the four years at Chicago as the most formative time for her scholarship. When T. S. Eliot visited America in 1946, he invited the Chinese couple for dinner and thanked Zhao for her translation of *The Waste Land*. While at Chicago, Zhao worked on a dissertation about Henry James, a key transitional figure between literary realism and modernism in English literature. She collected so much material on James that one Chicago professor later ranked Zhao Luorui a third-place collector of Henry James archives in America. At a time when Henry James was not yet well known, this interest showed Zhao's own excellent literary taste.

Life before 1949 and after was a dramatic change for Zhao Luorui. In the wider society, the communists sought to destroy the "old China" and rebuild a new social order through the nationalization of key resources, such as land, capital, and labor allocation. Communists also eradicated free market enterprises such as commercial guilds and private businesses. In the countryside due to brutal land reforms, the gentry class which used to be a pillar of its civil society was completely wiped out through violent executions. The communist rule directly penetrated into rural villages by installing the most politically loyal cadres as watchdogs for any social activity outside of direct government control. Social trust and interpersonal networks were undermined after a series of political movements. This period also nurtured a political culture that rewarded betrayal and impersonal political loyalty to the Chinese Communist Party.

After the U.S.-Korean War broke out in 1951, the communist regime propagated nationalist fervor against "American imperialism." As Spence says, "Given momentum by the anger and excitement of the Korean War, a second mass campaign was directed at domestic 'counterrevolutionaries.' "[23] Massive rallies were launched in large cities against Chinese individuals who had Western, and especially American, connections. These campaigns later grew in brutality, intensity, and thoroughness, targeting some most widespread sects, such as Yi Guan Dao ("Way of Basic Unity Society").[24] Jonathan D. Spence notes that public media were used to disintegrate the old social order: "Propaganda networks were also developed, consisting of trained experts who could work through the media and through small discussion groups to encourage compliance with the government policies. One function of these cadres and propagandists was to break down the often tight personal, emotional, and family bonds."[25]

As the U.S.-Korean War escalated, the Chinese communist regime launched an "intellectuals' reform and thought reconstruction" movement. Teams of communist cadres moved into the faculty residential area of Yenching University. T. C. Chao and other well-known faculty members became targets of public struggle meetings. As department chair, Zhao Luorui not only had to criticize her own "capitalist thoughts," but she also needed to participate in all kinds of political meetings. In 1952, all Christian colleges in China were ordered to close down, surrendering space and staff to nationalized higher education institutions. Yenching University came to an end. Zhao Luorui was reassigned to a faculty position in Beijing University. When hearing that Wu Ningkun had been demoted to teach at Nankai University in Nanjing, as a much inferior arrangement, Zhao Luorui began to sob, showing immense regret for having personally asked Wu Ningkun to return from his otherwise promising future in America. Wu wrote in his memoir about this moment: "She had persuaded me to quit my doctoral dissertation and return to China. Now I was at the disposal of others, with political odds against me. How could she not show regret? Back then, she had such great ambition to expand Yenching's faculty of the English department, using the faculty model at the University of Chicago as a blueprint. Now this ivory-tower that she helped to build with her extraordinary talent was falling apart. Wonderful dreams became an illusion in the mirror. How could she not mourn?"[26]

Driven by its egalitarian ideology, China's new communist regime had to swiftly change the opportunity structures in society, leveling power from previous privileged classes to the mass. Two generations of Chinese Christian intellectuals nurtured by the Protestant mission since the 1910s faced increasing marginalization in their well-developed areas of expertise. These included

Western scholarship and the liberal arts. Earnest to show their patriotic devotion to the Party-State that saved China from semicolonialism, many Chinese intellectuals compromised and failed to defend academic freedom. As history unfolded, few could protect themselves from the harm of radical politics.

The U.S.-Korean war catalyzed a long process of radicalized religious policies. First, the Chinese government cut off all foreign financial support for Christian institutions in China. Second, 151 church leaders met in Beijing for a conference to discuss how to associate with foreign mission organizations from then on. Zhou Enlai suggested that true patriotic Christians must sever all social ties with foreigners, especially Americans. These participating Protestant leaders issued their own United Declaration of Chinese Christian Churches, embracing Zhou's demands. The third and next step was a campaign to expose reactionaries from within the church, in preparation for merging all Protestant denominations into a single unified body. Finally, after churches formed the Three-Self Patriotic Movement, they were asked to hold public denunciation meetings (also known as "struggle meetings") to further cleanse any residual Western imperialism.

The nationalization of Christian colleges took place along with the disintegration of a wider ecology of Protestant establishment. Populist political forces resisted Western art and scholarship. In the radical campaigns that followed, academic disciplines also underwent an overhaul, with humanities and social sciences abolished.[27] Chinese intellectuals who had overseas degrees in disciplines such as English literature, sociology, and religion were ostracized. Since 1954, notable liberal leaders of the Protestant church launched the Three-Self Patriotic Movement.[28] And by 1955, the most fruitful decades of world missionary enterprise in China had ceased.

In 1956, the director of the Bureau of Religious Affairs filed a status report on the state of Chinese Protestantism, emphasizing its strategic importance since the majority of Protestant leaders were highly educated and influential. The same report admitted government policy failures during radical politics when some leaders suffered brutality and injustice.[29] In the same year, Mao Zedong openly invited intellectuals for discussions and critiques of government policies. This was known as the "Hundred Flowers" policy. What followed was a period of relaxed and open discussion and even criticism of the new government's policies. A year later, this liberal climate ended abruptly when another campaign of "rectification" began. Church leaders felt the pressure not just only to publicly verbalize their loyalty to the state but also to engage in heavier criticism and self-accusation against their own churches. What was later known as the Anti-Rightist Movement penetrated every village and urban workplace with radical politics by alienating certain liberal-leaning individuals. In all these policy fluctuations, Christians gradually lost their sense of alertness as a canary in the cage would:

Christians groped the way through the maze of revolutionary propaganda, not knowing if the command to fight "the four pests" of flies, rats, mosquitoes, and sparrows included rooting out unpatriotic elements in the churches, or if the government's decree on the Fight-the-Locusts campaign should be augmented by mobilizing Sunday worship services and Sunday schools as propaganda mills. . . . It became a cruel Kafkaesque game of victims beating themselves with a rod fashioned from the dark suspicion, innuendo, and rumors directed at them.[30]

What the Anti-Rightist campaign did was a complete shutdown of dialogue between Chinese Protestants and the state. Even privately held religious beliefs, not just practices, were effectively criminalized. Two years later, Mao's Great Leap Forward (1958) closed public places of worship so that all labor force be directed into full-steam production. Although later historians record that missional activities happened even in prisons and labor camps, small clusters of believers could only secretly gather and worship.[31] In the Chinese society, more divisions were sowed, pitting people against each other in a bid to curry favor with the authorities. Any disagreement on Mao's whimsical policies risked being considered "rightist" or "counterrevolutionary" by fellow Christians and party officials. For example, 240 church leaders met in Nanjing to purse "rightist elements" among their churches in 1958 in order to show support for socialist construction. Meeting without government permission and preaching against socialism were banned. Later many clergy also launched another movement with an unmistakably idolatrous name: "Hand-the-Heart-to-the-Party" campaign. Similar rhetoric began to personify the party as a paternalistic entity who deserved acts of honor and filial piety.

In the Anti-Rightist Movement, more intellectuals spoke up for freedom of speech but were penalized and sent to labor camps. Wu Ningkun was one of them. He had to endure decades of harsh labor before a reunion with his old friend Tsung-Dao Lee in the 1980s. By then, Lee had won the Nobel Prize in Physics. What followed the Anti-Rightist Movement was the Great Leap Forward and the Great Famine. But even in the midst of political uncertainty, Zhao Luorui and her husband Chen Mengjia tried to make their patriotic loyalty evident to the communist authorities. For example, after a few years of relative peace, Chen Mengjia felt the need to praise Mao Zedong. As he wrote, "Chairman Mao's two speeches marked a milestone in a few decades concerning Chinese literary art and science. It is a trumpet call to the forthcoming cultural revolution."[32] He added that it made him realize with pride and excitement that "a new, healthy and lasting morale is taking shape."[33]

In the same month as Chen Mengjia wrote this, however, he also published several critiques of China's literary reform, protesting that "the plan to simplify Chinese characters came around too quickly, without consulting experts or the mass."[34] He challenged the plan for being "unscientific" and done in "haste," while advocating for the preservation of traditional Chinese character-writing. After Chen Mengjia spoke up with a purely professional opinion, he was inevitably classified as a "Rightist." Chen suffered persecution in public struggle meetings and was sent down to rural Henan for reeducation through harsh labor. When more radical cleansings happening around him, Chen Mengjia sensed the dawning of an Orwellian terror. He once uttered in despair to his friends, "This is 1984! It is coming." Since that event, he became mentally ill. Zhao's father, Yenching theologian T. C. Chao also became the target of public humiliation. Zhao Luorui was accused of "capitalist thinking" and "downplaying politics" in her academic discipline. She also suffered emotional breakdowns and had to be hospitalized. It was not until the Central Propaganda Ministry asked Zhao Luorui to be on the committee for a book *History of European Literature* that the fate of her family took a positive turn. This book later became a classic textbook for the discipline. At that time, Zhao was among the only two top-tier female professors in China. In 1962, she and a committee of scholars were convened by communist leaders to start a translation project of Walt Whitman's works.

Zhao Luorui spent a few peaceful years using her expertise while caring for her husband. Nobody foresaw another fatal wave of political change. In 1966, Mao Zedong's Cultural Revolution began. Red Guards, who were mostly teenagers wearing red armbands, roamed the streets of cities, raiding homes of those who owned properties and attacked those who they thought were wearing "bourgeois" clothes and accessories. In this campaign designed to overthrow established authorities, middle-school teachers and university instructors found themselves on the center stage of public humiliations through "struggle meetings," a technique of communist cleansing. Betrayals and whistleblowing happened frequently. For example, Chinese American historian Wang Youqin documents that as part of their reeducation intellectuals were required to sleep in dorms, where even words uttered in dreams at night were monitored and reported as evidence of anti-revolutionary crimes.[35] On August 5, 1966, CCP issued a document to annul the previous "Forbid Violent Beatings" announcement issued by Liu Shaoqi in June. Tortures, suicides, and murders led to a massive death toll. For example, it is estimated that nearly 1,800 people lost their lives in Beijing in the two months after August in 1966.[36] Radical Red Guards even wrote August 1966 into many poems and articles as "Red August," a way of lauding their achievements of successfully demolishing historical antiques, raiding bourgeois homes, and killing anti-revolutionaries.[37] As the movement went on, historians note more lawlessness: "the Party carried out purges; closing schools, freeing students from their classes to conscript them to ideological training camps, and hounding scholars, now considered 'stinking' social debris."[38]

As a former Rightist and collector of expensive antique furniture, Chen Mengjia became targeted by Red Guards. He was made to kneel in the open yard of the Institute of Archaeology in the hot summer days, while Red Guards spat in his face. In the end of the public humiliation, Zhao Luorui and Chen Mengjia were forced to move into ramshackle housing, and their writings and belongings, including a collection of Ming dynasty furniture, were looted. After a few more public beatings, the 55-year-old poet-scholar Chen Mengjia had mental breakdowns that pushed him to attempt suicide multiple times. Sadly, Chen eventually took his own life. This tragedy devastated Zhao Luorui, who sank into chronic depression and even schizophrenia. Zhao's father also suffered persecution and lost his academic position. As one American journalist writes, "The Zhao family, like most Chinese, was reduced to poverty, and upkeep was minimal."[39]

By September 1966, all the churches were closed down. The Red Guards campaigned across China to stamp out any trace of religion, especially Western-imported ones. Images of Buddha, crucifixes, and other symbols were destroyed in their publicly demonstrated revolutionary rage. Destruction became a virtue, and emotions were often frenzied. At the end of each ritual of demolition, Red Guards performed a ritual of holding up the *Little Red Book of Chairman Mao*, citing it as the only authorized scripture. As historian Lamin Sanneh writes, "The party updated the Heavenly Mandate of the Confucian tradition with a hefty dose of Marxism-Leninism."[40] Ironically, "Antagonism to Christianity as a foreign religion coexisted incongruously with the exclusive espousal of the foreign ideology of Marxism."[41]

During these ten years of utter disaster, some China observers in the West continued to look at China's social experiment with optimism. For example, historian at Cambridge University Joseph Needham, who was deemed the greatest scholar of Chinese civilization, wrote in 1972 that the Chinese revolution had remade a society that was "further on the way to the true society of mankind, the Kingdom of God" than its Western counterpart: "It would seem that the China which broke the heart of missionaries has accepted the spirit of Christ from another source, namely, Marxism."[42] His writing became hugely influential. He added, "I think China is the only truly Christian country in the world in the present day, in spite of its absolute rejection of all religion. . . . Where is Christ to be found? . . . Where the good are, where good things are done. . . . That means appreciating what is happening in China at the present day."[43] In other occasions, Needham commented that Maoism was God's saving power in China.[44] Another scholar Raymond Whitehead echoed the phrase about Maoism being "God's saving power" in China.[45] Scholar of Catholicism Richard Madsen also concluded that "the good predominates heavily over the bad."[46] He also believed that the salvation of God had been ushered in by the Chinese revolution. As China embraced the message of revolution in the place of salvation, sinologists and experts on Christianity in China could hardly reach any agreement on their understanding of the new reality. As historians note, "At the one extreme we find interpretations such as that of Harold Rigney's book *Four Years in a Red Hell*. And on the other, we have the example of Christian Maoists proclaiming the realization of the Kingdom of God in China. Between them there exists a full range of histori- cal and theological interpretation."[47]

Since the 1940s, Zhao Luorui's literary interests followed the latest trends of the English-speaking West, introducing names such as T. S. Eliot, Henry James, and Walt Whitman to a wide Chinese audience. During war time, Zhao Luorui sacrificed her own career when she could not be on the same uni- versity faculty as her husband. Before the founding of China's new regime, Zhao also obeyed her father's call to return. She was the fruit of two genera- tions of Christian intellectual yearning for a flourishing China that embraced a healthy exchange between East and West. For pragmatic reasons, Zhao Luorui tolerated Marxist-Leninist guidelines in her academic institution. Why did she choose to work on Walt Whitman? The answer was not revealed until 1995 when a Western journalist interviewed Zhao in her home and asked why not only Chinese writers such as Guo Moruo and Ai Qing but also the communist regime found Walt Whitman so appealing.[48] According to Zhao Luorui, Whitman was considered "America's poet of comrades" by Chinese communists.[49] And there was a political interest in turning this comradeship into something in line with Marxist ideology. For this reason, a high-ranking official in the Communist Party, Chun Tunan, had also translated selected poems from Whitman's *Leaves of Grass* into Chinese during the 1950s. Apparently, Zhao Luorui knew that she had carved out a niche with less political hazard.

But neither patriotic optimism nor political deliberation shielded Zhao Luorui from the inevitable change in an evolving power dynamic in the communist regime. Becoming a member of the intellectual establishment did not save her from being hard hit by the storm of Mao's Cultural Revolution. After the Cultural Revolution ended, Zhao Luorui was able to resume her research, specializing in American literature. Her translation of Walt Whitman's *Leaves of Grass* demonstrated much resilience and professional- ism. Although Zhao never manifested her Christian faith, she regained her interest in a camp of American literature that both the communist regime and Chinese academics found appealing. She was a pioneer whose legacy helped sustain strands of East-West literary connections in an age of Chinese xenophobia. It was due to Zhao Luorui's efforts that translation of Western literature has expanded from Enlightenment figures to more contemporary writers like Eliot and Whitman. Zhao Luorui left a lasting legacy for later generations of Chinese scholars who are interested in Western scholarship.

For example, Yang Zhishui, the editor of *Dushu* magazine, accredited Zhao for helping him grow in editorial professionalism when it comes to critiques of translated Western poetry.[50] From 1979 to the present, *Dushu* has been a monthly Chinese literary magazine which introduces ideas from modern Western philosophy as well as postcolonial theories such as Orientalism. It has been received as the most influential publication among educated Chinese in mainland China.

But it was not for another decade before Zhao Luorui reappeared in public. She did, however, maintain correspondence with scholar friends in America. In 1982, Zhao wrote in a personal letter to Ed Folsom about her life in China. "Here in China we are trying to get used to the good fortune of being allowed to work again. I am glad that I am in pretty good health so that the last years of my life need not be wasted. . . . I can never forget the education I received at Chicago."[51] She also discussed the difficulties in translating Whitman. "There is so much spontaneity and originality in him that one really must enter into his whole personality to do him at all competently."[52] In 1983, Zhao was restored to her former faculty position in the English department of Beijing University. In 1988, a *New York Times* reporter visited Zhao Luorui in her home and wrote about the life of this renowned but tragedy-stricken female scholar. He documented:

> Her desk is small, a table really, its grainy rosewood polished by her palms, the frayed bindings of dictionaries, the tissue-thin paper she fills with tiny ideograms. For the last ten years, Zhao Luorui has sat here, at this desk carved four centuries ago during the Ming dynasty, putting Walt Whitman's boisterous, individualist, prodigious *Leaves of Grass* into Chinese.[53]

In this interview, Zhao lamented that "thirty-five years of my life were lost. . . . I've poured everything into Whitman."[54] She explained that her theory is that "translators will be faithful to the written form and spirit." But even when one cannot be faithful to both, "you have to be faithful to the content." Toward the end of the interview, Zhao's words revealed the appeal of Whitman to herself: "The individual means everything to Whitman. . . . The individual should have a change for self-development." While visiting relatives in America, she always spent time in libraries, reading manuscripts by Walt Whitman. In 1991, Zhao Luorui's own rendition of *Leaves of Grass* was published in 1991 by Shanghai Translation Press. Since then, she has been considered the foremost translator of Whitman in China. In the same year, the University of Chicago gave her a Professional Achievement Award at the institution's centennial celebration. Her next public appearance was in 1993 when she visited the Chinese University of Hong Kong for two weeks as a research fellow.[55] She lived three more years after that.

The life story of Zhao Luorui captures how the century-long Protestant establishment in China disintegrated under communist rule. As historian Daniel Bays writes, "In the first half of the 20th century, the foreign missionary movement in China matured, flourished, and then died."[56] The fruits of this missionary enterprise, mostly educated Chinese who had overseas training and degrees, were left to endure intensifying persecution. There was tremendous waste of talent and collective trauma. Individuals were simply powerless to face the overwhelming violence by a whimsical political apparatus. Tragedies within Zhao Luorui family did not awaken her into resistance. No evidence showed an awakened gender awareness in her. Perhaps that is asking too much since the entire Chinese society was drenched "in a sea of dark blue or gray, as women and men wore the same Mao jackets and cut their hair short."[57] Stories of women's resistance came to the public awareness much later, such as that of Lin Zhao who returned to the Christian faith while imprisoned and tortured.[58] Even Zhao Luorui's father, China's most prominent Protestant theologian T. C. Chao, later confessed to a German biographer that he had lost the faith toward the end of his life.[59] Until today, it remains a mystery whether Chao was being intentionally ambiguous in order to avoid political risks. But a deep sense of disillusionment occurred about what Christianity had to offer after China's communist revolutions.

NOTES

1. T. C. Chao's oldest son Zhao Jingxin was working at the China Airlines in Hong Kong and returned to Beijing in January 1950. Her second oldest son Zhao Jingde was working for the U.S. Geological Survey when U.S.-China relationship worsened. He was once considered a communist by the United States and failed to return. Zhao's youngest son Zhao Jinglun was studying in Harvard University but had to quit the program and return in 1951.

2. Ian Johnson, *Wild Grass: Three Stories of Change in Modern China* (New York: Vintage Books, 2005), 129–30.

3. Ningkun, Wu, *A Single Tear: A Family's Persecution, Love, and Endurance in Communist* (New York: Back Bay Books, 1994), 5.

4. Ibid. In the 2000s, Wu Ningkun met Tsung-Dao Lee again after the latter had achieved the Nobel Prize in Physics.

5. Paul A. Cohen, *China Unbound: Evolving Perspectives on the Chinese Past* (New York: Routledge, 2003), 148–49.

6. Bays, *A New History*, 149.

7. Ibid., 159.

8. Quoted in Yu Yingshi, "Preface: Remembering Yenching University in 1949," in Wu Ningkun, ed., *Lonely Harp* (Taipei: Asian Culture Publishing, 2008), 9.

9. Anonymous, "Red China and the Self-Understanding of the Church: Marxism-Leninism-Mao Tse-tung Thought and the Philippine Revolution," in Lutheran World Federation/Pro Mundi Vita, ed., *Christianity and the New China*, 2 vols. (South Pasadena: Wm. Carey Library, 1976), 1:3. Quoted in Janz, *World Christianity and Marxism*, 177.

10. Donald E. MacInnis, *Religion in China Today: Policy and Practice* (Maryknoll: Orbis, 1989), 264, 313.

11. Arthur Lewis Rosenbaum, "Christianity, Academics, and National Salvation in China: Yenching University, 1924–1949," *Journal of American-East Asia Relations* 13 (2004–2006), 27.

12. Zhao Luorui and Zhao Jingxin, "Our Father Zhao Zichen," *Collected Works of T. C. Chao*, vol. 1 (Beijing: Shanghwu Printing Press, 2003), 4.

13. Ibid., 5.

14. Chao, Tzu-Chen. "Strengths and Weaknesses of China's Church." In *Collected Works of T. C. Chao*. vol. 3 (Beijing: Shanghwu Printing Press, 2003), 131.

15. All children of T. C. Chao (Zhao Zichen) became well-known scholars. Second child Zhao Jingxin (1918–2017) graduated from Yenching University in 1941 with a degree in economics and taught as faculty in Beijing's Foreign Trade University. Third child Zhao Jingde(1919-2009) obtained a PhD in geology from the University of Chicago in 1948 and worked in the U.S. Geological Survey. Youngest son Zhao Jinglun(1923–2015) graduated with a PhD from Vanderbilt University in 1978 and later worked as a fellow at the Harvard University and other U.S. institutions.

16. Chen Mengjia, Wen Yiduo, Xu Zhimo, and Zhu Xiangyi were known as "four great poets" of the New Moon School.

17. Qian Mu, *Memoir of Parents, Teachers and Friends at Age Eighty* (Shanghai: Shanghai Sanlian Press, 2005).

18. T. C. Chao produced over 3,000 poems that were burned by ransacking Red Guards during the Cultural Revolution. In fact, Zhao Luorui's name was taken from a poem by Li Bai, China's most well-known poet from Tang dynasty.

19. Chen Mengjia, "Preface to Selected Translations of William Blake's Poetry," *Collected Works of Chen Mengjia* (Beijing: Zhong Hua Shu Ju, 2006), 169.

20. "A Short Biography of Zhao Luorui: A Republican woman translator who suffered hardships and schizophrenia," *Wanxiang History*, May 9, 2019. Online Resource. https://zhuanlan.zhihu.com/p/65127208

21. Zhao Luorui, "T. S. Eliot and The Waste Land," *New Current Affairs*, 1940 issue.

22. Quoted in "Zhao Luorui: The Translator of T. S. Eliot's The Waste Land," Chinese University of Hong Kong, China Research Center "Grassroots History" Archives. Online resource. http://mjlsh.usc.cuhk.edu.hk/Book.aspx?cid=4&tid=3951

23. Ibid.

24. Ibid., 534.

25. Spence, *The Search for Modern China*, 537.

26. Wu Ningkun, "A Woman of Talent: Remembering Professor Zhao Luorui," *Chinese and Foreign Book Digest*, 10, 2007. Online Resource. http://edubridge.com/erxiantang/l2/zhaoluorui_wuningkun.htm

27. Han, Minghan. *The History of Chinese Sociology* (Tianjin: People's Press, 1987), 172.

28. See Wallace C. Merwin and Francis P. Jones, eds., *Documents of the Three-Self Movement: Source Materials for the Study of the Protestant Church in Communist China* (New York: National Council of the Churches of Christ in the United States, 1963).

29. MacInnis, *Religion in China Today*, 111–14.

30. Sanneh, *Disciples of All Nations*, 250.

31. Bays, *A New History*, 176. Li Ma and Jin Li, *Surviving the State, Remaking the Church: A Sociological Portrait of Christians in Mainland China* (Eugene: Pickwick Publications, 2017), chapter 1.

32. Chen Mengjia, "Two Hopes," in Chen Mengjia, *Collected Works of Cheng Mengjia* (Beijing: Shang Wu Shu Ju, 2006), 202.

33. Ibid.

34. Ibid., 241–42.

35. Wang Youqin, *Victims of the Cultural Revolution*. Unpublished report, 491. Online resource. http://ywang.uchicago.edu/history/

36. The overall death toll during the ten years of Cultural Revolution is estimated to be around 1.72 million. See Chen, Yongfa. *Seventy Years since China's Communist Revolution*, vol. 2 (Taipei: Lianjing Press, 2001), 846.

37. Wang, *Victims of the Cultural Revolution*, 89.

38. Sanneh, *Disciples of All Nations*, 250.

39. Johnson, *Wild Grass*, 130.

40. Ibid., 251.

41. Sanneh, *Disciples of All Nations*, 243.

42. "A Christian Perspective on the Chinese Experience," *Anticipation* (Geneva: August 1973), 24, 28, 29. Also in "China and the Churches in the Making of One World," *Pro Mundi Vita* 55 (1975): 16–17. Quoted in Sanneh, *Disciples of All Nations*, 251–52. These documents, representing Western theological views of China in the 1970s, came from a 1974 colloquium in Louvain sponsored by the Lutheran World Federation and by the Catholic organization Pro Mundi Vita.

43. Quoted in Vita, "China and the Churches in the Making of One World," 28.

44. Ibid., 21.

45. Raymond I. Whitehead, "Love and Animosity in the Ethic of Mao," in Lutheran World Federation, *Christianity and the New China* (New Yrok: Ecclesia Publications, 1976). 79. Also see Raymond I. Whitehead, *Love and Struggle in Mao's Thought* (Maryknoll: Orbis, 1977).

46. Richard Madsen, "The New China and the New Self-Understanding of the Church," in *Lutheran World Federation, Christianity and the New China* (New Yrok: Ecclesia Publications, 1976), 175, 179.

47. Janz, *World Christianity and Marxism*, 123–24. Also see Harold Rigney, *Four Years in a Red Hell* (Chicago: Regnery, 1965).

48. Price, Kenneth M. An Interview with Zhao Luorui. *Walt Whitman Quarterly Review* 13 (1995): 59–63.

49. University of Iowa, Faculty and Staff News, December 8, 2000, vol. 38, no. 8. Online Resource. https://web.archive.org/web/20070106103124/http://www.uiowa. edu/~fyi/issues/issues2000/12082000/walt_whitman.html

50. Yang Zhishui, "Master Luorui: Journal Entries during Ten Years of *Dushu*," in *Wen Dao Lu: A Collection of Yang Zhishui's Prose* (Zhejiang Guji Publishing, 2017), Kindle book, location number 1429 to 1590.

51. Letter to Ed Folsom, dated April 29, 1982. Quoted in Ed Folsom, *Whitman East and West: New Contexts for Reading Walt Whitman* (Iowa City: University of Iowa University Press, 2002), 4.

52. Ibid.

53. Edward A. Gargan, "Walt Whitman Sings Anew, but Now with a Chinese Lilt," *New York Times*, February 6, 1988. Quoted in Ed Folsom, *Whitman East and West*, 7.

54. Ibid.

55. Chinese University of Hong Kong website, http://www.cuhk.edu.hk/rct/30th/bio/lz.html

56. Bays, "From Foreign Mission to Chinese Church."

57. Kwok, Pui-lan, "Christianity and Women in Contemporary China," *Journal of World Christianity* 3 (1) (2010): 1–17.

58. Lin Zhao (1932–1968) attended a missionary school and then studied at Peking University. She actively participated in communist land reform and zealously worshipped Mao as her "father." But when she criticized the Great Leap Forward policies, Lin was sentenced to twenty years in prison. It was during a time of torture when she recommitted to her Christian faith. See Xi, *Blood Letters*.

59. Glüer, *Christliche Theologie in China*. [Christian Theology in China: T. C. Chao 1918–1956] (in German).

Chapter 6

Does the Motherland Love You Back?

On the night of January 31, 1967, a few months after Mao announced his Cultural Revolution, 29-year-old Gu Shengying committed suicide. She was China's finest pianist, who had won top prizes in many international competitions. Tragically, her mother and younger brother also died with her by suicide that same night. Official archives hid the cause of Gu's death for decades. Her life story has been obliviated. What happened to this young and promising artist was only revealed by biographers and historians many years later. This chapter contains disturbing stories of other contemporary Chinese Christians who also committed suicide during intense violence. Historian Daniel Bays writes that "as China plunged ahead into the mindless destruction and social chaos of the Cultural Revolution in 1966, Chinese Christians drank deeply from the same bitter draught of which all Chinese must partake."[1]

Gu Shengying was born in Wuxi of Jiangsu Province in July 1937, a week before the Japanese military launched a second offensive in northern China. Her name "Shengying" literally means "Holy infant" in Chinese, indicating her Christian family background.[2] Gu's father served as an interpreter and Nationalist Party military official. Her mother was well-educated, with a degree in French literature from Datong College in Shanghai. Their affluent upper-middle-class family provided the young girl with an elite modern education. For Gu Shengying, Christianity has become a cultural component of the family tradition led by her father who converted in the 1910s, a high time of Protestant mission in China. Nurtured in an appreciation for Western culture, the household took personal interest in the cutting-edge areas of cross-cultural advancements, Western literature, and piano performance, respectively. Take music, for example. The Shanghai Conservatory was founded in 1927 as a Western-style art academy. In Republican-era Shanghai, music acted as two social markers. Historian Richard Curt Kraus once wrote that "thousands of missionaries came to China with pianos for thumping out hymns to save heathen souls."[3] Nevertheless, besides its Western origins, a piano was expensive, well beyond the means of most Chinese families. So, this instrument became a quintessential status symbol for the new bourgeoisie.

Gu Shengying started learning piano at age five and was tutored by a few top Chinese musicians, including the prominent Christian music theorist Ma Geshun who composed a Chinese symphony like an original Chinese piece *The Messiah* (*mi sai ya*) and a collection of psalmody.[4] A work published in 2017 states, "The music education Gu Shengying had was unparalleled at that time. Her pure 'bloodline' in the musical discipline and rare talent created an irreplaceable piano genius."[5] She also developed piano techniques by performing the finest music of the Western world, including that of Mozart and Chopin. As for her formal education, Gu Shengying also attended one of the best Christian schools in Shanghai. As a fellow classmate Ding Zilin, a female professor and later organizer of the Tiananmen Mothers, recalled decades later, in 1944, almost all pupils in this school came from wealthy Christian families who picked them up by private chauffeurs every day.[6] Ding recollected that Gu was raised in a Christian home.

After the communist regime, the liberal arts were not immediately abolished as Western colonial artifacts. In fact, the regime adopted pragmatism to allow different streams of influence, as was the case in the Soviet Union, where limited room was made for the arts. Chinese authorities also preserved the talents nurtured in the Republican era to boost its international image. Nevertheless, in a time of workers' strikes and warfare, Gu Shengying's upper-middle-class upbringing and elitist Christian education in Shanghai exemplified the rising wealth gap in the Chinese society, an important dimension that factored in the appeal of a growing populist-socialist movement.

In 1952, at age fifteen, Gu made her debut public performance, playing Mozart's Piano Concerto in D Minor with the Shanghai Symphony Orchestra. As critics wrote, "[Gu] demonstrated exceptional musical talent and through diligence created a unique style characterized by great depth of feeling, sensitivity and poetic expression."[7] She was known to integrate heroic passion with scholarly mellowness in public performance. Afterward, she was admitted into the Central Music Academy as a graduate student and studied under a few Soviet master pianists. Her instructor once commented that since Gu invested ten to twelve hours a day in practice, she actually spent twice as much time honing her craft as the professional trained musicians in Soviet colleges. Friends and colleagues also recall her intense schedule of practicing piano. Apart from musical art, Gu Shengying also read Chinese and foreign classics, ranging from fiction to plays. She also drew poetic impulses from visual arts. At the height of her international fame, Gu Shengying joined a world tour to Europe. In Poland, the home country of Frédéric Chopin, the government and host organization presented her a plaster cast of Chopin's left hand as a way to honor her excellent techniques at playing his works. A Bulgarian critic wrote that "the music of Chopin exhibits unreproducible beauty in her performance."[8]

Before long, Gu Shengying became a tokenized figure for China in the European arena of competition: "The success of triumphing over European musicians was especially sweet, and China gave ample credits to Soviet advisors who helped train young Chinese artists."[9] It motivated the twenty-some Gu to perform better, showing an unreserved devotion to her motherland, in the hope that the communist regime could consider her family's political stance favorably. As Richard Curt Kraus writes, "Their skills made them important for China's industrialization,"[10] and "cultural nationalism is expressed by vigorous efforts for Chinese to win prizes in international music competitions."[11]

Because of her compliant personality, Gu Shengying always abided by the rules and expectations around her. In 1954, she joined the Communist Youth League (CYL), enabling her to win a "Progressive Youth" title from the city-level CYL committee. She later served on the city's cultural bureau committee and the Chinese Musicians Association. Whenever there was need to serve the workers and peasants, she willingly joined in. For example, Gu Shengying performed three times a day for the People's Liberation Army during Spring Festivals. On behalf of China, Gu Shengying toured the Soviet Union, Switzerland, Belgium, Poland, Hungary, Bulgaria, and Finland. At international contests, she recorded these words in the diary: "Always perform at a high level and win glory for the Motherland and for the Chinese people!"[12]

Despite her musical talent, exceeding diligence and strenuous demonstration of political loyalty to the Communist Party, Gu Shengying's life took a tragic turn due to events in her father's past. In 1957, Gu's father was sentenced to life-term imprisonment due to his political association with a former vice mayor of Shanghai Pan Hannian, two decades before.[13] When the authorities came to arrest Gu's father, the whole family was frightened. Mr. Gu said to his daughter, "Remember to practice your piano. Love the country and love the people."[14] Gu Shengying replied quietly but with sorrow and indignation, "Father, I love the motherland, but I love my father more!" Gu's father was taken to Qinghai, a remote and underdeveloped city in northwestern China. In the same year, Christian composer Ma Geshun and translator-scholar Fu Lei, who both had close ties with Gu Shengying, were also denounced as Rightists.

Chinese conductor Li Delun recalls that due to stress related to her father's arrest, Gu Shengying "looked like a sick person, pale and spiritless; but as soon as she began to play, it was like she changed into a totally different person, passionate and strong."[15] In October 1958, when Gu Shengying finished a performance in Poland, a business agent came to her with a contract, promising international fame and fortune. However, Gu declined the offer, saying that "as an artist of the People's Republic of China, all my activities should follow the arrangements of our nation."[16]

During these tours in other countries, Gu kept a diary for self-evaluation and improvement after each performance. Her rhetorical style in diary writing was similar to many women's memoirs about their sent down experiences in the countryside. Several recurring themes include the detailed drudgery of work, feelings of exhilaration at new experiences, a growing sense of capability and self-reliance, and regular salutation to Mao and the official ideology. As if addressing a public audience or guessing the diary would be censored in the future, they demonstrated a highly politicized awareness. The result is a lack of intimacy and authentic self-dialogue. Though in her twenties, Gu Shengying never mentioned sexual attraction or anything of the sort. Life to her was one of regiment and constant display of political loyalty.

Though devastated by her father's arrest, Gu Shengying still participated in the Sixth Global Youth Piano Contest in Moscow and won a gold medal for China. It was the first time a mainland Chinese musician ever won a top prize at an international contest. A fellow musician recalled that her photo taken at the contest resembled a famous painting of Jesus' prayer at Gethsemane.[17] "As a true artist, Gu Shengying had a noble character and patriotic zeal. Even in the days of political exclusion and humiliation, Gu still poured out her heart for the motherland while performing overseas."[18] From the Soviet Union, she also bought back a collection of paintings by an ancient Chinese artist. The president of China's Central Music Academy Zhao Feng once commented that very few of China's musicians were able to appreciate ancient paintings by the Eight Immortals.[19]

In 1958, Gu went to compete at the Tenth Congress of International Music Competition in Geneva, Switzerland, and received the highest honor in piano performance for women.[20] Many European media, including Swiss National Television, broadcasted the awards to the public. This earned her great fame as "China's poet pianist." In 1964, Gu won another award in the Queen Elizabeth International Piano Contest held in Belgium. International critics hailed her as "a true born-to-be Chopin performer and piano poet" who remarkably integrated sophisticated techniques with deep thinking while performing.[21] A Chinese musician commented that "she had interpreted Chopin's Scherzos with simplicity, fluidity, and lightness of touch."[22] Also during this time, the state appraisingly tokenized a group of unmarried young women, known as Iron Girls, in Dazhai of Shanxi Province. Their work in this agricultural model included repairing high-voltage wires.

But these awards and recognition did not prevent the fate of Gu Shengying's family from becoming more precarious. During the political persecution against Gu's father, her mother lost her job, and her younger brother quit school due to scarlet fever. The livelihood of this family fell on twenty-year-old Gu Shengying, who earned a wage equal to an associate professor in Chinese colleges. Meanwhile, in essays and letters, she seldom mentioned the hardship at home. When she wrote home from abroad during contests, Gu Shengying mostly talked about people and events that had to do with piano performance. She simply had to hold herself together for sake of the whole family. But over time, frequent international tours not only extracted the best of her musical performance, but they also brought mental strain on the young musician. Her diary during this time showed an intense and almost obsessive perfectionism in performance and a strong fear of failure that would lead to the family's persecution.

It is important to point out that even this intense struggle Gu Shengying experienced could not be compared to what the rest of the country was suffering during the Great Leap Forward. An ideological campaign, haphazard experimentation, and draconian measures against migration of the poor was compounded by natural disasters that left tens of millions to starve to death and the economy shattered. Among the masses,

> [g]lowing output reports coming in from around the country reassured everyone that the hoped-for Communist prosperity was imminent. But the dining halls soon foundered on the larger problems engendered by the Leap: widespread false reporting of massively inflated productivity by local leaders afraid of being characterized as laggards; excessive government requisitions of grain, in part based on these false reports and in part the result of callous decisions at the top; administrative chaos in huge new structures run by inexperienced cadres; the state decision to repay all debts to the Soviet union, which in 1960 broke off fraternal relations with China partly over the unorthodox strategy of the Great Leap; and bad weather.[23]

As required by the changing political climate and Gu's own eagerness to show her political loyalty, Gu Shengying changed the elitist style of piano performance and adopted the communist "mass line." She began to perform in places outside the music hall, such as factories and parks in order to "immerse into the mass." There she was forbidden to play Chopin, Liszt, or Shumann. The designated repertoire was usually revolutionary songs such as "Sing a Mountain Song to the Party," "The Sky in Liberation Zone," "Lift High the Revolutionary Flag," or "Proletariats of the World United." As usual, she willingly complied. In a letter to a friend, Gu wrote, "I agree with what you said that 'it's a long-term task to change our thought and emotions.

Frequenting the countryside and factories are doing good to people like us who always preferred something foreign, something ancient and something single-handed.' "[24] It is important to note that Gu Shengying, just like Zhao Luorui, had given way to such a heightened class consciousness that her religious consciousness and gender identity faded. We have no evidence of what she was actually wrestling with. A form of "bourgeoisie-guilt" was probably accumulating in her because her expertise was the fruit of an elitist, cosmopolitan, modernizing mission, which found itself in frequent tension with recurring populism and nativism. The new virtue was demonstrated by disliking Western scholarship and music. For Chinese artists who were in survival mode in this time, their primary identity was that one of patriotic devotion to China, and this prohibited them from escaping new forms of bondage.

In April 1963, Gu wrote in another letter showing that her life had been revolving around political study, but she realized its importance. She wrote, "Capitalist thoughts and old habits may sprout and spread again when socialist thoughts have not yet taken root in us. . . . I deeply sense the Party's high standards that are becoming more and more specific. Education is timely and class struggles are serious."[25] In the same year, Gu also devoted an entire recital to Chinese composers including a medley titled "Chairman Mao Comes to Our Village."[26] Influenced by her Soviet mentors, Gu Shengying was able to adapt her piano performance to a style that was patriotic yet alien, revolutionary yet elitist. But no matter how hard she tried, this high-form art did not have a social base in Chinese society. A new ruling class formed, with many communist leaders coming from China's interior; they regarded urban China as decadent and foreign. The compromises made by Gu Shengying did not extend any credits to her family. Like her obviously Christian name, Gu's piano expertise was later viewed by the populist revolutionaries as something too foreign in Mao's China. As a contemporary of Gu Shengying and a member of the Shanghai Conservatory recalls: "Because of the Conservatory's leadership, we had received a bourgeois education, which had cut us off from the lifehood of the New China—its peasants, soldiers, and workers."[27] These musicians of Western persuasion were seen as failing the central goal of the revolution, which was "to bring dignity and well-being to the oppressed."[28] Historian Richard Curt Kraus writes that "the piano was likened to a coffin, in which notes rattled about like the bones of the bourgeoisie. . . . it is *the* Western musical instrument, only tentatively tooted in a society busily rejecting Western influence."[29]

By 1965, the entire climate in the art industry had undergone dramatic changes. The most popular shows were a musical called *The East Is Red* and a ballet *The White-Haired Girl* (*bai bamo nv*), which was later adapted into Beijing Opera and a film.[30] The year before, on celebrating the Fifteen Anniversary of the People's Republic of China, premier Zhou Enlai directed a thirty-five-song musical called *The East Is Red* with over 3,500 actors. It began with the prelude *The East Is Red* and ended with all in attendance singing *The Internationale*. In the prelude, symbols such as sunflowers and the sun represent Mao as a Creator. The lyrics repeatedly praise Mao with "He is the Great Savior of the people. He seeks happiness for the people." Part one, entitled "Dawn from the East," implies a hope. The succeeding four parts chronicle the history of the revolution. The subject of history, "the people," is endowed with life by Mao (represented as the Light of Life). In the twelfth song "Red Army Soldiers Miss Mao Zedong," a song about how the party leads the army, includes the lyrics: "I looked up to the guiding lamp/ my heart missed Mao Zedong/ Thinking of you while getting lost/ I have found the direction/ Thinking of you in the dark/ I have light on my way. . . . Thinking of you in adversity/ I have strength/ Thinking of you in victory/ I have brightness in my heart." These figures of speech mimic Christian devotion to the Savior. The theme of part five is "Burying the Dynasty of Chiang Kai-shek," in which an old chaotic order is completely replaced with a new order. In the end, all nations unite and worship together. A universalism with Hegelian-Marxist historical dialectics merge into the narratives of Mao and the Chinese revolution. "The Internationale" was used to sum up the human commonwealth. This narrative structure follows a Messianic consciousness in traditional Western Christian theology inherited by Marx. It has a "creation-fall-chaos-redemption" theological structure. All these were not accidental. During the rehearsal for this musical, Chinese premier Zhou Enlai proposed that "the portraits of Marx and Lenin should be placed to the left side of the veil. There also needed to be two flags rising in front of these portraits—one Party flag and one red flag with the portrait of young Mao Zedong, showing that it is under these two flags that China's revolutionary army is marching on."[31] The Marx-Lenin-Mao link completes the creation of the new world and a united humanity.

The White-Haired Girl is based on legends circulating in rural China, depicting the misery suffered by local peasants, especially women. Stories of a dozen women stretched from the late Qing to the 1930s, a span of what Old China looked like. This ballet performance won the praise of Mao and became one classic of revolutionary China. Everyone who grew up in the 1960s was familiar with its music. This ballet and many other revolutionary shows condemning the old society while praising the new effectively became the standard for all performing arts in China. A historical narrative of the Chinese Communist Party as a savior of China was demanded of all artists. Before the Cultural Revolution, symbols about Mao like "the sun from the east" and "the helmsman" represented a motivating force with roots in traditional mythical worship and life origins. They continued the representation that compared emperors to the "sun" or "heaven" in ancient history. But the term "helmsman" was a product of modern history—in the beginning of nation-building after the American revolution, the nation began to be referred to as a "boat," and the leader of the nation was a "captain" or "helmsman." This imagery replaced the allegory of the nation as "the mystic body" or "Leviathan" since the Middle Ages. In early communist China, Mao and the party were said to be the full representation of three systems of truth.

The life of a revolutionary artist needed to be politically correct and busy. Gu Shengying's diary during this time showed a hectic schedule. She became exhausted between formal performances and playing to the masses in countryside and factories. Sometimes she was asked to perform for welcomes of key communist leaders. But Gu always cheered herself up by repeating the purpose of these tasks. In foreign countries, performers rarely adjust their program according to the needs of the audience; but rather contrarily, the audience choose the performer according to their preferences. But being a musician in communist China had to serve the people. She reasoned, "Performing to the worker comrades is a more correct experiment than having students and professionals in the audience."[32] She reminded herself of the goal that "I will strive to revolutionize and become a true revolutionary, a communist soldier and a communist party member."[33]

But according to her biographers, it is puzzling why a talented and educated musician like Gu Shengying who had gained international affirmation would change her own commitment so much to the extent that she self-revolutionized.[34] It could be that Gu did it all to compensate for the lack of political loyalty as determined by her father's case. At a time when everything needed to revolutionize in order to secure legitimate survival, Gu Shengying had to twist her own values. As one of China's most famous musicians, she had long suffered the political pressure to join the Chinese Communist Party. In 1964, the Sino-Soviet split brought more uncertainty and stress for Gu, who had been mentored by Soviet musicians.

Unfortunately, history did not present Gu Shengying with a smoother path. When Mao Zedong launched his Great Proletarian Cultural Revolution, it was aimed at overthrowing top leaders of the Communist Party by agitating the youth of the nation, mainly college and middle-school students. These young Red Guards enthusiastically traveled all cross China, reading from a red book of Mao's words on class struggles and ransacking people's homes to rid of the Four Olds, including ideas, culture, customs, and habits of the exploiting class. Christians were most likely to become targets of such violence. Moreover, Red Guards liked to make public spectacles of victims through these mob activities, resulting in thousands of suicides. As historian Daniel Bays writes, "In countless places, Christians were put through such abuse that many did not survive the ordeal."[35] Over a decade of history of

Chinese Protestantism since 1967 became undocumented except for scattered anecdotes and individual testimonials.

In the summer of 1966, as secondary-school pupils rose to strike down their teachers in Beijing, Gu Shengying began to fear for worse things to come. China under Maoism entered into a Hobbesian state of large-scale violence, or rather, a collective madness. The day before she returned from Beijing, Gu had a long chat with a friend at the Central China Music Academy. They talked about Vietnamese work songs and other personal affairs. Before departing, Gu Shengying gave all her winter clothes to this friend. After returning to Shanghai, Gu began to live a more secluded life and limited her outings to Shanghai Orchestra Society for political study sessions. But in September, the shocking news came that Fu Lei and his wife, neighbors and good friends of Gu Shengying, committed suicide together in their home. Fu had once tutored Gu in Chinese literature when she was young. As events later unfolded, Chinese intellectuals in higher education and arts became the focus of political persecution by radical revolutionaries.

On January 31, 1967, Gu Shengying suffered another public struggle meeting held at Shanghai Symphony Orchestra. At the time, she was a member of Shanghai City Revolutionary Committee, a new association emerging from what was known as the "January Power-Change Storm." Radicals dragged her onto the stage and struck her face. They pulled her hair and cursed her as "a classic white-collar professional," "a traitor with foreign connections," "a revisionist," and "offspring of historical anti-revolutionaries." They also made Gu keel down before a statue of Mao to confess. A colleague of Gu stepped on her fingers. Another mocked her by putting a spittoon on her head. Toward the end of this public humiliation, the abusers announced that Gu would be the main target for public confession and another struggle meeting the next day. They threatened to beat Gu's mother and brother too. As Li Delun later recalled, "these acts may not lead to tragedy, but to Gu Shengying who was as pure as crystal, the humiliation was too much for her to bear."[36]

That very night, Gu Shengying lost all hope. The last shred of strength to move on with life was gone. Along with her mother and younger brother, Gu committed suicide in their home using a gas stove.[37] They left a farewell letter to Gu's father, alluding to a reunion in heaven one day. The examining doctor wrote a death announcement in haste and ordered cremation of the bodies. Since Gu's father was still in prison, nobody collected their ashes after cremation. It was not until eight years later, in 1975, when Gu Shengying' father finished his prison term and returned to Shanghai that he learned about the death of these family members.[38] He began collecting anything that had to do with Gu Shengying. Since then, Gu's father became the curator of a small, private Gu Shengying Memorial Museum in Shanghai.

As scholar and ethnographer, Wang Xeuqin writes, in the beginning of Mao's Cultural Revolution, "schools in all of China have been turned into detainment centers, prisons and slaughter houses"[39] where most leading figures of universities also suffered violent beatings.[40] Many committed suicide through a variety of methods, ranging from drinking pesticide, wrist-cutting, jumping down the building, touching electric outlets, lying down on railroads and other horrors. The rash of suicides among Chinese intellectuals during Mao's Cultural Revolution was a neglected part of history. According to historian Neil J. Diamant, it was a unique phenomenon because "the extant literature does not give the impression that peasants or workers responded to political attacks by taking their own lives."[41] Rather,

> intellectuals sometimes reacted to violence directed at them by committing suicide, a final gesture of defiance against the miscarriage of justice very much in the Confucian intellectual tradition . . . by 1966 the family was no longer a secure refuge from national politics: politicized, class-conscious children might attack parents, and ideologically literate spouses might "draw a line" and ostracize their partner should they be attacked. When the private sphere of family and home was attacked with unprecedented thoroughness . . ., intellectuals under assault felt they had no place to which to turn. One result of this was suicide.[42]

Among the victims, a group of Christian intellectuals stood out. They belonged to a highly educated generation with overseas study experiences prior to 1949. Almost all of them made the decision to return to the motherland out of a patriotic passion. Some had the hope that Christianity and Communism would coexist under a regime that promised religious freedom. But what started in 1952 went downhill for them. As historians summarize, "In the middle and late 1950s, China divided the world into imperialist, socialist, and nationalist countries. One important aspect of China's foreign policy was to win over and unite with nationalist countries in Asia, Africa, and Latin America, to expand its anti-America united front, to isolate and strike against the imperialist bloc headed by the United States."[43] By the time Red Guards' violence struck in 1966, these Chinese intellectuals had already suffered a few rounds of communist political campaigns such as the Three-Anti and Five-Anti campaigns (1951–1952) and the Anti-Rightists Movement (1957–1959).

The wave of violence in August 1966 became the last straw for many. One example was the prominent Chinese novelist Lao She, a baptized Christian since 1922.[44] He had advocated for Sunday School reform and the necessity of indigenous Chinese leadership in the church. From 1924 to 1925, Lao She taught Chinese language at the University of London. Influenced by British writers such as Charles Dickens, Lao She began a career of literary creation where a variety of Christian characters emerged from his novels. Nobel Prize literature winner Pearl Buck praised him as the most Chinese writer.[45] In 1951, Lao She wrote about his struggles to accept the norm of verbal abuse and physical violence.[46] In his "excitement and cheer over things in society," Lao She viewed denunciation meetings as something new and strange. He explained: "The meeting began with an announcement about the campaign and the crimes of those evil bullies. Rows and rows of people sitting down the stage shouted slogans like 'Down with the evil bullies!' and 'Embrace the People's Government!' "[47] He was utterly overwhelmed by the unison of voices "sounded like a crashing wave of the ocean," which meant to him "the voices of the people." When crowds of people shouted for physical attacks, Lao She found himself and other intellectuals influenced by this rising sentiment, shouting out the same verbal violence.

Unfortunately, even these expressions of political loyalty did not save Lao She from his own public humiliation. Radicals targeted him because of his overseas experience and intellectual status. He could not bear it. On August 23, 1966, Red Guards publicly beat him and twenty-eight others for three hours. They were made to kneel on the ground, and students surrounded them with accusations and violent gestures. Another writer then stood up to charge Lao She with acts of treason because he had accepted American dollars.[48] The Public Security Bureau detained him until midnight and asked him to return the next day for another struggle meeting. Early the next morning, he left home unnoticed and drowned himself in Taiping Lake. Lao She tragically ended his life without knowing that he would be nominated for the Nobel Prize in literature that same year. When Lao She's son went to pick up his ashes at the cremation center, he was told that they had been discarded.[49] But even at the last moment of his life, Lao She was most concerned to show his loyalty to the Communist regime. Lao She's last words that night to his wife were: "The People understand me. The Party and Chairman Mao understand me. Premier Zhou understand me best!"[50] The disillusionment they expressed was not about their new regime and beloved motherland, but about their failure in proving their loyalty to the Communist Party.

Another notable Chinese intellectual who committed suicide was Liu Dezhong, lecturer in the Foreign Language Department of Fudan University. Liu's mother was German and his father Chinese. Both parents were devout Christians who raised Liu in the faith. In early October 1966, the Red Guards raided Liu's home and shaved off half his wife's hair to humiliate her. Soon afterward, Liu and his wife dressed themselves in decent new clothes and hanged themselves together using a newly purchased white rope. When the Red Guards found their dead bodies, they also saw that on their table, a Bible was turned to the Gospel of Matthew. There was a piece of paper with two lines in English: "When an earthly refuge fails me, can I find a shelter in the love of Christ?" At that time, the usage of English was seen as a sign of treason, so to the Red Guards this paper note confirmed the disloyalty of their actions. In other instances, although many used suicide to prove their innocence, the Red Guards and their backing political authorities interpreted the fact of suicide to be the sure proof of a counterrevolutionary traitor.

Because nationalist identities are often constructed in opposition to what is defined as "foreign," it inevitably entails intolerance, both domestically and abroad. It often underpins imperialism, war, racism, and intolerance, and sometimes even forges an engine of revolt against foreign presence (anti-foreignism). Chinese nationalism, as an ideology of the nation-state under the Chinese Communist Party, has become the civil religion. Citizens are required to sacrifice all else in order to further the image of the nation. In this way, nationalism may slip into institutional abuse. The personification of the nation by way of the metaphor of "motherland" enhances the legitimacy of such abuse. The rationale goes that just as a mother gives birth to a child and that child owes everything to the mother, the motherland may claim everything from the citizen. As a result, this ideology leads to a deprivation of men and women's identity and integrity.

Similar collective suicides triggered by large-scale violence in China happened a few decades before. In 1900, when an alliance of eight foreign powers used violent force against the Boxers in Beijing, as many as 570 Chinese women committed suicide after they sensed the imminent threat of rape.[51] Woman revolutionary leader He Xiangning once lamented this mass suicide incident as a national shame.[52] During Mao's time, historians later also notice the surge of mass suicide among homosexuals.[53]

The tragic collective suicide of Gu Shengying and her family was a silent retreat from a chaotic reality that promised no further earthly consonance. The legacy of Gu Shengying resembles that of the archaeologist Chen Mengjia, husband of Zhao Luorui. Although Gu did not author books to leave behind or pass on her piano techniques to students, her story reminds later generations of a brief cultural renaissance in communist China. It continues to inspire Chinese artists who strive for the unity of our common humanity through global cultural exchange.

Until the time of writing, some texts still mention Gu Shengying's death as "due to an illness."[54] The same tragedy of suicide was repeated among seventeen professionals that affiliated with Shanghai Music Academy.[55] In the midst of these waves of intellectual suicides, the public demonstration of apathy was chilling. Writer and literary critic Ba Jin observed that "people had no sympathy when seeing an acquaintance trying to jump down a building."[56] Even worse, the choice of "suicide" were used by radicals who conveniently attribute the cause of death as a confirmation for these individuals' "crimes."[57] Gu Shengying did not leave writings that reveal her state of mind to later generations. However, one of her biographers Li Delun offers a fitting analysis:

Although some intellectuals with independent thinking might awaken and improve themselves under such hardship, Gu Shengying was different. She was only a pianist, and like many artists who are simple and kind, she conformed to the mainstream ideology, hoping to gain approval from the Communist Party and follow the pace of her time. But when all her efforts were shattered, she was left with no console.[58]

It was not until recent years when the Chinese public had a feverish interest in the history of Republican China that Gu Shengying was remembered as "a born Chopin performer and a poet of the piano."[59] In 2019, Chinese media covered an event when the city of Shanghai unveiled a new memorial wall near Gu Shengying's former residence to commemorate her as China's first prize-winning pianist at international contests.[60]

It may appear that not much in the brief life of Gu Shengying had explicitly articulated the gender and religious aspect of living under the communist regime. But that is exactly the point—most of this period's polemics have been dominated by politicized and confrontational identities that little room was there for a continuation of previous narratives. Although the next chapters would introduce Christian women who were able to survive this oppressive stage of the regime and resumed their agency in social affairs, this history is incomplete if we exclude Gu Shengying's tragic life. Her suicide was a final social action against a totalitarian regime that many educated Christians eventually took. Society at large was concerned about whether counterrevolutionary attitudes could be curbed in all institutions. People have been diligently searching for an invisible enemy that may become embodied and emerge as a new bourgeoisie. Even the issue of gender inequality was also brushed aside, compared to the early 1950s. In fact, the CCP-directed Women's Federation was dissolved in 1966 on the grounds that at a time of class struggles, women's issues were the same as men's.[61] But there are larger layers of reality that became increasingly gendered. Just as the Great Leap Forward and its aftermath deprived many youth of their education and career choices, the Cultural Revolution also affected young men and women in gender-differentiated ways. Hershatter explains:

Gender was a far less visible organizing axis. Still it was not absent. Women's mode of dress signified their class allegiance. Red Guard girl students dressed like male soldiers, with cropped hair, armbands, and wide belts. There was a missionizing zeal in their adoption of this military aesthetic: groups of Red Guards seized women pedestrians on city streets in the fall of 1966, cutting their braids, slicing up skirts and form-fitting pants, and warning violators of this new dress code not to mimic the fashion habits of the bourgeoisie. When Wang Guangmei, the wife of China's president, was hauled before a huge political rally to be criticized for her revisionist politics, Red Guards humiliated her by dressing her in a satirically exaggerated version of bourgeois women's attire: a form-fitting dress and a necklace of ping-pong balls.[62]

Gu Shengying suffered similar public humiliation. But instead of uniting together, young women of this time were intensely divided by class ideology, with one group launching mob violence against whoever appeared to be an outlier of the movement. Role models for women under Mao's Cultural Revolution were established in the eight communist ballets produced by Jiang Qing, the former actress on Republic era screen and later wife of Mao Zedong. One particular household name from the ballet plot was The White-haired Girl, who was seized and sexually assaulted by a landlord in Old China, and was rescued by the Eighth Route Army who fought for a New China. The women heroines in these widely viewed public dramas all showed an awakening political consciousness in a victim-turned-survivor story line. Male party cadres were portrayed as benevolent rescuers, who fought for these women's freedom. The final message, which was almost an emotional alter call, was always that women should become revolutionaries too. Gail Hershatter summarizes:

> No cultural productions during the Cultural Revolution were set in the present or addressed inequalities that persisted under socialism. The main message they imparted to women was not a new one: class divisions are fundamental, the roots of women's oppression are found in class oppression, the road to emancipation is to work alongside men to make revolution and build socialism.[63]

After Mao's death, his wife Jiang Qing was arrested, tried, convicted and imprisoned until her death by suicide in 1991. Public criticisms against Jiang Qing were made along gendered lines, "invoking a saying from imperial times that when a woman seized political power, chaos would result."[64] Along with this kind of public commentary was a popular rejection of militant and activistic femininity. Women who grew up during this era largely refrained from viewing gender inequality as the result of structural injustice in society. The bankruptcy of a class-driven view of women did, however, give way to a more multifaceted approach in the post-reform era. Religion was not absent from this history; quite the contrary, Maoist rituals constituted a political religion that encapsulated public life.

NOTES

1. Bays, *A New History*, 179.
2. Contemporaries of Gu Shengying testify that she was baptized at a young age. See Chen Mingyuan, "Remembering Big Sister Gu Shengying: Mass of an Atheist,"

The Independent Review, February 12, 2009. Online resource. http://www.duping.ne
t/XHC/show.php?bbs=11&post=945377

3. Richard Curt Kraus, *Piano and Politics in China: Middle-Class Ambitions and the Struggle over Western Music* (New York: Oxford University Press, 1998), 4.

4. Ma Geshun was a professor at the Shanghai Conservatory of Music and one of the most significant choral conductors in twentieth-century China. See Chen Ruiwen, "Sinicizing Christian Music at Shanghai Community Church," in Zheng Yangwen, ed., *Sinicizing Christianity* (Leiden: Brill, 2017), 301, 305. Gu Shengying accompanied Ma Geshun when Messiah was showing across China in 1954. See Cao Shengjie, "We Remember Professor Ma Geshun," *Heavenly Wind* (official magazine of the Three-Self Patriotic Movement) Issue 2, 2016. http://www.jdjcm.com/jiaohui
/2019.html

5. Cao Liqun (ed.), *Missing Documents: A Gu Shengying Reader* (Guilin: Lijiang Publishing, 2017). Kindle book.

6. Ding Zilin, "Three People Deeply Imprinted on My Memory," *Human Rights in China*, April 8, 2001. Online resource. https://www.hrichina.org/en/content/4665

7. Lily Xiao Hong Lee et al., *Biographical Dictionary of Chinese Women*, vol. 2 (New York: Routledge, 2002), 182.

8. Cao, *Missing Documents*. Kindle book.

9. Kraus, *Piano and Politics in China*, 130.

10. Ibid., px.

11. Ibid., 198.

12. "Shanghai Story," *Sohu*, June 7, 2009. Online resource. http://www.sohu.com
/a/319209298_659409

13. Pan was a Chinese Communist Party leader in Shanghai and vice mayor of Shanghai in 1949. But in 1955, Pan was accused of counterrevolutionary crimes and sentenced to a fifteen-year prison term.

14. "Shanghai Story."

15. Cao, *Missing Documents*. Kindle book.

16. Ibid.

17. Guangren Zhou, "The Unforgettable Piano Poet: Gu Shengying," year unknown. Online resource. http://www.yufamily.org/src/ZhouGuangren_Unforgeta
bleGuShengyingPoetOfPiano.php

18. Ibid.

19. "Shanghai Story."

20. Meng Bian, *The Formation and the Development of Piano Culture in China* (Beijing: Yuehua Press, 1996). Yun Sun, *The Cross-Cultural Influence of the Formation and Evolution of Piano Pedagogy at the Shanghai Conservatory of Music*. Doctoral of Musical Arts dissertation, The City University of New York, 2012. Mo Xu, *The High Finger Piano Technique in China: Past, Present and Future*. Doctoral of Musical Arts essay, University of Iowa, 2018.

21. Cao, *Missing Documents*. Kindle book.

22. Zhu, Xiao-mei, *The Secret Piano: From Mao's Labor Camps to Bach's Goldberg Variations*, translated by Ellen Hinsey (Seattle: Amazon Crossing, 2007), 71–72.

23. Hershatter, *Women and China's Revolutions*, 141–42.

24. Letter to Mr. Diao from Gu Shengying, January 27, 1962. Included in Liqun, *Missing Documents*. Kindle book.

25. Letter to Mr. Diao from Gu Shengying, April 25, 1963. Included in Liqun, *Missing Documents*. Kindle book.

26. "Gu Shengying and Bo Yibin Perform Concerts of Chinese Music," *People's Music* (August-September 1963): 63. Quoted in Zhu, *The Secret Piano*.

27. Zhu, *The Secret Piano*, 68.

28. Ibid.

29. Kraus, *Pianos and Politics in China*, pvii.

30. Di Bai, "Feminism in the Revolutionary Model Ballets: The White-Haired Girl and the Red Detachment of Women," in Richard King, ed., *Art in Turmoil: The Chinese Cultural Revolution, 1966–76* (Vancouver: University of British Columbia Press, 2010), 188–202. Also see Bo Jia, *Gender, Women's Liberation, and the Nation-State: A Study of the Chinese Opera the White-Haired Girl*. Dissertation at Rutgers University, 2015.

31. Weizhi Zhou, "Recollections on Zhou Enlai," on *Yan Huang Chun Qiu* website, http://www.yhcqw.com/50/8342.html. Weizhi Zhou was a musical composer and producer of *The East Is Red*.

32. Gu Shengying's Diary, July 10, 1964. Included in in Liqun, *Missing Documents*. Kindle book.

33. Ibid.

34. Cao Liqun, "Remembering Gu Shengying," *Ai Yue* magazine, September 19, 2008. Online resource. http://ny.zdline.cn/h5/article/detail.do?&artId=5070

35. Bays, *A New History*, 185.

36. Cao, *Missing Documents*. Kindle book.

37. Unlike Beijing where residents rely on burning coal for heating, Shanghai had installed more advanced gas stoves for its residents. But from June to September 1966, gas stoves became the main tool for people in Shanghai to commit suicide. Other notable people who ended their lives this way include Professor Li Pingxin at East China Normal University, Professor Li Cuizhen at Shanghai Music Academy, and poet Wen Jie at Shanghai Writers' Association. Across China, many suicides happened with couples or families ending their lives together. Examples include translator Fu Lei and his wife, Professor Liu Shousong at Wuhan University and his wife, Professor Liu Dezhong, at Fudan University and his wife, Professor Huang Guozhang at Shaanxi Normal University and his wife.

38. Liu Manqin, "The Death of the Famous Female Pianist Gu Shengying," *Zhengming* 23 (September 1979): 14–19.

39. Wang, *Victims of the Cultural Revolution*, 51.

40. Ibid., 272.

41. Diamant, *Revolutionizing the Family*, 308–9.

42. Ibid.

43. Danhui Li and Yafeng Xia, *Mao and the Sino-Soviet Split, 1959–1973: A New History* (Lanham: Lexington Books, 2018), 230.

44. "Christian Lao She: How Church Experiences Changed His Fate," *Tencent News*, February 22, 2019. Online resource. https://new.qq.com/omn/20190222/201 90222B1ATQ3.html

45. Ibid.

46. Lao She, "New Society Is a New School," *People's Literature*, October 1, 1951. Quoted in Hu Jieqing (ed.), *Lao She's Career as a Writer* (Tianjin: Baihua Literary Press, 1981), 247–49.

47. Ibid.

48. Yang, Mo. *The Diary of Yang Mo* (Beijing: October Literary Press, 1994), 5.

49. Shu, Yi. "Two Last Days of My Father's Life," in Shu Yi (ed.), *The Death of Lao She* (Beijing: International Culture Publishing, 1987), 62.

50. Ibid., 61.

51. George Lynch, *The War of the Civilizations: Being the Record of a "Foreign Devil's" Experiences with the Allies in China* (London: Longman's Publishing, 1901), 140.

52. Hershatter, *Women and China's Revolutions*, 55.

53. Li Yinhe, "Regulating Male Same-Sex Relationships in the People's Republic of China," in Elaine Jeffreys, ed., *Sex and Sexuality in China* (New York: Routledge, 2006), 84.

54. Lee, *Biographical Dictionary of Chinese Women*, 183.

55. Cao, *Missing Documents*. Notable figures who committed suicides include Professor Yang Jiaren and his wife, chair of Piano Department Li Cuizhen, Music Theory Professor Shen Zhibai, and department chair of String Instruments Chen Youxin.

56. Ibid.

57. Ibid.

58. Ibid.

59. Lee, *Biographical Dictionary of Chinese Women*, 182.

60. Yang Jian, "'Culture Walls' Recall History on Yuyuan Road," *Shine News*, April 6, 2019. Online resource.
    https://www.shine.cn/news/metro/1904062573/ He Qi, "Shanghai story shop seeks stories about Yuyuan road," *China Daily*, August 23, 2019. Online resource.
    http://www.chinadaily.com.cn/a/201908/23/WS5d5fb96da310cf3e35567990 .html
    Lin Shujuan, "Injecting Vigor into Old Communities," *China Daily,* June 28, 2019. Online resource.
    http://www.chinadaily.com.cn/global/2019-06/28/content_37485772.htm

61. Zheng Wang, *Finding Women in the State: A Socialist Feminist Revolution in the People's Republic of China, 1949–1964* (Oakland: University of California Press, 2017), 112–39.

62. Hershatter, *Women and China's Revolutions*, 245–46.

63. Ibid., 249.

64. Ibid., 250.

Chapter 7

The Party Could Still Use You

From the late 1950s to 1960s, many educated Chinese Christians with expertise or overseas experiences became targets of suppression and mob violence during Mao's intensifying campaigns. The previous chapter introduces the unusual phenomenon of suicide among educated Chinese. Admittedly, many also survived even the harshest persecution. In this chapter, I focus on two Chinese women who not only survived but were also able to rise to the center stage of public life after the Cultural Revolution. These women are public health advocate Lin Qiaozhi and writer-scholar Xie Wanying (also known as Bing Xin). Unlike other women pioneers whose names were obliterated, Lin and Xie were tokenized in the official history of Chinese regime.

When the communists took rule, Lin Qiaozhi worried about the future of medical science in China. Confused and disturbed by new ideological movements, she read the Bible more diligently.[1] Unlike many other Chinese intellectuals who gravitated toward political power, Lin always kept a distance. For example, when Lin received an invitation to be publicly present at the new regime's inauguration ceremony in front of the Tiananmen Square on October 1, 1949, she declined, claiming that the occasion had nothing to do with her profession and that she preferred to stay with patients in the hospital. In 1950, when the communist regime began a nationwide land reform and ordered obstetrician-gynecologist Lin Qiaozhi to join the campaign, she told a communist leader that "as a Bible-believing Christian, I have decided not to participate in any activity that has nothing to do with ob-gyn medicine."[2] In the early 1950s, when many well-known Chinese intellectuals joined the Chinese Communist Party, Lin Qiaozhi told Chinese Premier Zhou Enlai that as a Christian, she could not become a communist party member.[3]

Lin Qiaozhi was born on Gulangyu, a treaty port and pedestrian-only island off the coast of Xiamen in southeastern China. Since her birthday was two days before Christmas, Mr. Lin considered his third daughter as a gift from God. They named her Qiaozhi, meaning "nimble and innocent." When Lin was five, her mother died of cervical cancer. It was the first trauma that led her to realize how important women's health can be to the family. Lin Qiaozhi was brought up by her father and older brother. Lin's father went to Singapore in pursuit of a college degree and returned to work as a translator and writer in Gulangyu. A devout Christian, Mr. Lin believed that women should also be educated. He regularly took his children to church and told them Bible stories. Despite financial difficulties in the family, Lin Qiaozhi obtained a good education through a girls' mission school founded by British Presbyterians. Lin's English was more fluent than her Chinese. She also excelled at math, a subject that most young girls in her school found difficult.

When Lin Qiaozhi reached age ten, she entered the Xiamen Women's Normal School, where a British missionary Mary Carling mentored her spiritually. Carling encouraged Lin to read *The Story of a Soul* by Thérèse of Lisieux, which became an important work for Lin's spiritual journey. Having read it so many times, she could recite certain paragraphs by heart. Lin told Ms. Carling that this book helped her appreciate more about Jesus welcoming little children in the Bible. She also understood that doing things that appear mundane with great love is in itself a big mission. At age thirteen, Lin Qiaozhi received baptism in her local church. Other teachers also recognized the gift of Lin's nimble hands, and they suggested that she could become a physician. Influenced by her father's faith, Lin Qiaozhi read in the gospels and the book of Acts about the way Jesus and his followers practiced healing power while spreading the Good News.[4] Ms. Carling encouraged Lin that given her academic abilities, she should pursue further education.

After working for two years in her hometown as a primary school teacher, twenty-year-old Lin took the premedical entrance exam in Shanghai. During the test, a female classmate fainted due to nervousness-induced heatstroke. Stopping writing the exam, Lin immediately came to her aid. She placed the classmate in a cool place and performed cooling methods on her. Although this incident affected her test results, Lin's unfinished exam still showed her fluent English and academic abilities. At the medical school, students were expected to communicate with many foreigner physicians and to read research materials, so English was a key consideration. Impressed with her selfless and calm demeanor, the college bent the rules and admitted her to the program.[5] Within her family, Lin's stepmother and second oldest brother opposed her decision to study medicine. The main reason was that they considered twenty-year-old Lin's chance of getting married would decrease if she studied for a few more years. Lin Qiaozhi was determined that she would rather remain unmarried than miss this opportunity. Lin's older brother was her main supporter. Upon leaving her southeastern hometown for Peking,

Lin Qiaozhi was motivated by her father's farewell reminder to her that "one would better become a famous physician if not a good premier."

In her fifth year of study, Lin's father died of a cerebral hemorrhage. Lin's older brother continued to support her financially. After eight years of medical training, Lin was one of two to receive the Wen Hai scholarship award for graduates.[6] In 1929, Lin Qiaozhi won a scholarship to enter Peking Union Medical College (PUMC), sponsored by the Rockefeller Foundation in 1917. Historian Robert Bickers writes of the excellence of this medical institution: "Rockefeller funding transformed this from the workable but mediocre standard that was generally the norm in underfunded missionary institutions into something quite out of the ordinary, even by international standards: a Johns Hopkins for China, an elite institution."[7] He also notes that students at PUMC mostly came from wealthy Chinese families who could afford the fees, which were five times of other schools.[8] It was at PUMC where Lin Qiaozhi excelled and obtained a doctor of medicine degree accredited by the New York State University. Lin also became the first indigenous female physician in the Department of Obstetrics and Gynecology of PUMC hospital. Her specialized areas included fetal breathing, female pelvic diseases, gynecologic oncology, and neonatal hemolytic disorders.[9] Because tradition-minded administrators of the PUMC hospital considered professionalism and motherhood conflicting roles for Chinese women, they made a policy against women physicians getting married while in their position. This became a large reason for Lin's preference to stay single.

Lin Qiaozhi was widely known for her genuine care for patients. Once she explained her philosophy of care to students: "Physicians are treating real living human beings. Medical care is not mechanical work, and doctors cannot become technicians. They need to treat patients face-to-face and offer adequate care."[10] When she was training nurses, Lin told them that with Christ's love, all mundane tasks of caring for patients could become enjoyable. She considered it a negligence and dishonor for medical staff to ignore antenatal check-ups for pregnant women.[11] This includes striving to respect the patients' needs. On one Christmas eve, when all physicians in Lin's hospital were celebrating, a pregnant woman had a critical bleeding condition. Lin was an assistant physician with no surgery experience. In order to save the patient, she had to forgo the rules of the hospital, just as she did decades before at the premedical exam. Lin succeeded and in just six months she was promoted to the full title of residential physician, which usually required up to five years of professional training.

When teaching nurses and young physicians, Lin Qiaozhi also paid much attention to how much care they had for patients. To illustrate, she gave the grade of "Good" to only one medical student in an entire class during a particular year. Other than getting the answers right, this student left a comment on the medical record that "the patient had bean-size sweat droplets on her forehead." Lin affirmed this observation as caring and responsible. Other times, Lin stressed that medical staff need to respect the dignity of patients. Once a medical student forgot to pull the shade around a patient during examination, Lin walked over and reminded her to "protect the patient."[12] When an intern physician scolded some women in labor pain for shouting too loudly, Lin asked this doctor to apologize. She made a policy forbidding any verbal offense from medical staff to women who were about to deliver, for the latter were in an intense state of emotional anxiety and pain. Lin reminded her staff that it was out of great trust that patients came to the hospital for medical assistance, and that the actions of medical professionals should not fail them.

At that time, China's infant mortality was three to five times of that in Western countries such as the United States, the United Kingdom, and France.[13] The risk of women dying in childbirth was so high that there was a widely used saying that by having a baby, a woman "makes a tour around the entrance of hell." At a time when Western medicine was frowned upon, Chinese ob-gyn physicians like Lin Qiaozhi made a historical contribution to alleviating this common plight of women. When working in PUMC hospital, Lin Qiaozhi also strove to treat patients equally. When some nurses reminded her that some VIP patients were in the waiting room, often wives of certain politicians or foreign ambassadors, Lin always replied: "Only serious conditions deserve special treatments."[14]

The 1930s were a time of professional development for Lin Qiaozhi. In 1932, Lin went for advanced training at the London School of Medicine and Dentistry and the School of Medicine at the University of Manchester. She also spent a year in Vienna as a visiting scholar. When the Japanese war broke out in 1937, Lin was an associate professor at PUMC. She befriended famous writer Xie Wanying and delivered Xie's three children in the same hospital. Years later, Xie included a character based on Doctor Lin in her novel *About Women*,[15] and she wrote praising words about Lin's contribution: "She helped nurture numerous fighters of the nation!"[16]

In 1939, Lin did research in the Pritzker School of Medicine at the University of Chicago. Her research publications were under the name Lim Kah T'I. Prior to this, Lin's English publications had been included in academic conferences in Birmingham, Great Britain. Lin was also named an honorary member of the Chicago Academy of Nature in 1940. Although faculty and friends in the University of Chicago urged her to stay in America, she was determined to return to war-torn China. Although her hospital had been closed by Japanese military, Lin was determined to resume clinical practice from her residence in Beijing. She lowered the registration fee and reduced medical fees for impoverished patients. Between 1940 and 1951, she kept a total of 8,887 medical records through this small home clinic.[17]

Lin sometimes rode on the back of a donkey to see patients in rural areas. Once after helping a family in poverty deliver their child, Lin not only waived their payment but also donated money to the husband so that he could buy nutritious food for the new mother. During this decade, however, her medical research was paused.

In 1956, after the government took control of PUMC and renamed it as Beijing Obstetrics and Gynecology Hospital, it allowed Lin to become the first female director of an obstetrics and gynecology department. She was also appointed vice chair of the Chinese Medical Association and a deputy director of the Chinese Academy of Medical Services. The communist regime recognized her professionalism and included her in the new nation's political life, such as the National People's Congress and the Political Consultative Conference. It was widely known that Premier Zhou Enlai and his wife had high praise for Lin Qiaozhi. But Lin herself was not overly excited about the honors granted by communist leaders. She once said, "I cannot do without patients. I feel upset if I haven't seen patients for one day."[18] Because of her time-tested devotion to patients, many women called her a "living Guanyin (Buddha)," a widely used term for someone with superhuman compassion. Due to political censorship, however, her lifelong Christian faith was largely unknown to the general public.[19]

Lin's professionalism became a form of resistance during China's Great Leap Forward starting in 1958. Communist cadres asked the hospital to simplify procedures, including the handwash steps of sterilization. Many medical staff dared not to oppose this command, for fear that they were seen as not "revolutionary" enough. But Lin Qiaozhi defended that this method was a tested one in medical circles and changing it would lead to a high risk of infection. Because she insisted on following professional medical advice, the political authorities gave in. Also, from 1958 to 1960, Lin organized a wide census on women's cervical health in Beijing that included over 90,000 subjects. The study was later repeated with a million women in China's twenty cities. This was the first and biggest gynecological research project conducted in China.

During Mao's Cultural Revolution, PUMC hospital was renamed an "anti-imperialism" hospital, and communist cadres put up a public exhibit to "denounce the religious aggression of foreign imperialism." Directing physicians of each department were pulled down from their positions of leadership. Lin Qiaozhi was also demoted from her director position. Denounced as an "anti-revolutionary academic authority," she was demoted to the rank of a nurse, whose job included cleaning toilets and spittoons. Radicals also imposed limitations on her whereabouts. They forbade Lin from wearing traditional dresses and demanded she move out of hospital housing. Unlike other Chinese intellectuals who felt humiliated, Lin Qiaozhi remained positive in attitude and grateful for being able to remain in the medical system. She willingly cleaned every corner of the hospital. Lin reminded herself the same thing she used to tell other nurses in training that with the love of Christ, all these mundane chores could be enjoyable. When some came to ask her to join the anti-American campaign, Lin replied: "It was Americans who trained medical doctors for us, and my skills were taught by Americans."[20] The vice mayor of Beijing heard about this comment and demanded Lin to read a letter of "thought work" in the hospital staff meeting. Lin refused to follow his commands but only spoke about her love for the motherland.[21]

For a time in the late 1960s, Lin lost hope that she would ever return to practicing as an ob-gyn doctor. When a former student called her for advice on treating patients, Lin felt honored to be asked. In April 1969, the Revolutionary Committee of Union Hospital announced a decision to rectify Lin Qiaozhi. She was restored to her job and continued to treat all patients equally. Once the daughter of Peng Zhen, a high-ranking but toppled communist official, came to the hospital for treatment, Lin Qiaozhi received her despite opposition from other staff who feared political risks. When the wives of Premier Zhou Enlai and Chairman Mao Zedong came, she showed no favoritism either. In February 1971, Zhou Enlai received Lin Qiaozhi at the People's Great Hall, a sign of her political security. Fortunately, Lin did not suffer physical torture as many Chinese intellectuals did. When many Union College professors were sent down to cowsheds with their salaries suspended, Lin Qiaozhi still received a wage. She divided it and shared with many families.

In the 1970s, Lin was also appointed the vice chairwoman of the National Women's Federation. She also directed the founding of a national medical network for rural areas and trained many "barefoot" doctors and midwives in these areas.[22] From 1973 to 1977, she served as a consultant to the World Health Organization and also visited four European countries as the deputy chief of a Chinese delegation. While in Britain, Lin suffered a brain hemorrhage and was hospitalized for six months before returning to China.

Even after she was confined to the bed due to another hemorrhage in the 1980s, Lin wrote a proposal to set up a medical research center, which materialized in the Ob-gyn Research Institute under the Chinese Academy of Medical Science. She also wrote a 500,000-word volume *Gynecological Tumors*, a fruit of six decades of medical research. By then she had also published three other books, *Family Heath Advice*, *Encyclopedia of Family Child-Rearing*, and *General Knowledge for Rural Women and Children*. About the prospect of illness and death, Lin referred to her Christian faith as a source of peace: "As a doctor, I have seen too many births and deaths. I am not afraid of death, for the Bible says 'I will go to see Him.' "[23] Even China's communist media outlet *China Youth Daily* printed this testimony.

Unmarried throughout her life, Lin Qiaozhi made herself available for others' needs. In 1974, Lin donated her savings of 30,000 *yuan*, a large sum at that time, to fund the hospital's kindergarten and preschool. Just days before her passing in 1983, Lin helped deliver three infants in the hospital.

It is said that Lin Qiaozhi helped deliver over 50,000 babies in lifetime, though she had no children of her own. For this reason, Lin is also remembered as "Mother of Ten Thousand Babies" and "Doctor of Mercy."[24] Many parents name their children to commemorate the doctor. For example, names like "Jing Lin" and "Nian Lin" means "Respect Lin" and "Remember Lin." Gulangyu, her hometown, set up a Lin Qiaozhi Memorial Hall, where a white marble statue of Dr. Lin stands in the botanical garden. In 1990, China's National Postal Services issued a memorial stamp to honor her.

Lin Qiaozhi's life story shows that it was possible for Christian professionals to survive the most intense political era of Maoism by living a testimony of professional and spiritual integrity. She could have suffered more severe persecution for her unwavering Christian faith if not for the friendships and protection from key communist leaders. Her posture toward the communist regime was consistently one of respectful distancing. Though her nonpartisan example of medical professionalism won recognition from top communist leaders, she never gave her full devotion to what the totalitarian ideology required. Lin definitely was an outlier among educated Chinese who found it necessary to prove their political loyalty to the regime. Maybe her role in medicine also protected her from experiencing total disillusionment during the Cultural Revolution. A way to live out her faith has always been through medical professionalism, however trivial the tasks were. Even during the high time of class struggles, Lin Qiaozhi did not annul her gratitude for American missionaries who nurtured and trained her. She refused to distort history to feign a superficial display of patriotism.

As previously mentioned, Xie Wanying is a contemporary of Lin Qiaozhi. One of the most prominent Chinese writers, her pseudonym Bing Xin is a household name in China. She lived through modern China's most tumultuous century. Xie's fame as a young novelist and activist during the May Fourth Movement in 1919, a founding moment for Chinese communism, later shielded her from suffering severe political suppression. Due to her longevity, Xie earned the reputation of "Century Elderly" and "grandmother" of modern Chinese literature.[25]

Xie Wanying's father was a commanding officer of the Qing Imperial Navy, so her family relocated frequently. The couple had a daughter followed by three sons. Every time his wife delivered a child, Mr. Xie found a female doctor from a missionary-founded hospital, referred by his own brother who was a convert in the family. Months after Xie Wanying was born in 1900, her family had to move from a southern port city to bustling metropolitan Shanghai. A few years later, they relocated again to a coastal city in Shandong Province when Xie's father was made Head of the Naval College. With her mother often sick in bed, Xie followed her father to work. These experiences left deep and positive imprints on Xie, as she became very observant of nature and people. Mr. Xie did not bind her daughter's feet and often dressed her in boy's clothes. Later Xie Wanying even desired to become a naval official like her father. She reflected: "It was easy for me to become a tomboy."[26] But Xie soon later realized that her gender was "an obstacle in following them."[27] In 1911, before the outbreak of the Republican Revolutions, Xie's father resigned and the family returned to Fuzhou. There Xie started formal education at a girls' school. Two years later, her father was appointed director of the Naval Studies Bureau of the Admiralty in Beijing, and they were northbound.

Xie was also influenced by her grandfather, a member of the patriarchal gentry who befriended Western-trained scholars. One among them translated over 170 novels from English and French to benefit a whole generation of Chinese readers including Xie Wanying. From her youth, she had access to her grandfather's collection of Western literature and read Charles Dickens's *David Copperfield* and Alexandre Dumas's *La Dame aux Camelias*. Scholar-translator Yan Fu also taught and influenced the progressive tendency of Xie's father at Beiyang Navy Officers' School. At the same time, Xie Wanying received classical Confucian education at home, reading Chinese classics such as *A Dream of Red Mansions* and *Water Margin*. As previous chapters detailed, China was at the crossroads of breaking from its Confucian tradition.

In 1918, Chinese writer Lu Xun published *Diary of a Madman* as a determined condemnation of the Confucian tradition. In this short story, a fictional figure spent days and nights reading into Chinese history and classics, and then this madman "began to see the words between the lines, the whole book being filled with the two words—'Eat People'." Historian Daniel K. Gardner summarizes the essence of Lu Xun's work:

> Dressing itself up in the pieties of goodness and righteousness, Confucianism, in actuality, cannibalized and destroyed people; its hierarchical structure, which insisted that children be filial, that women be subordinate, and that inferiors be obedient to superiors, robbed people of their autonomy and vitality, and crushed the human spirit.[28]

Because of his analytical lens into the spirit of the Chinese people and ethos, Lu Xun has been hugely influential among young people of the time. Literature was a salvific means to awaken the soul that has long been in a moral hibernation. A careful reading of Lu Xun's works may reveal echoes of the Christian message.[29] "Although never a member of the Communist Party, [Lu] he was canonized as a patron saint of the Chinese communist revolution."[30] He was an active contributor to the woman's question, like other reformist intellectuals. For example, in 1923, Lu Xun gave a speech to female students at Peking Normal University. In discussing Henrik Ibsen's stage play *A Doll's House*, the renowned writer posed a question that later stirred up heated debate: "What happens after Nora leaves home?" Later, even Mao Zedong himself considered Xun a great thinker on the cultural front and a revolutionary. Research on Lu Xun has become a premier academic discipline. His works have been edited, annotated, and printed many times over.

It was during this literary renaissance when Xie Wanying graduated from the American Congregationalist Bridgman Academy for Girls in Peking and enrolled at the Peking Union College for Women.[31] In these Christian institutions, although Bible study was mandatory and some of her family members were Christian converts, Xie remained indifferent to worship and rituals. Burdened by social problems, she switched from medicine to literature. When the May Fourth Movement happened in 1919, Xie Wanying was the secretary for the Students' Association at Union College. She later wrote, "It was the thunder of the May Fourth Movement that 'shocked' me onto the path of writing."[32] Xie worked occasionally on propaganda pieces and published her first novel, *Two Families*, which was initially published in a local newspaper. Using the new vernacular style of Chinese language, this novel told of how feudalistic families distort young people. It immediately became popular. Xie pioneered a genre of "social problem fiction," dealing with social injustice, generational conflicts, and feminism. For the first time, she used a penname Bing Xin, meaning "Pure Heart," taken from a famous poem from the Tang Dynasty.[33] It later became such a household name that few people in China were aware of her real name:

> Bing Xin's reputation as a Chinese writer is largely based on her ability to represent the condition of ordinary women in enduring narratives that are socially complex and emotionally convincing. As a May Fourth participant who came to write in an increasingly political atmosphere, however, she was often compelled to relate her own version of feminism to the pressing demands of Chinese nationalism.[34]

Xie Wanying resorted to Christianity when she tried to incorporate a new cosmologic framework into her writing. In 1921, she wrote a poem "The Dusk" with these lines: "O God, endless wisdom, fathomless marvels, who possess all the knowledge. Is it me, or is it someone else? No one, except you, who instructed Jesus Christ through your splendor."[35] As scholars of her earlier poetry write, "Bing Xin felt extremely grateful for God's love, . . .

love became an imperative component of her social remedy."[36] Two of her most important works, *Stars* and *Letters of Young Readers* best demonstrate her philosophy. Luijun Bi highlights that "[t]he central didactic theme . . . is her notion of universal love, which is depicted as a bridge for any gap and a remedy for any social problem."[37] Later a scholar affirmed the theme of love in Xie's works "with the love of 'nature' as longitude and the love of mother and child as latitude, . . . this is the basis for all her works—there are no other words which are better than Bing Xin's to describe 'love' successfully and completely."[38] Another recent scholarly volume comments that "by depicting women and children's lives, her essays spread feminist ideas and advocated for women and children's rights."[39] Gradually, among China's literary critics, her unique approach was dubbed "Bing Xin style," which combines poetic expression with narrative realism. The renowned Chinese scholar Shu Shi once gave the following highly positive comment:

> Most authors writing in vernacular Chinese were still searching for a style suitable to the new form, and many of them were crude; some were vulgar. Miss Bing Xin had been giving a good grounding. . . . She had brought to the new medium a delicacy and refinement which made her writing fresh and direct.[40]

During this time, Union College was amalgamated with Yenching University. Xie was baptized on campus, but she recalled her decision being a response to peer pressure. As the best student in the class in a Christian college, Xie felt: "If I had not been baptized, they would also not be. I said it was easy, then I was. I do not value much religious rituals but only am convinced of behaving as a person who does not violate the creed."[41] Nevertheless, it would be a mistake to consider Xie a nominal Christian because she indeed embraced most key Christian values such as the goodness of God, the self-sacrifice of Jesus, and human responsibility for serving each other. Her life and works expressed these convictions well.

In 1923, Xie Wanying won a scholarship to attend Wellesley College in America for a master's degree in literature.[42] Her thesis was an English translation of the poems of a famous women poet of the Song Dynasty. While in America, Xie witnessed how blacks in the southern states were not allowed to worship with whites. She had doubts and grievances about such incompatibility with the teachings of Jesus. She even spoke out against racial discrimination, in an article titled "Mourning Dr. Dubois": "If apartheid is practiced in God's church, is it still a religion that promotes freedom, equality and fraternity?"[43] In her novel *Photo*, Xie Wanying also criticized the American church's treatment of Chinese believers. She unflinchingly pointed to missionary privilege: "Foreigners in China are much comfortable than the Chinese in foreign countries at least from a material aspect, don't you think so?"[44] Xie once reckoned that "the religious thought in my life is completely derived from the beauty of nature. . . . Seeing the beauty in flesh and blood form often makes me awe the admiration of creation."[45] During this time, Xie Wanying also developed "a lifelong fondness of the stories of St. Paul," particularly his conversion account in the Bible.[46] Without complying with traditional exegesis, Xie connected St. Paul's filial devotion to God with the theme of motherly love. "In Bing Xin's evocation of the biblical topic, the body of a Chinese woman is placed in the special position that St. Paul occupies to establish his mission and canonical authority."[47]

After graduating in 1926, Xie Wanying returned to teach at Yenching. By then, she had published many popular works in Chinese: *Superman* (1921), *A Maze of Stars* (1921), *Spring Water* (1926), *Letters to Young Readers* (1926). The last collection gained her wider fame and popularity. In the next decade of her career as a Yenching professor, Xie would publish more stories including *The Past* (1931), *Winter Girl* (1931), *Bygone Country* (1933) and a few anthologies. In 1929, she married another Yenching faculty Wu Wenzao, who had graduated with a doctorate from Columbia University.[48] The two young scholars had known each other from the same trip to study in America. The president of Yenching, American missionary and educator John Leighton Stuart presided at their wedding ceremony. By this time, Xie has published four collections of essays, earning a wide readership and reputation. Yenching University build an on-campus dwelling for her family, which was a way of paying respect to esteemed scholars. Xie and Wu raised three children and experimented with an egalitarian education philosophy at home and teaching them kindness and equal treatment to all people.

During the anti-Japanese war, Xie Wanying used a male pen name to publish a collection of short stories *About Women*, which was initially published in a local Chongqing journal *Weekly Review* in 1941. Then she added more stories and published revised editions in 1943, 1945, 1992, and 1993 by various publishers. The history of successive editions suggests the enduring popularity of this collection. In this important evolving work, Xie developed her own literary voice, one of lyrical and ironic style, enabling her to challenge the status quo and patriarchal authority. In *About Women*, for example, critics point out that in the early stories, "the sophisticated male narrator that disguises the gender of the author functions subtly to undermine male authority and its appearance of total mastery."[49] So instead of directly presenting images of women, her stories engage readers to a deeper and even dramatized self-reflection on problems involving gender and modernity. The later stories of this collection shift to portraying the adversity of everyday life. She also enlightened female readers to grasp a broader cultural-political tension that gender conflicts were embedded in. Mao Chen surmises, "Like her Western counterparts, such as Joyce and Faulkner, Conrad and Woolf, Bing Xin ultimately employs her modernist breakthroughs to express a more comprehensive view of a specific moment in historical time."[50] Critics consider Xie as a "feminist rhetorician" who "creatively used the vernacular . . . create a new discourse resistant to the dominant ideology."[51] Furthermore,

> [h]er feminist commitments, which need to be presented to the Western reader as unique to this particular writer, as well as her political commitment to Chinese nationalism—especially during the period leading up to the Japanese Occupation during World War Two—were crucial to her literary reception in her own time, and placed an indelible stamp on the form and content of her fiction.[52]

In 1946, after Japan surrendered, Wu Wenzao worked as a representative of the Republican government to Japan. Xie was invited to teach at Tokyo University, along with her family. She became the first foreign female professor in postwar Japan and taught anti-war Chinese poetry. The six years in Japan became a formative experience toward cosmopolitanism for their children. One day when their eight-year-old youngest son united Chinese children to scare Japanese children, Xie scolded him severely, teaching him that children are innocent in wartime. In 1951, two years after the founding of the new Chinese regime, Xie and her family returned to China. Then she wrote *After the Return*, which Xie herself considered as "a new turn of my creative life."[53] China's state-run publishers all raced to publish her new works, including *Selected Prose and Short Stories of Bing Xin*, *We've Awakened the Spring*, *The Little Orange Lamp*, and *Late Clearing*. Among these, *The Little Orange Lamp* was included in the national Chinese language textbook. In 1953, Wu Wenzao was assigned a faculty position at Central China Ethnic College. The central government allotted a special building fund for Xie and her family to live on campus. The next year, Xie was elected as a delegate to the National People's Congress.

But as history unfolded in 1957, Wu Wenzao was classified as a Rightist. It was not until 1961 that Wu was reinstated. After the early 1960s, overwhelmed by political engagements, Xie wrote very little. Her earlier works on love and nature ran directly counter to the nation's Marxist ideology about class struggle. During the Cultural Revolution, her home was ransacked by Red Guards, and she was sent to live in a cow's shed. In 1970, now seventy years old, Xie was sent down to rural Hubei for reeducation through harsh labor. One of her biographers later wrote to defend the value of her works:

> In twentieth century Chinese literature, Bing Xin occupied a unique place. She did not follow suit by writing about political struggles. Instead through her experiential and intellectual contribution, she called on people to nurture

a kind of love and promoted a philosophy of love. . . . Because of her unique voice, many kind Chinese people felt some warmth on earth. . . . Many people attribute depictions of social injustice and darkness to Bing Xin's shallowness, or they blame on this kind woman for writing about disharmony and conflicts in Chinese families. These are not only unreasonable but arbitrary wrongdoing to her. Why can't we embrace a Greater love and a philosophy of love?[54]

In 1972, American president Nixon's visit to China changed the fate of many Chinese intellectuals. Xie and her husband were allowed to return to Beijing. Together with Chinese sociologist Fei Xiaotong, the couple were given some translation projects, such as *The Outline of History* by Herbert G. Wells and *World History* by three American historians. Between 1964 and 1978, she produced almost no creative writing.[55] Xie did, though, translate some foreign literature, such as Indian author Rabindranath Tagore's *The Gardener, Gitanjali, The Collected Poems of Tagore*, and works of other writers such as Mulk Raj Anand and Kahlil Gibran. Among them, Tagore had a deep influence on Xie's later writing. Critics write, "Bing Xin borrows Tagore's poems and genres for her own use in a very new way and exalt them into cosmopolitanism, or rather, a kind of recognition of modern values like love, equality and abundance and of an awareness of female autonomy, whch is absent in Tagore's literature."[56] As scholars comment, "her translation retained the poetic device to the greatest extent; it also showed cultural relations in intercultures."[57] After a hospitalization at age eighty, Xie Wangying resumed writing and published her third volume of *Letters to Young Readers* in a children's periodical. For Xie Wanying, motherly love and childhood innocence became two noncontroversial themes in her later works. She also carefully participated in the nation's public life. Apart from being a regular committee member with China's Writers Association, the National People's Political Consultative Conference, and other political occasions, the only moment Xie Wanying voiced her independent thinking was in the mid-1980s when she signed an open letter of petition in support of political reform. In 1999, Xie Wanying passed away at the age of ninety-nine.

In the course of seven decades, Xie Wanyu produced a variety of works, ranging from poetry and novels to essays, earning the reputation to be China's most prolific writer of the twentieth century. In her honor, Fuzhou city founded a Bing Xin Literature Museum, attracting over 30,000 visitors each year. Until today, China's heavily censored state media often release TV programs that read and analyze Bing Xin's life and writings.[58] For decades, Chinese textbooks in primary schools included works by Bing Xin on the themes of motherhood and parenting.

Because of Xie Wanying's recognized literary status as a student activist during the May Fourth Movement, which was enshrined by the Chinese

Communist Party, the regime considered her worth keeping. Nevertheless, although Xie pioneered the genre of "social problems fiction," she tempered it significantly in the later career by keeping to noncontroversial children's literature. Her works centered around the theme of motherly love. This may well be a survival strategy under strict censorship. She effectively restores motherhood as a central component of a woman's virtue. Her approach was to treat motherhood as a general common good. Thus, maternal duty was glorified and elevated to a vocation. Her works were popularized with the permission of the regime because they assisted in maintaining good order and prosperity of family and state. It did not bother Xie that not all women are mothers. By focusing on only the theme of motherhood as tolerated by the Chinese regime, the renowned feminist writer in her later career took on an unfortunate exclusivism and helped consolidate a domestic ideology.

In terms of gender consciousness, Xie also deviated from her early signature style of portraying ordinary women in socially complex narratives. While hailing motherhood as the highest calling for women, she unintentionally diminished the value of women's vocation beyond motherhood and devalued women who are not mothers. Using literary imagination, her works nevertheless lure women back to the confining realm of the family. In highlighting the purity of motherhood, Xie Wanying completely reversed herself on the nature of womanhood. No longer were resistance to patriarchy, a form of authoritarianism, considered laudable. Women were now characterized by peaceful domesticity. Accompanying these qualities of virtue and moral goodness was the assignment of piety to femininity. The passion of speaking up against injustice was an avoided topic. Even Christianity has been hollowed out of this theme of domestic piety, because Chinese state media, including the book-publishing industry, strictly censored against the mention of any benefits by Christianity. A more generous and liberating discussion about "womanhood" is lost.

Xie's earlier inability to separate feminism from politics seems to have paved the way for her later apolitical tendencies. Though struck by the storm of Maoist revolutions, Xie did not produce works like her earlier *About Women* that engaged with the political context. She shifted to what was known as children's literature because it was assigned by the party-state. They wanted to maintain her reputation as a cultural icon as a "kind and virtuous grandmother," while leaving little room for her genuine creativity. As a result, unlike Xie's earlier works that gave readers access to a turbulent history, her later publications presented a detached idealism. This change points to an underlying reality facing many Chinese intellectuals who survived Mao's era—their independent thinking was hushed. Xie Wanying's reconstruction of gender followed a path of devolution from challenging status quo to acquiescing to the enduring injustices Chinese women were suffering under communism.

NOTES

1. "Lin Qiaozhi: Guardian Angel of Mothers and Babies," *China Daily*, August 7, 2011.

2. Hui Feng, "Lin Qiaozhi Refused to Participate in China's Inauguration Ceremony," *DW News*, February 11, 2011.

3. Yi Ming, "Christian Doctor Lin Qiaozhi," *Chinese Good News*, a public Wechat public channel, May 8, 2017.

4. Guowei Wright, "Lin Qiaozhi: The Steady Pulse of a Quiet Faith," in Carol Lee Hamrin, ed., with Stacey Bieler, *Salt and Light: Lives of Faith that Shaped Modern China* (Eugene: Wipf and Stock Publishers, 2008), 119.

5. Yusheng Wang, "Exemplary Physician and New Woman Lin Qiaozhi," *China Science and Technology Education* 4 (2013): 76.

6. In the late 1920s, 400 *yuan* was roughly a year's wage for a new in-residence physician.

7. Bickers, *Out of China*, 260.

8. Ibid., 263.

9. "Lin Qiaozhi: Guardian Angel," All-China Women's Federation website, December 12, 2007.

10. Quoted in *Beijing Chronographies: Healthy and Hygiene Chorograph* (Beijing Press, 2003), 518. Also see Jinghe Lang, "Lin Qiaozhi on Prevention of Prenatal Illnesses," *Guangming Daily*, May 17, 2017. https://www.sohu.com/a/141119752 _115423

11. Jinghe Lang, "Remembering the Pioneer of China's Ob-Gyn Science," *Chinese Journal of Obstetrics and Gynecology* 12 (36) (2001): 710.

12. Jing Jie, "Fear Life to Protect Life," a blog article on Sina.com, May 6, 2013. Reposted at http://www.kyhs.net/swwz/11249.html?pwtafc=dgimt3

13. Beijing Local History Compilation Committee, *History of Beijing: Public Health* (Beijing: Beijing Press, 1946), 455.

14. Ibid.

15. Bing Xin, "Remembering Doctor Lin Qiaozhi (1983)," *Full Collection of Bing Xin*, Volume 7 (Fuzhou: Haixia Literary Press, 1994).

16. Quoted in "Lin Qiaozhi: Guardian Angel of Mothers and Babies," *China Daily*, August 7, 2011. https://cpcchina.chinadaily.com.cn/2011-08/07/content_1 3919297_2.htm

17. "Medical Staff during the Anti-Japanese War," *People's Political Council*, September 2, 2015. http://www.rmzxb.com.cn/c/2015-09-02/568068.shtml

18. "Lin Qiaozhi: Guardian Angel of Mothers and Babies."

19. Wright, "Lin Qiaozhi: The Steady Pulse of a Quiet Faith."

20. "As the Only Academic in China's Academy of Science, She Refused to Join China's Inaugural Ceremony and Just Wanted to be A Good Coctor," Wanjia Web, December 11, 2017. https://www.wanjiaweb.com/node/3840

21. Ibid.

22. "Barefoot doctors" (*chijiao yisheng*) were folk healers who provide rural health care to villagers in China. Most of them were farmers themselves but had middle or secondary school education which enabled them to know more about medicine.

23. Quoted in Zhang Qinping, *Lin Qiaozhi: A Biography* (Beijing: Baihua Literature and Art Press, 2006), 390. Also see Wright, "Lin Qiaozhi: The Steady Pulse of a Quiet Faith."

24. Zhu Ying, "Angelic Lin Qiaozhi," *Shanghai Daily*, August 12, 2018. https://archive.shine.cn/sunday/now-and-then/Angelic-Lin-Qiaozhi/shdaily.shtml

25. Mao Chen, "In and Out of Home: Bing Xin Recontextualized," in Philip F. Williams, ed., *Asian Literary Voices: From Marginalized to Mainstream* (Amsterdam University Press, 2010), 63–70.

26. Bing Xin, "My Childhood," in Bin Xin, *Selected Works of Bing Xin in Seventy Years* (Shanghai: Shanghai Literary Press, 1996), 199.

27. "Recollecting on a History of Men by Women Writers," *Fenghuang Book Review*, December 24, 2014. http://book.ifeng.com/shuzhai/detail_2014_11/24/1204893_0.shtml

28. Daniel K. Gardner, *Confucianism: A Very Short Introduction* (New York: Oxford University Press, 2014), 113.

29. David Jasper, "Seeking Christian Theology in Modern Chinese Fiction: An Exercise for Sino-Christian Theology," *Religions* 10 (7) (2019): 422. Open access resource: https://www.mdpi.com/2077-1444/10/7/422/htm

30. Zhang Longxi, "Revolutionary as Christ: The Unrecognized Savior in Lu Xun's Works," *Christianity and Literature* 45(1) (Autumn 1995): 81.

31. Bing Xin, "Autobiographical Notes," *Renditions: A Chinese-English Translation Magazine*, Special Issue on Bing Xin, 32 (Autumn 1989): 84.

32. Quoted in Mishi Saran, Weiwei Chen, and Francie Latour, "Rediscovering Bing Xin," *Wellesley Magazine*, Fall of 2009. http://web.wellesley.edu/Alum/Magazine/bingxin.html

33. Ancient Chinese poet Wang Changling (698–756) wrote "my heart for you is as pure as ice in a jade kettle."

34. Chen, "In and Out of Home: Bing Xin Recontextualized."

35. Bing Xin, *The Dusk*, March 1921. Retrieved from http://www.bingxin.org/index1.htm Quoted in Bi, "Bing Xin: First Female," 23–29.

36. Ibid., 23–29.

37. Ibid.

38. Huang Renying, *A Study of Modern Chinese Women Writers* (Shanghai: Guanghua Press, 1933), 187.

39. Bo Wang, *Inventing a Discourse of Resistance: Rhetorical Women in Early Twentieth-century China* (Tucson: The University of Arizona Press, 2005), 142.

40. Quoted in Chen, "In and Out of Home: Bing Xin Recontextualized."

41. Quoted in Daonan Li, "Bing Xin's Christian Faith and Real Life," *China Christian Daily*, May 17, 2019. http://chinachristiandaily.com/news/china/2019-05-17/bing-xin-s-christian-faith-and-real-life_8358

42. This private women's liberal arts college was a destination for young girls from upper-middle-class Chinese families, such as Soong Mei-ling (also known as Madame Chiang Kai-shek) and her two sisters. See "Wellesley College's Famous Alumnae," *The Huffington Post*, June 26, 2015.

43. Ibid.

44. Ibid.

45. Bing Xin, "Another Newsletter 25 to Young Readers," quoted in "Wellesley College's Famous Alumnae," *The Huffington Post*, June 26, 2015.

46. Yan Haiping, *Chinese Women Writers and the Feminist Imagination, 1905–1948* (New York: Routledge, 2006), 78.

47. Ibid.

48. Wu Wenzao received his PhD from Columbia University and specialized in adapting the discipline of sociology to the Chinese context.

49. Chen, "In and Out of Home: Bing Xin Recontextualized."

50. Ibid.

51. Wang, *Inventing a Discourse of Resistance*, 124, 130.

52. Chen, "In and Out of Home: Bing Xin Recontextualized."

53. Xin, "Autobiographical Notes," 87.

54. Binggen Wang, "How Bing Xin and Wu Wenzao Educated Their Children," *China Readers Newspaper*, July 18, 2012. http://www.wenming.cn/wmzh_pd/rw/rw dt/201207/t20120718_762416.shtml

55. Xie published 23 books from 1920 to 1964, and later 12 books from 1978 to 1994. She translated one volume of poetry in 1965.

56. Tanfeng Zhang and Linxin Jiang, "Bing Xin Studies in the English Speaking World: A Critical Survey," *Comparative Literature: East & West* 23(1) (2015): 1, 71–89.

57. Ke Yi-man et al., "Localization of Free Verse in China: A Case Study of Bing Xin's Short Poems," *Journal of Literature and Art Studies*, 8(3) (2018): 366–72.

58. "Twentieth-Century Chinese Cultural Celebrities," a documentary series, Central China Television (CCTV), 2008. This program in China's state media has a rare mentioning that Xie Wanying wrote about themes including "God's love." "Uncover History: Bing Xin and Wu Wenzao," *Hubei TV Station*, May 23, 2016.

Part III

THE ERA OF DEVELOPMENTAL COMMUNISM

INFLUENCERS, WHISTLEBLOWERS, CELEBRITIES

In 1987, the legalization of Bible printing in China was a turning point for Chinese Protestantism. Then the Tiananmen incident left a spiritual vacuum for most Chinese. Meanwhile, many short-term missionaries entered China by using tourist visas. These three factors created the condition for a wave of mass conversion among the Chinese since the early 1990s. Shortly afterward, the urban work unit system disintegrated, leaving millions jobless while relaxing state surveillance for urban residents. Growing market economy and free entrepreneurship created new commercial space for urban evangelism. China's entry into the World Trade Organization (2001) ushered in a globalization era when exchanges across national borders became frequent for the Chinese. A new generation of Chinese diaspora preachers became active in evangelizing mainland Chinese. The antagonism between the Three-Self establishment and fast-growing house churches also led to dividing influences overseas.

In 2004, China's economy was officially reconfigured into a developmental mode as private property rights were rewritten into the constitution. Soon afterward, urban housing market boomed, and more commercial space opened up for urban churches to expand in membership. While churches in China provided alternative resources for rising social problems such as rocketing divorce rates and family conflicts, a new wave of conservative evangelicalism from America also began to enter through missionary activities. Such expansion collided with rising nationalism since the 2008 Beijing Olympics. Since the authoritarian rule of Xi Jinping (2012), state-sponsored nationalism, popular anti-Christian sentiments and tightened religious policies created a hostile environment for Chinese Protestantism. In 2014, even many Three-Self churches also experienced a setback with the cross-removal campaigns. But since private property rights are still largely observed by the regime whose legitimacy rests on economic performance, there is still considerable space for religious practices. With the popularization of communication technology such as social media, Christian presence even became more visible but not less controversial. For example, the broader climate of consumerism and stardom culture allowed Christian celebrities to express their religious beliefs through their social media platforms.

Chapter 8

Bibles, Hymns, and Competing Influences

The 2000s saw a golden age for the public influence of Chinese Protestantism, both domestically and abroad. Two distinct Chinese women brought competing narratives of religious freedom and persecution to the international stage: Cao Shengjie and Lü Xiaomin. In April 2006, when American media *The Gospel Herald* interviewed the host of a large Chinese Bible exhibit held at the Crystal Cathedral in Los Angeles, it presented a new face of the Chinese church: Cao Shengjie. She was the president of China Christian Council (CCC), an arm of the Three-Self church system. This news story reported that "China Bible Ministry Exhibition . . . has given tremendous contribution to reinforce communication between Christianity in the West and in the East," and Cao herself played a catalyzing role.[1] Just a year later, in 2007 the Gospel for China Conference took place in Hong Kong, commemorating the 200th anniversary of Robert Morrison's entry into China as the first Protestant missionary. It was the first large Protestant mission event closest to mainland China that was attended by mainland church leaders since the founding of the communist regime. Before this event, the conference had been a recurring event in America, organized by a Chicago-based magazin *Christian Life Quarterly* (*shengming jikan*). On this platform, Chinese Christians were introduced to a hymn-writer and house church evangelist Lü Xiaomin, who has gained rare celebrity status through her collection of Canaan Hymns. In order to understand how Cao Shengjie and Lü Xiaomin each emerged to advance competing influences, it is necessary to review what happened to Chinese Protestantism since China opened up again to the outside world.

China and the United States normalized diplomatic relations on January 1, 1979. In February, Deng Xiaoping visited America. Months later, a top leader of the Three-Self Patriotic Movement named Bishop Ding Guangxun led a Chinese Religious Delegation to participate in the World Conference of Religion for Peace. It was the first time that mainland Chinese religious leaders stepped outside of China since the founding of the communist regime. Bishop Ding spoke publicly in New York, thanking American Christians for praying for believers in China during decades of severed China-U.S. communication. When refuting claims about the communist regime's intolerance of religious groups, Ding also said that "Some of your prayers were based on misinformation, but I wouldn't worry about it because Gods knows best."[2] Bishop Ding thinks that "the Three-Self Movement represents God's act of mercy in giving Christians a new chance in China. It is simply a movement to make the Church in China truly Chinese."[3] He challenged Western Christians' misunderstanding that the "patriotic" church collaborates with the communist regime while the "nonconforming" house churches are elevated as "martyrs." Theologically speaking, Westerners also consider the Three-Self groups as advocates for either liberal or liberation theology. Ding also critiques the euphoric identification of China with the Kingdom of God as endorsed by many Western missionaries in the Maoist era. He does not think that a new humanity, a new heaven, and a new earth has been born in China.[4] Ding rightly argues that Chinese Protestant theology is deeply conservative. Oddly enough, by this he, in fact, means pro-socialist and progressive. He affirms that Jesus' teachings include a fundamental critique of systemic injustice, such as "the domination of the powerful over their victims, the common people."[5] He thinks that official Chinese Protestantism is embodied in materiality, at once concerned with not just the spiritual but also the material well-being of people. It is also post-denominational by transcending traditional boundaries. But the outsiders notice that "Chinese Protestantism . . . has been profoundly transformed at the hands of an alien ideology. For four and a half decades, the seed planted by Western missionaries has grown under the constant influence of Chinese Marxism. Today those missionaries would perhaps scarcely recognize the outcome."[6]

In early 1980s, after twenty-plus years of separation from the outside world, when foreign Christians reentered China again as tourists with the first legal guided tours, they were surprised to find the Christian faith still alive. After the CCC was founded in 1980 as an umbrella agency for all Protestant churches, Three-Self churches reopened and functioned as safe contact points for Western Christians to meet local people. Before 1987, Bibles were strictly banned in China, so families that owned one copy would share it with other believers or copy some portions for memorization. Sometimes a church group would need to borrow the only Bible from another village for their whole neighborhood to use. In the early 1980s, a detailed study of Protestant growth in one province found that some 800 worshippers gathered on a given Sunday, that "a few in attendance were Party cadres, and one out of 800 had a Bible."[7] Many of these early Bibles were smuggled into China by Western Christians. The most well-known project was led by Open Doors. In 1981, this organization launched Project Pearl, a plan to transport 1 million Bibles to the south seashore of China by tugboats and barges in one night. Believing villagers collected them with fishing nets, and then dried them up in the sun. Some copies were confiscated and burned by authorities, but the majority were placed in the hands of local believers.[8]

The regime progressed in its tolerance toward Christianity. By way of revising the Chinese Constitution in 1982, the communist regime reaffirmed religious rights under Article 36, followed by the publication of Document 19 on religious policies. This document essentially rolled back the excesses of the Cultural Revolution militancy against religion. In it, the party said that religion continues to exist in China because "the people's consciousness lags behind social realities," so it is wrong to attempt to eliminate it. It even declared that churches must be rebuilt, clergy educated, and believers protected. Soon afterward, over 4,000 Three-Self Protestant churches were reopened or rebuilt. Countless house churches began to grow in size, though they still maintained a culture of secrecy. By 1986, more and more high-ranking officials offered endorsements or even subsidies for church reconstruction projects. As Daniel Bays observes, "An avalanche of information" on Christianity were made available by overseas evangelists in the 1980s, including books, pamphlets and tracts, audio tapes, videos, and so on.[9]

In the 1990s, foreign investment was welcomed into the coastal zones of China. Among the influx of Western businessmen, diplomats and journalists, many came with a secondary mission to evangelize. What later was dubbed "business as mission" became another entry strategy for foreign Christians. Since the Chinese laws forbade open proselytizing, many foreigners had to work within legal boundaries by finding "cover jobs," such as English teachers hired by universities. They relied largely on casual occasions and private conversations to testify about the Christian faith. Despite the progress they made, it was still hard for them to develop long-term discipleship and mentorship programs without being noticed. If they were discovered providing Christian teaching and training programs, the government would evict them from China and bar their return. Consequently, due to state surveillance, political evictions, and missionary mobility, missionary work during this time tended to be irregular and short-term. By then, Three-Self churches formed a negotiation model of interaction with the government.[10] Although previous religious policies forbade foreigners from attending any church gatherings, including those held at Three-Self churches, these boundaries later became quite porous. Even for some strict Three-Self churches that tried to maintain the foreign-local boundary, they set up segregated seating for foreigners and checked their passports at entry points.

When China resumed sending out its Christian delegation to the United States in the late 1990s after four decades of disconnection, Cao Shengjie acted as the president of the CCC. She informed the Western world that religion now has "a deep root" and plays "a positive role" in mainland China.[11] Within China, Cao Shengjie has been a long-standing voice advocating for women's rights as defined and sanctioned by communist ideology, yielding to the church's broader patriotic mission of serving the motherland. Meanwhile, she has cautioned against a direct importation of Western feminist theology. Within China's Christian circles, Cao Shengjie's pro-communist posture has earned her a controversial reputation. The life of Cao Shengjie reflects, on a smaller scale, how Protestant Christianity survived the most suppressive era of communist control. Born in 1931, Cao Shengjie was given up for adoption and raised by a Christian family in Shanghai. Both her adoptive mother and grandmother were devout churchgoers. Cao was baptized as an infant in an Anglican church. Later, the principal of her Christian elementary school gave her the name "Shengjie," which literally means "holy" in Chinese. At home, both Cao's mother and grandmother wanted her to serve the church when she grew up.[12] They also tried to instill the idea of celibacy into the young girl. At age five, once a week, Cao was already an excellent Bible storyteller serving through Evangelical Broadcast Radio in Shanghai, founded in 1933 by local businessmen and missionaries.[13]

After 1937, the Japanese invasion and warfare put Mr. Cao's family business on the fringe of bankruptcy. Due to stress, Cao's father fell ill and passed away in 1943. At school, children were required to learn Japanese, even in Christian schools. The mixed feelings of fear and hatred fueled Cao's early nationalistic sentiments. She longed for the day when she could "tear up and destroy all Japanese textbooks."[14] As she recalls, "I almost wanted to squeeze anything Japanese out of my head, so it was out of a nationalist desire that I eventually lost the grasp of a foreign language which took five years for me to learn."[15] Meanwhile, her financially struggling family (her mother and grandmother) had to pawn jewelry and fur coats to make ends meet. In middle school, Cao relied on financial assistance from the school to continue her formal education. She was often under tremendous pressure to achieve first place in class in order to maintain the financial aid. Also, in high school, Cao found out that she was adopted. Since then, she carefully navigated relationships with parents in two families.

From 1947 to 1949, Cao Shengjie had the impression that many teachers in her Christian school were progressive in their thinking. Later she learned that a few were communists who used morning chapel time to spread anti-war speech.[16] Even though some classmates joined underground activities at St. John's University, Cao always withdrew. "I felt fearful towards the Communist Party and considered these activities too dangerous."[17] When she graduated from high school, Cao was determined to enter seminary despite peer pressure. Her views of future choices were framed by a sacred-secular dualism, where the former was definitely better. She avers, "I was shaped by a thinking in the Chinese church that pitted theism and atheism against each other."[18] When Cao took the entrance exam for Central Theological Seminary in Shanghai, she was confronted by an essay question "Explain whether religion is the opium of the people." Cao had no idea that this statement came from Karl Marx, and she supplied an elaborate and definite answer "No." The seminary admitted her. Over the next three years, Cao Shengjie was exposed to theologies other than the fundamentalist and Pentecostal traditions in her own church. Anti-communist tendencies were palpable in her seminary, as a political science faculty at St. John's, Donald Roberts, taught students that Marxism originated as a Christian heresy known as gnosticism.[19] The president of the seminary also lamented with tears about the future of the church under a communist regime.[20]

By 1952, the national Three-Self committee pushed for a conglomeration of eleven seminaries in eastern China, headed by Nanjing Jinling Theological Seminary. Cao Shengjie transferred to finish her degree at Jinling. Soon, however, all college students were protesting against American imperialism after the U.S.-Korean War broke out. Radicals also organized rallies against "anti-revolutionaries." When Cao heard people in a crowd once crying out "Kill him!" she was greatly disturbed. She wondered, "How could Christians shout out 'Kill him'?"[21] Cao was overwhelmed with a sense of powerlessness and a loss of moral direction with regard to good versus evil. Soon, progressive and pro-communist students on Christian campuses joined the revolution. When Cao Shengjie saw many old acquaintances from her church quit school to become revolutionary cadres, she was shocked to find that "many church people supported the new regime and the revolution with their actions."[22] For example, two-thirds of students in Jinling Theological Seminaries left to join the revolutionary force.[23] Some of these unfortunately lost their faith, as she later learned:

> Among most of us who stayed, we wanted to serve the church but had little knowledge about the present situation. What does the patriotic movement's "Three-self" (self-governance, self-propagation) really mean? Can we stand while Christian influence in staffing, economic and social realms was declining?[24]

When Cao Shengjie graduated from Jinling in 1953, she was fully convinced that a new China required a new church. Partly it was due to her participation in some public "denunciation" meetings where church leaders were put on the stage to expose the ills within the church. There were a few major questions under discussion: Was the Chinese church a political entity? Were indigenous churches controlled by foreign powers? What was the relationship between mission-sending societies and their governments? Was the Bible ever used in anti-communist propaganda? Cao became more and more convinced that churches in China had been politicized to favor the Nationalist Party despite the latter's corruption. She also saw a certain legitimacy in identifying foreign missionaries as imperialists wielding power over the indigenous. These thoughts came to Cao Shengjie as new revelations of reality.

Since 1954, Cao Shengjie began to emerge as a younger female leader from the indigenous Chinese church. When the first China Christian National Conference was convened in Beijing, she was among the four recording secretaries. Cao remembered this meeting to be an "unprecedented solidarity within Chinese Christianity."[25] Nevertheless, she also recorded examples of nonconforming leaders such as Wang Mingdao who criticized leaders of the Three-Self Movement as "false apostles."[26] Wang continued his resistance by publishing scathing criticism against the movement's modernist-leaning theology, leading to Wang's arrest in 1955. Cao Shengjie mentioned Wang in her writing:

Once Premier Zhou Enlai went to a conference in Geneva, where a rumor was spread wide about Beijing's execution of thirty-nine preachers. Among these the first name was Wang Mingdao. Some people told Wang that he should speak up and clear the misinformation. But Wang not only failed to so, but he became even more bold in spreading it.[27]

Cao referred to Chinese theologian T. C. Chao (Zhao Zichen) who once described all the conferences he had attended in the pre-TSPM era to be "rent by disunity from within."[28] But after the movement began, even to someone as widely respected as Chao, the Three-Self patriotic vision was the "only clear, common and uniting goal for all."[29] From her side of the experience, Cao Shengjie was convinced that Chinese Christianity was entering into "the great march for the whole Chinese nation to construct a new China."[30]

Previously in 1957, Mao Zedong's anti-Rightist campaign devastated many church leaders who had embraced communism. Cao wrote that "it did hurt many people who could have walked the 'Love the Nation and Love Christianity' path but instead suffered unnecessary harm."[31] After the Great Leap Forward, since all labor was allocated to industrial work, churches struggled financially. Later, local governments ordered congregations to hold combined services, further cutting down the number of meeting locations. In the early 1960s, church buildings were mainly used to hold political meetings. As Cao later describes, "Although given some economic compensation, these meetings had many people smoking, and smoke filled the sanctuary. It was hard for Christians to see their holy worship space turned into something so noisy and messy. Their religious sentiments were hurt."[32] The fact is, more and more people in China considered it time for Christianity to pass away. "Christians were pressured and thus unwilling to come to church, especially the younger group who feared for their future."[33] It was also the policy of the Communist Party that children should not be allowed in churches, because the church and the party were competing for the loyalty of youth. Cao acknowledged in her memoir that this prohibition was not lifted until the 1990s.[34]

In 1962, Cao was appointed the secretary of China's Three-Self Patriotic Protestant Movement Committee (TSPC). She worked alongside Wu Yaozong, one of the founding figures of the Three-Self Movement. By then, she realized that the situation in new China had changed so much that it was not as she expected. People also began to question Cao's earlier commitment to celibacy. As she recalls, "I sensed that since my earlier path was no longer feasible, and I was getting older, maybe I should consider the possibility of marriage."[35] At age thirty-four, Cao married a staff at the Young Men's Christian Association in 1965. Later she learned that many church staff who had vowed celibacy walked the same path. Around this time, even high-ranking leaders of the Three-Self Movement felt insecure about what was ahead. Everyone was looking for a way to cope with uncertainty. Cao wrote that once Wu Yaozong came back from a conference in Beijing and shared a disturbing incident with her:

> Wu told me that Chairman Mao once jokingly said to him, "Your God is no longer!" This was a very harsh comment to Wu and he was speechless. As a national leader and having seen Christianity shrink daily, Wu was distressed. More than once he used "stepping into thin ice or an abyss" to describe his state of mind. Wu feared that he might also need to be accountable for what goes wrong in the future.[36]

During the Cultural Revolution, Cao Shengjie's pregnancy helped her escape some of the political attacks. She recorded once when Wu Yaozong was ordered by radical leaders to confess his role as "head of all ox-demons and snake-gods," Wu went home and wrote a confession. She seldom saw him afterward. Later Cao Shengjie was sent down to a suburban farm in Shanghai for six months and then to a chemical factory for "re-education through labor work."[37] She did factory work for eight years. Religious activities came to a full stop nationwide. As Cao wrote, "My spirit was low because I could not see any future for Christianity. What I could not fathom was why after coming around to love this nation through patriotic education in the 1950s, after following the Party and reconstructing our motherland, we all became the bad guys, ox-demons and snake-gods?"[38] It was a time of mob violence when Red Guards raided homes and attacked people. The radicals also forced family members and neighbors to betray each other. Cao wrote the following in her memoir:

> In that time when people were exposing and criticizing each other, I did not fabricate any "false testimony" with regard to facts. But in order to protect myself, I joined excessive struggle meetings that I am not proud of. Most of these people now have passed away, and I can only plead God for forgiveness.[39]

She also wrote that while Three-Self churches disintegrated, many believers held secret meetings in their homes. House churches thus came into being and had their own leaders. She elaborates, "They passed hand-copied Bibles among them, and actively evangelized on funeral occasions."[40] In 1979, Protestant churches in China were allowed to reopen. In 1980, Cao was appointed the vice general director of the CCC headquartered in Nanjing. When Shanghai Academy of Social Sciences set up an Institute of Religion, it invited Cao Shengjie to join as a research fellow. She conducted research in Zhejiang Province, where Protestantism was booming. In 1985, Ding Guangxun worked with other social forces to found the Aide Foundation, which later became the only legal Bible-printing enterprise in China. This foundation also formed a network connecting with Americans who hoped to serve in China. Over the next seven years, hundreds of Americans went to teach in China's postsecondary and higher education institutions. As Cao recalled, "Their goal was cultural exchange and [they] had to comply with the 'no proselytism' rule while in China, but they became friends of the Chinese people."[41]

After the death of Mao and Chinese Communist Party's Eleven Plenary Conference, Three-Self churches were allowed to reopen. Cao Shengjie returned to work in Shanghai's Academy of Social Sciences. At a meeting in 1982, Ding Guangxun asked participants to share their experiences over the past decade, hoping that the common suffering could become a source of solidarity, but nobody spoke up.[42] They mainly discussed the way forward, including how to print Bibles and reopen worship space. The two decades after the 1980s marked an unusual phase of growth for Protestant churches in China, both registered and unregistered. By 1986, Shanghai alone saw the reopening of twenty-two Three-Self churches. In Cao Shengjie's own words, "after decades of suppression, once re-opened, Christianity must experience a burst."[43] She also frowned upon "foreign infiltration" such as the Project Pearl, smuggling millions of Bibles near the east coast.

In the 1990s, the growth of Protestant Christianity in China was primarily a rural phenomenon. Historians attribute this to "the greater momentum of rural Christianity coming off the decade of the Cultural Revolution."[44] But given the devastation done by land reforms and collective farming, a more probable explanation is the relaxation of social control through the system of rural communes after market reform first took place in villages. These changes enabled clusters of believers to gather again without being criminalized. A similar growth in China's urban centers happened only after the second wave of market reform in 1992 when the *Danwei* system began to disintegrate. When the regime relaxed restrictions on assembly, China's rural regions soon saw a house church revival with tens of thousands converting to unofficial Protestant groups in agricultural provinces such as Henan. There a few large Christian networks emerged, including Jesus Family and Fangcheng Fellowship.[45] *Financial Times* reported that this wave of believers were "overwhelmingly poor, rural, uneducated, female and elderly."[46] *The Independent* describes Fang Cheng as a clandestine group "which claims up to 500,000 followers."[47] These newly formed house churches inherited the rhetoric that lambasted the Three-Self Patriotic Movement as betraying the authentic Christian faith by having sided with an atheistic and oppressive regime since the 1950s. Labeling themselves as faithful and nonconforming house churches, they gained a pride to be in the unofficial camp of Chinese Protestantism that was experiencing visible numerical growth. Occasional harassment and suppression by local authorities in these regions also reinforced this persecution complex.[48]

Growth in Three-Self churches has also been visible. By 2003, in addition to the 45,000 registered official churches, around 40,000 groups affiliated with the Protestant Three-Self Patriotic Movement were still waiting to register.[49] The demand exceeded the supply of worship space and pastoral resources. By 2005, China's official statistics reported more than 18 million Protestant believers, a twenty-fold growth compared to the figure for 1949. Among them, women made up more than 70 percent, making them the Protestant majority in China. The Three-Self system included an increasing number of women into their seminaries.[50] With China's increased openness through the entry into the World Trade Organization, both Three-Self churches and house churches saw opportunities to expand their influences overseas. Seminaries, denominations, and Christian institutions in America also developed divided loyalties, some favoring a persecution narrative spread by house churches and others embracing the fact that Chinese Christians as represented by the official brand of Christianity have achieved a higher level of religious freedom.

In America, *Christian Life Quarterly*, a Chinese-language magazine based in Chicago was among many platforms that discounted the legitimacy of Three-Self churches. It has been organizing the Gospel for China Conference for over a decade, usually with thousands of attendances. As a recognized platform to share knowledge about the most famous pastors and leaders in the Chinese faith community with a growing Christian population, it essentially transformed a subculture into a mainstream. The previously low-profile Chinese church became one that elevates its own celebrities, including dissident-turned-evangelist Yuan Zhiming and hymn-writer Lü Xiaomin. Some former Three-Self church pastors also gave testimonies at the Gospel for China Conference telling how the state-run church system had always been infiltrated by the communist regime.

Lü Xiaomin gained fame among house churches in China before she stepped into an international sphere of influence. Since the late 1990s, her collection of Chinese praise music known as *Canaan Hymns* became widely popular among an expanding Christian population, both domestic and overseas. Wherever these hymns are sung, the story of its composer Lü Xiaomin was told and retold. Two features that inspired people are Lü's lack of formal education and her house church background. To many, the former trait affirmed the divine inspiration of these hymns, and the latter associated a deeper Christian devotion.

In 1970, Lü Xiaomin was born into a peasant family in Fangcheng of rural Henan Province.[51] In an interview, she said, "My parents are simple farming folks. My mother never went to school and my Dad studied for only a year or two. He barely reads."[52] The family are Hui people, China's largest Muslim group.[53] Poverty made her parents almost give Lü away when she was two years old. In eighth grade, she quit school and returned home to help with farming. Her aunt was a house church believer who invited Lü to join local church gatherings. Lü prayed to God for healing of her chronic health problems, including sinusitis and stomach disease.[54] When that prayer was answered, she decided to be a Jesus follower.[55] Lü joined a Pentecostal house church near her village.[56]

A few years later, when Lü was nineteen, she began composing hymns, or more accurately, singing out songs of praise. The first hymn came to her one night after she returned from church. Overwhelmed by a strong devotion to God and unable to sleep, she found herself singing out loud at night: "The Holy Spirit touched me the moment I consecrated myself to God. That's when I sang my first hymn."[57] She relayed the song to her older brother who was surprised to find that Lü was able to sing out both the lyrics and melody at once. He helped Lü record her first song and showed others at the village church. It gained an immediate acceptance among local believers and also spread to house churches in other places. Knowing that the song-writer was an uneducated peasant girl, local believers enthusiastically attributed Lü Xiaomin's sudden musical abilities to the work of the Holy Spirit. Later Lü received a cassette tape recorder as a present, and she began to capture these special moments of composing. Others helped her write them down in simplified Chinese musical notation, so that local churches could use the new hymns.

As a member of an actively evangelizing Pentecostal church, Lü Xiaomin wanted to become a traveling evangelist herself. She also wrote many hymns with outreach themes when the church sent her out to evangelize in adjacent areas.[58] In 1992, Lü's church leader in the Fang Cheng Fellowship asked her to leave home and go preach the gospel in Anhui Province.[59] She replied that because her father was still an unbeliever, she would not travel that far from home. Lü was determined to bring her whole family to Christ.

A few months later, Lü Xiaomin's house church gathering was disrupted by local authorities. She and many others were detained for weeks. By that time, Lü had composed fifty hymns that were widely used in churches. She gained enough confidence to see herself as a hymn-writer and evangelist. During this time in detainment, Lü also sang her own hymns and preached to others in the detainment center. A new hymn "In Such Special Time" came into being: "In such special time, we can exercise our faith. In such special time, our faith can grow." She wrote down the lyrics on toilet paper and gave it to visitors. During a short time, Lü's seven non-Christian cellmates had converted. In the next nine days, Lü composed eight more hymns: "Lord, You Look After Me," "Although I Can Not See Moonlight," "I Desire Nothing Else," "Fear Not," "Lord, We Know Deeply," "You Are Never Wrong," and "Longing for Freedom." These later became the No. 51 to 58 songs in *Canaan Hymns*. All together she came up with two dozen new hymns. By then, Lü's hymns exhibited a consistent style of being short, musically simple and rhymed like Chinese folk songs. They have a unique spontaneity which reflects the process that Lü Xiaomin uses—she makes up songs based on Bible verses while praying and meditating. When inspirations come, it usually takes her minutes to conceive a new hymn. Even uneducated people could learn these hymns easily, and churches could use them without any instrumentation. Thus, "[t]hese hymns have spread the immense land of China in the blink of an eye."[60] Even in tribal villages of Yunnan Province, missionaries were surprised to find that the local Christians were singing Lü Xiaomin's hymns.[61]

The *Canaan Hymns* became so widely used that even China's official Three-Self churches also began to include Lü's hymns into their official publications, although not without criticism. For example, in 1999, *Tian Feng* magazine, the official publication of the Three-Self Patriotic Movement, scrutinized Lü Xiaomin's hymn 195 titled "Lord, Have Mercy on China, Hold Back Your Anger." They questioned whether its lyrics fit with Christianity's role in serving socialism.[62] It is true that many of Lü's hymns reflect a tension between China's political suppression and growing Christian devotion. Many focused on themes such as hardships and "enduring state persecution."[63] Although for a time local authorities frowned upon the underground publications of *Canaan Hymns*,[64] these songs were eventually allowed in Three-Self church liturgy.[65] Scholars tend to think that because Lü's hymns embody the "Three-Self principles" advocated by the official church, they are considered as compatible with government-sanctioned Christianity.[66]

In the early 2000s, Lü Xiaomin became widely known among a growing wave of new Chinese converts, both domestic and overseas, through a documentary *The Cross: Jesus in China* (2003) produced by China Soul for Christ Foundation headed by Yuan Zhiming, a Tiananmen movement participant-turned-pastor living in the United States.[67] This widely popular documentary promoted Lü Xiaomin to a saintly pedestal. By then, Lü had composed over 900 hymns that later became the collection *Canaan Hymns*. Orchestral adaptations of her hymns have been made by famous musicians from the Chinese diaspora.[68] In the documentary, Lü also shared that God has given her dreams to evangelize in countries as far as the land of Africa. She began to tour around the world and was one of the most sought-after speakers in mission conferences.

American Journalist David Aikman also featured Lü and many other house church leaders in his book *Jesus in Beijing*. Aikman suggests that if up to 30 percent of the population in China are Christian, then China is in the process of becoming a "Christian nation."[69] Such a vision followed the "third wave" of democratization (1974–1991), which has given evangelicals new incentives and opportunities for expansion and influence in the global South. Some scholars claim that the growth of house church Christianity offers "the Leaven Effect," hinting its implication for China's democratization.[70] Overall, positivism was in the air when it comes to the prospect of Protestant revival in China. To a certain extent, China observers were right in noting an emerging, deep spirituality among house churches. But its integrity has yet to stand the test in an increasingly open Chinese public sphere.

In media publicity, Lü Xiaomin's life story as an uneducated peasant girl, her inspiring musical experiences, and evangelistic ambition are inseparable parts of her public persona. As her reputation grew, Lü's contribution to Chinese Christianity also became a divisive topic. Those who took pride in this young female oral musician applauded her as the most prolific hymn-writer in China and an epitome of deep house church spirituality. Someone also gave her the title of "China's songbird."[71] Her hymns are considered as "the pulse of seventy million Chinese Christians"[72] and "a gift from God to the Chinese church."[73] However, those who scrutinized the theology of *Canaan Hymns* claimed that these were all amateur performances since Lü had neither theological nor musical education. Despite such division, Lü's *Canaan Hymns* did become one of the most widely printed Christian publication in China.

Incidentally, around the same time as Lü Xiaomin traveled in the United States to testify for the persecuted yet reviving house churches in China, Cao Shengjie was also touring America on a branding mission for the Three-Self church. From 2004 to 2007, the Two Councils planned for six Bible exhibits in Hong Kong, the United States, and Germany. These exhibits took up most of Cao Shengjie's time during these years. She utilized many overseas friendships to push through dialogues and to make even more new contacts. Through good relationship with the Billy Graham Evangelical Association, in 2005, Cao Shengjie and two other Chinese women leaders were invited to the Presidential Breakfast at the White House. In 2007, she also met with Douglas Coe outside of Washington, DC. In April 2006, the Crystal Cathedral in Los Angeles hosted the China Bible Ministry Exhibition, as presented by the CCC. In an interview with the media, Cao Shengjie stressed the importance of "legality" and "openness" of foreign involvement in China mission:

> Whether . . . you want to donate money or you want to send Bibles, everything is good, but you must do it openly and legally with dignity. I think for all the things that Christians do, whether before God or before man, we should not do secretly, because you may be arrested and you may leave a bad impression when others hear about it.[74]

Cao explained that this was a historical lesson from Western missionaries who entered into China "with political agenda." In cases when foreign mission workers get arrested and foreign media asks CCC, she candidly said that "I really don't know what has happened." She refers to the media's coverage of such self-inflicted consequences as "propaganda of the press." When the media asked about her views on "unregistered churches," Cao willingly accepted these groups as long as they have "true Christian faith." When refuting the widespread claim that China has "religious persecution," Cao surprisingly affirmed the equal status of unregistered churches. "We don't think there are 'underground' churches. There are church groups that are not registered, but you cannot categorize them into 'above-ground' or 'underground.' These churches are equal in front of God."[75] She also explained that every Christian believer in China can gain access to Bibles, because since 2005 China has printed around 40 million copies distributed through a network of 70 hubs.

While the Three-Self church has occupied the official channels and platforms for promoting its discourse, a growing consumerist culture in post-WTO China also opened up informal ways for emerging unregistered churches. Take Lü Xiaomin's growing popularity, for example. Because her hymns were so widely used in Chinese-speaking congregations, even some Three-Self churches began to include them in liturgy. On occasion, her hymns also created a cultural phenomenon in the wider mainland Chinese society. In 2012, famous Chinese director Feng Xiaogang used Lü's hymn "The River of Life, the River of Joy" as the theme song of his movie *Back to 1942*.[76] These words of joy and affecting melody created warm resonance within Christians and non-Christians alike: "The river of life, the river of joy/ Slowly flows into my heart/I will sing a song, a heavenly song/All the dark clouds and worries vanish away." A year later, China's largest state cable TV station, China Central Television (known as CCTV), also included Lü's hymn "I Love My Home" being sung by a Christian family.[77] In a country where Christianity has been censored in major media outlets, these cultural incidents were rare and boundary-breaking. They gave opportunities for the fast-growing churches to have their voices heard.

By 2016, the ever-growing collection of *Canaan Hymns* included over 1,680 hymns. Although critics say that these hymns are influenced by Yu Opera and folk music traditions in rural Henan, they also became very popular in overseas Chinese churches.[78] Scholars evaluate these hymns as "genuinely inculturated . . . with a folk lilt, Chinese harmonics, and an imagery that blends rural China with biblical themes."[79] In America, Australia, Singapore, Taiwan, and other places around the world, many Chinese-speaking churches are adding *Canaan Hymns* to their liturgy because the songs incorporate a house church spirituality with themes of persecution and sacrifice. Among these hymns, the most well-known one is probably "Five O'clock in the Morning in China" that contains the lyrics: "Everyone gives their sincere love, wholeheartedly for China." When overseas Chinese Christians sing this song, their hearts go out to the motherland where religious freedom for Christians is restricted. It always creates a sense of solidarity and a yearning to learn from the deep devotion of Christians in mainland China. At a conference in Taiwan in 2015, Lü Xiaomin shared that she has the habit of praying at five o'clock every morning and this song came to her during a morning devotion.[80] Nevertheless, critics continue to point out that Lü came from an uneducated, Pentecostal background and her hymns are only amateur. Others also point out that some hymns even mimic Cultural Revolution-era propaganda songs.[81]

After gaining great fame, Lü Xiaomin often turn public events into opportunities for new song-making. The Beijing Olympics, the crash of a Malaysian airline, and the need for blood donations all became events over which Lü uttered a Christian voice by song writing. Occasionally, this approach was seen as hasty and inappropriate. In 2017, two young Chinese missionaries were killed while teaching Mandarin at a language school run by a South Korean in Pakistan's most volatile province.[82] After the killing, Pakistani authorities accused these two young Christians of being preachers who had misused business visas. This incident led to divisive public discussion on Chinese media with some criticizing house churches for putting people's life at risk and others elevating these two young people to martyrs who were paving the road "back to Jerusalem." Mainland Chinese Christians' outlook of seeing themselves at the center of God's next revival has distilled new energy in the fundamentalist "Back to Jerusalem" movement that began in the 1940s. The vision was to bring the gospel westwards in the direction of Jerusalem, a crucial step that would usher in the Second Coming of Christ. In the midst of the public debate, Lü Xiaomin made a new song with these words: "The blood of missionaries/was shed in places that it should be/Their touching stories/were spread on earth." This new hymn falls in an enduring theme of evangelistic zeal and persecution that has always been prominent in Lü's composition. Critics challenge her endorsement of the "Back to Jerusalem" movement, which has accumulated numerous controversies in the past decades.[83]

During the coronavirus crisis in 2020, Lü Xiaomin wrote a song "Wuhan, Wuhan, You Are Not Alone" which included these words: "Thousands of Angels are walking towards you. God has made Aaron stand between heaven and earth, and the plague shall disappear. You shall meditate during this disaster, for the Lamb of the Passover has been sacrificed for you." Although this newly composed hymn tried to bring a Christian voice into the public health crisis, some conservative Christian critics responded that, as usual, Lü had committed serious theological errors in its content. Heated discussions have taken place on Chinese-language social media.

Ironically, although leaders of the Three-Self system and house churches have developed antagonistic rhetoric about each other's lack of legitimacy, they often mirror-image each other. Both groups are out of touch with a generation of educated Chinese who grew up under the "open door" policy of Deng Xiaoping and has been influenced by antiauthoritarian intellectual works. In particular, when it comes to a theology about the church, mission, and the role of women, they are more similar than they are different. For example, Three-Self churches base their institutional legitimacy on the power of assembly granted by the communist regime. Inevitably, their top-level leaders had to actively participate in the affairs of the Chinese Communist Party. Community-level pastors operate in a diffused field of power, with only sparse authority to teach and counsel from the officiated pulpit. In comparison, house churches lack official legitimacy but have achieved exponential growth in membership by relying on recruitment via close-knit networks. Once included into a house church network, a believer travels into a field of power with authoritarian leaders at the top of the hierarchy. So, in both of these organizational ecologies, power abuse became rampant as Three-Self churches conform to regime power and house churches reinvent their own authoritarian structures.

An additional challenge for leaders from house churches is their tendency to seek a different kind of nationalistic discourse, either based on persecution under communism or China-centered missional revival. In both instances, churches find themselves immersed in broader cultural narratives. For example, at around 2008, when Beijing held its first Olympics, Lü Xiaomin's new hymns took a nationalistic turn. Earlier, she had written patriotic lines such as "Chinese heart" and "the Chinese shall rise."[84] But this time, a nationalistic pride for China's rising international status was evident through the lyrics of Olympics 2008: "Today's China is flourishing, rich, strong, beautiful and glorious/. . . Olympics 2008 is in Beijing, Revival in China."[85] The discourse of Christian nationalism permeates both pro-communist Three-Self churches and anti-establishment house churches.

The same dynamics also apply when it comes to the role of women in the church. Although Three-Self churches acknowledge the ordination of women and have more female pastors than male pastors, its understanding of women's role still needs to conform a communist interpretation. For example, Cao Shengjie only began to pay attention to women's role in the church since 1984, when she led a Chinese delegation to visit Australia. From talking to female leaders of the church there, she realized that churches in Australia had many restrictions with regard to a women's role. Cao recalled this incident as follows.

Australian churches were very conservative, especially the Anglican church where there were many restrictions. . . . While other places had approved women in office, this area lagged behind. Once in a seminar, Australian women poured out their hearts in telling us their humiliation. Most church administration were done by women, but these women's efforts were not appreciated. The church would not approve them to be pastors. Some seminaries only had one female. On this point, churches in China have obviously surpassed them.[86]

The issue of women's status in the church was a regular theme on the lips of female leaders in the Three-Self establishment. In 1994, for example, Gao Ying, vice president of the Nanjing Union Theological Seminary, once lamented at the regression of women's status within the church. She advocated that "women's emancipation is an ongoing progress and we have a long way to go both to achieve greater leadership participation and partnership equality."[87] In 1995, Cao as vice president of the CCC gave a speech at the United Nations' Fourth World Conference of Women, in Beijing, affirming the communist regime's advancement of women's status in society and in the church.[88] Because of her writings and public speeches on this issue, many consider Cao Shengjie as "one of the most important female leaders in the mainland Chinese church" who continues to emphasize the importance of women's work.[89]

But compared to Christian advocates in Hong Kong, Cao was a step behind. The former group had been exploring a postcolonial feminist theology which allowed them to challenge the construction of Western and Eastern ideologies as binary opposites.[90] In 1944, the Anglican Communion passed the ordination of its first woman, Florence Lei, triggering a pushback in the broader Church of England. In the end, Lei was pressured to resign. In 1948, an international committee was convened, calling for the recognition of women in pastoral ordination. Its memorandum reminded all that the pressure to embrace the full equality of women in the church came from the mission frontier where conversion waves were "often made by women evangelists" long before any sacraments were administered to these new believers by formal clergy.[91] This document placed the Chinese church and women's issues on the cutting edge of history. It reminded readers of the historical Order of Deaconesses. It even challenged the Western church that it might have been out of step with the real work of God in the world. Later, even at the most political inconvenient times, these women leaders have also spoken up against Chinese nationalism. For example, at the historical junction of Hong Kong's handover to China, Rose Wu, former director of the Hong Kong Women Christian Council criticized leaders who supported the status quo.[92] In comparison, Cao Shengjie has been defending the Chinese communist regime's religious policies regarding Christianity.[93]

When house churches are concerned, the vast majority of leaders never formally reckoned with the issue of women's leadership because of the combination of fundamentalist theology and patriarchal governance. To them, male leadership and biblicism are two marks of theological "conservatism." As in the West, theological fundamentalism in China has been a reactionary stance against theological modernism. The rigidity of this tradition was reinforced by communist suppression from the 1950s to the 1970s. When social control relaxed and house churches expanded in size and number, theological fundamentalism remained a dominant view among unregistered Protestant groups. Given the marginalized status of these groups, such a tradition exerts a particular "psychological strength," which is "derived from such an understanding of the Bible as a historically accurate record of God's will."[94] It is a biblicist-historicist understanding that seeks for theological certainty with the risk of becoming rigid and authoritarian.[95] Although many churches began as small Bible fellowships led by Bible *women*, when these groups expand and institutionalize, the power is always transferred to male leads who were deemed more fit to make decisions. Tales of iconic male leaders such as Wang Mindao, Watchman Nee, and John Sung were retold from one generation to another, stressing the association between male leadership and revivalism.

However, house churches have also demonstrated their practical adaptability when the gift of women leaders like Lü Xiaomin gained public fame. Some Pentecostal groups founded by women also encouraged their leadership.[96] The mystery, secrecy, and assumed revivalist heroism go along with a hard-to-estimate size of unofficial Protestantism.[97] Western observers of the Chinese church are preoccupied with numeric growth and anti-communist resistance. For example, while China's own Public Security Bureau gives a figure of 25 million Christians in total in China, *World Christian Encyclopedia* estimated 89 million house church Protestants in China.[98] When something of this invisible but grander scale is happening in communist-ruled China, one tends to consider it the work of God. As female leaders in the Three-Self establishment and house church system, both Cao Shengjie and Lü Xiaomin have been adamant that their respective lineage was doing "God's work." They were placed at a historical conjuncture when globalization has made cultural influences pluralistic. Therefore, each field of power, whether Three-Self or house churches, has become diffuse with porous social boundaries. House churches now have more access to the Chinese diaspora when countering the monopolized narrative of the Three-Self establishment. But at the same time, gender equality remains a contested issue for both Cao and Lü in their respective field of power. In comparison, emerging house churche believers who take their conversion seriously are more susceptible to claims of conservativism. This became part of the preconditions for Christian Right activism in George W. Bush's America (2001–2009) to be reimported to China.

NOTES

1. Eunice Or, "Interview with President of China Christian Council Rev. Cao Shengjie," *The Gospel Herald,* May 1, 2006. https://www.gospelherald.com/articl e/church/9815/interview-with-president-of-china-christian-council-rev-cao-shengj ie.htm

2. Cao Shengjie, "An American-born Chinese Couple Pushed for Restored China-US Christian Communication," *Century Magazine*, May 22, 2019. https://ww w.thepaper.cn/newsDetail_forward_3403425

3. Quoted in Raymond L. Whitehead (ed.), *No Longer Strangers: Selected Writings of K. H. Ting* (Maryknoll: Orbis, 1989), 95–96.

4. Ibid., 96.

5. Ibid., 70.

6. Janz, *World Christianity and Marxism*, 148–49.

7. Ibid., 145–46.

8. Quoted in Nathan Faries, *The "Inscrutably Chinese" Church: How Narratives and Nationalism Continue to Divide Christianity* (Lanham: Lexington Books, 2010), 98–99.

9. Bays, *A New History*, 195.

10. Alan Hunter and Kim-Kwong Chan, *Protestantism in Contemporary China,* Volume 3 (Cambridge: Cambridge University Press, 2007).

11. "Chinese Christian Delegation Visits NCC and CWS, Reports Rapid Growth of Protestantism," *National Council of Churches News Service*, October 15, 2003. http://www.ncccusa.org/news/03chinesechristians.html

12. Cao Shengjie, *An Oral History of Cao Shengjie* (Shanghai: Shanghai Bookstore Publishing House, 2016), 8.

13. Ibid., 10.

14. Ibid., 14.

15. Ibid.

16. Ibid., 15.

17. Ibid.

18. Ibid., 21.

19. Ibid., 24.

20. Ibid., 25.

21. Ibid., 27.

22. Ibid., 30.

23. Ibid., 31.

24. Ibid., 32–33.

25. Ibid., 48.

26. Ibid., 49.

27. Ibid.

28. Ibid., 52.

29. Ibid.

30. Ibid.

31. Ibid., 83.

32. Ibid., 87.

33. Ibid., 88.

34. Ibid.

35. Ibid., 89.

36. Ibid., 92.

37. Ibid., 101–2.

38. Ibid., 103–4.

39. Ibid., 102.

40. Ibid., 134.

41. Cao, "An American-Born Chinese Couple Pushed for Restored China-US Christian Communication."

42. Cao, *An Oral History*, 107.

43. Ibid., 109.

44. Bays, *A New History*, 193.

45. Calum MaLeod, "Evangelists arrested as China targets church," *The Independent*, August 25, 2000. https://www.independent.co.uk/news/world/asia/evangelists-arrested-as-china-targets-church-711361.html. This article states that Fang Cheng "is named after another Henan county where the church's founder, Zhang

Rongliang, first preached." This leader was later sentenced to two years in a labor camp for "leading a cult."

46. Jamil Anderlini, "The Rise of Christianity in China," *Financial Times*, November 7, 2014. https://www.ft.com/content/a6d2a690-6545-11e4-91b1-0014 4feabdc0

47. Calum MaLeod, "Evangelists Arrested as China Targets Church."

48. See Ma and Li, *Surviving the State, Remaking the Church*.

49. Erik Burkiln, "The Greatest Need in the Chinese Church: The China Christian Council Confronts the Task of Theological Education," *ChinaSource* 5(1) (Spring 2003): 8–9.

50. Kwok, Pui-lan, "Christianity and Women in Contemporary China," *Journal of World Christianity* 3(1) (2010): 1–17.

51. In the 1980s and 1990s, Fang Cheng Fellowship became the center of a rural revival that spawned many house churches.

52. Quoted in "Xiao Min," Women of Christianity, https://womenofchristianity.co m/hymn-writers/xaio-min/

53. Starr, *Chinese Theology*, 356.

54. Ruth Wang, "'I Compose Hymns by Prayers,' Xiao Min, Composer of Canaan Hymns Shared Her Story," *China Christian Daily*, February 13, 2017. http://chinachr istiandaily.com/news/category/2016-02-06/-i-compose-hymns-by-prayers---xiao -min--composer-of-canaan-hymns-shared-her-story-_534

55. David Aikman, *Jesus in Beijing: How Christianity is Transforming China and Changing the Global Balance of Power* (Washington: Regnery Publishing, 2012), 109.

56. Starr, *Chinese Theology*, 355.

57. Quoted in a note from Xiao Min, *The Canaan Hymns* (Taipei: Hosanna Gospel Propaganda Association, 2003).

58. Aikman, *Jesus in Beijing*, 109.

59. Fangcheng Christian Fellowship was a network of Pentecostal house churches in Henan Province.

60. "Xiao Min," Women of Christianity, https://womenofchristianity.com/hymn -writers/xaio-min/

61. Ibid.

62. Aikman, *Jesus in Beijing*, 110.

63. Starr, *Chinese Theology*, 355.

64. Kate Zhou, *China's Long March to Freedom: Grassroots Modernization* (New Brunswick: Transaction Publishers, 2011), 141.

65. The typical hymns in the Chinese New Hymnal of China Christian Council are more formal because most are translated from Western hymns.

66. Thor Strandenæs, "The Never Ending Song: The Contextualization of Chinese Christian Hymnody," in Tormod Engelsviken, Ernst Harbakk and Thor Strandenæs, ed., *Mission to the World: Communicating the Gospel in the 21st Century: Essays in Honor of Knud Jorgensen* (Oxford Regnum, 2008), 158. Also see Starr, *Chinese Theology*, 358.

67. More information about Yuan can be found in the next chapter.

68. Starr, *Chinese Theology*, 356.

69. Aikman, *Jesus in Beijing*. This book's first edition was released in 2003.

70. Kim-Kwong Chan, "The Christian Community in China: The Leaven Effect," in David Halloran Lumsdaine, ed., *Evangelical Christianity and Democracy in Asia* (New York: Oxford University Press,2009), 43–86.

71. Ruth Wang, "You Are the Light of the World, Song for preachers, created by China's Songbird, Lv Xiao Min," *China Christian Daily*, December 15, 2015. http://chinachristiandaily.com/news/category/2015-12-15/you-are-the-light-of-the-world--song-for-preachers--created-by-china-s-songbird--lv-xiao-min_349

72. Xiao Min, "Women of Christianity."

73. C. Michael Hawn, "Landscapes and Soulscapes: How Place Shapes Christian Congregational Song," in Stanley Brunn, ed., *The Changing World Religion Map: Sacred Places, Identities, Practices and Politics* (Dordrecht: Springer, 2015), 2665.

74. Or, "Interview with President of China Christian Council."

75. Cao Shengjie, "Foreigners Have Misunderstandings about Christians in China," *China News*, April 18, 2006. http://www.chinanews.com/news/2006/2006-04-18/8/719216.shtml

76. A highly successful commercial filmmaker, Feng Xiaogang directed seventeen award-winning Chinese films. He is seen as a box office guarantee in China's entertainment industry.

77. Paul Golf, *The Coming Chinese Church: How Rising Faith in China Is Spilling over Its Boundaries* (Oxford: Monarch Books, 2013), 164.

78. Strandenæs, "The Never Ending Song," 156. Also see Paul L. Neeley, "Canaan Hymns," in Glen G. Scorgie, ed., *Dictionary of Christian Spirituality* (Grand Rapids: Zondervan, 2016), 591–92.

79. Starr, *Chinese Theology*, 356.

80. Wang, " 'I Compose Hymns by Prayers'."

81. Starr, *Chinese Theology*, 359.

82. "Risky Road: China's Missionaries Follow Beijing West," *BBC News*, September 4, 2017. https://www.bbc.com/news/world-asia-41116480

83. Organizers of this movement believe that God has called the Chinese church to preach the gospel to ethnic groups in Jerusalem. The movement leaders, such as Brother Yun, have been controversies with regard to their truthfulness. See Paul hattaway et al., *Back to Jerusalem: Three Chinese House Church Leaders Share Their Vision to Complete the Great Commission* (Downers Grove: IVP Books, 2003), 151. Among their vocal critics was Lin Xiangao, a prominent house church leader who exposed the lies told by Brother Yun. See Lin Xiangao, "China's Conman the 'Heavenly Man'," a blog article, January 1, 24. Reposted at http://bbs.creaders.net/rainbow/bbsviewer.php?trd_id=248001 Researcher Kim-kwong Chan points to the "movement" as a "hoax." See Kim-kwong Chan, "The Back to Jerusalem Movement: Mission Movement of the Christian Community in Mainland China," in Kenneth R. Ross, ed., *Mission Spirituality and Authentic Discipleship* (Oxford: Regnum Publishing, 2013), 172–92.

84. Strandenæs, "The Never Ending Song," 157–58.

85. Luke Leung, "New Song Olympics 2008 added to Canaan Hymns," *The Gospel Herald*, May 27, 2008.

86. Cao, *An Oral History*, 163.

87. Gao Ying, "The Place of Women in the Church in China," *In God's Image* 13 (1) (1994): 59.

88. Cao Shengjie, "Chinese Christian Women in Education and Development: Understanding the Compatibility of Faith and Action for Women in a Changing Society," *Church and Society* 86 (5) (May–June 1996): 76–81.

89. Yifan Lu, "Equal Discipleship: Exploring Chinese Feminist Theology," *The Ecumenical Review*, by World Council of Churches, April 22, 2019.

90. Angela Wai Ching Wong, *The Poor Woman: A Critical Analysis of Asian Theology and Contemporary Chinese Fiction by Women* (New York: Peter Lang, 2002).

91. "The Louvian Consultation," *Appendix: Contemporary Church, Contemporary China* by Herbert Dargan, Pro Mundi Vita, 54, 1975, 37.

92. Rose Wu, "1997 and the Destiny of the Hong Kong People," *In God's Image* 16 (2) (1997): 10.

93. Cao Shengjie, "The Current Situation in the Chinese Church," *Chinese Theological Review* 16 (2002): 57.

94. Fiorenza, *In Memory of Her*, 68.

95. It is important to note that the biggest difference between fundamentalism in China and the West is the former's apolitical stance. While fundamentalists in America have actively engaged in politics since the 1970s and have benefited from perpetuating the myth of a "Christian America," such is not the case for fundamentalist Protestants in China.

96. Nanlai Cao, "Gender, Modernity, and Pentecostal Christianity in China," in Robert Hefner, *Global Pentecostalism in the 21 Century* (Bloomington: Indiana University Press, 2013), 149–75. Also see Ma, *Christianity, Femininity and Social Change in Contemporary China*.

97. To this day, there has not been any reliable estimate of the Protestant population in China. This created both myth and opportunism for scholars and China mission practitioners to exaggerate numbers for media attention or fund-raising.

98. See China entry in *World Christian Encyclopedia*, 2nd ed. (New York: Oxford University Press, 2001).

Chapter 9

Exposing Abuses, Changing Narratives

For a few decades, house churches' elevation of male leaders has created a powerful field of tacit sexism. It is only a matter of time when the topic of sexual violence against women would come up as a contentious issue. In the early 2010s, two Chinese women in the diaspora Chinese church spoke up against sexual abuses, exposing past traumas and stirring up huge controversies. In 2011, retired Chinese American medical physician Lily Hsu published a book titled *The Unforgettable Memoirs: My Life, Shanghai Local Church and Watchman Nee*. Through interviews with the victims of sexual abuses by Watchman Nee, Hsu confirmed the validity of Nee's crimes for which he was once indicted by the communist government but which were dismissed by the house church community as an attempt to frame him. In 2014, former Tiananmen dissident and later Christian anti-abortion advocate Chai Ling released a public statement about her alleged rape by a famous evangelist and also Tiananmen leader Yuan Zhiming. Though each endured a prolonged controversy afterward, Hsu and Chai both challenged master narratives that have been at work in the recent history of Chinese Protestantism.

The first narrative came from the decades from 1950 through the 1970s when Protestant churches were either co-opted into a pro-communist apparatus or persecuted to go underground. Nonconforming leaders such as Watchman Nee and Wang Mingdao, as part of the latter group, have been endowed with martyr. In fact, Nee was widely considered a martyr due to his imprisonment and later death in 1972 in a labor camp. Over the next decades, even after regime tolerance increased and the Christian population had an exponential growth in China, stories about these leaders' piety and unyielding obedience to God became saga tales that provided moral legitimacy for the house church movement.

The second narrative was formed in the early 1990s after the Tiananmen Square protests, when notable activists who emigrated to the United States converted to Christianity. Some even became preachers and evangelists who later gained celebrity status aided by mass media platforms in the subculture of Chinese overseas evangelicalism. A similar tale of these former Tiananmen activists' resistance to regime power and obedience to God became part of their legacy. Their courage and piety made them larger-than-life figures, beyond reproach. Decades after the entangled beginning of Chinese Communism and Protestant Christianity, the dominant historiography of Chinese Christianity is still anti-communist.

Founded on the resistance toward two historical monuments under communism, namely the Cultural Revolution and the communist state's crackdown on the Tiananmen movement, both of these narratives reveal the Chinese church's longing for identity. For that purpose, persecution under communism remain at the core of a collective identity. It played a uniting role even between the Chinese Christian community and many conservative American Christians. And it was largely this meta-narrative that helped China-bound mission organizations in America to raise funds in support of their brothers and sisters in China. Just as the American missionary community was obsessed with tales of footbound seclusion in China around the early republic, mission organizations in America became similarly obsessed with dramatic suppression of Tiananmen activism when meeting with new converts from mainland China after the 1990s. The experiences of post-Tiananmen exile became a status symbol for many activist-turned-pastors.

The controversies around Lily Hsu and Chai Ling challenged these dominant narratives. They forced people to realize that there are multiple layers of power dynamics at work. Externally, male Christian leaders resisted an atheist regime, and such courage and heroism granted them much moral integrity. But internally, these same church leaders abused their power by exploiting the vulnerable within the church community. Sexual abuse of women is one issue, and there is usually financial malpractice, spiritual and emotional abuse as well. This important chapter in the development in Chinese Protestantism resembles a Katharine Bushnell moment when the abuse of women by powerful Christian men was taken into account in re-centering history.

Using a female voice through her book, Lily Hsu presents a subversion of a long-held view in the West with regard to China's most well-known Christian leader. Although almost a decade before Western scholars like Dana Roberts and Leung Ka-lun had written about Nee's failings in the 1940s, the 300-page account by Lily Hsu was based on her firsthand experience and interviews.[1] The book's English version was released in 2013. Lily Hsu not only sounded the alarm about sexual abuses that were long buried in what the West perceived as pious house churches, but she also offered insightful theological reflections on the personality cult surrounding Nee. In 2018, Lily Hsu expanded the book into a 700-page volume titled *For Whom the Siren Wails: Watchman Nee and the Local Church in China*. It included more of Watchman Nee's own writings and messages that showed a different side of him and were thus left out in his other publications.

Lily Hsu was born into a Christian family in Hangzhou. Her grandparents were the first Chinese converts led by missionaries of China Inland Mission. Hsu's mother attended Christian schools and worked as a nurse in a missionary-founded hospital in Suzhou. Her parents were both medical professionals. They divorced when Hsu was very young, and she was raised by her grandmother. Lily Hsu attended Christian schools and excelled academically. In the late 1940s, Hsu also actively participated in YWCA and was promoted to the president of its summer camps in 1947. That year, sixteen-year-old Lily Hsu was invited by a friend to a church meeting led by Witness Lee (or Li Changshou), a second-tier leader in Watchman Nee's Little Flock sect. Hsu was deeply moved by the spiritual devotion of this group, so she received baptism in the Shanghai Local Church.

Watchman Nee himself was converted in 1920 at an evangelistic meeting of Dora Yu (Yu Cidu), the earliest Chinese woman evangelist. Eight years later, Nee wrote *The Spiritual Man* (English translation, 1968). By 1930, Watchman Nee rapidly gathered followers from urban middle class and professional backgrounds. Unsatisfied with what he saw in Western-imported denominationalism, Nee led an anti-denominational trend and refused to let his followers call themselves by any particular name. People later used a biblical reference when referring to Nee's Local Church: the Little Flock. Even after Watchman Nee gained great fame, he did little revivalist preaching; rather, he disseminated his ideas through writings and publications, as well as the evangelistic efforts of his coworkers.

Between 1949 and 1951, Hsu actively participated in gatherings of core members of this sect led by Watchman Nee. "I wholeheartedly devoted myself into campus ministry. My heart had no desires other than the Lord Himself."[2] Her change was dramatic and total, turning away from previous hobbies and entertainment. In her own words, she wrote, "According to the teachings of the Local Church, I put down my favorite novels, movies and drama shows. . . . because 'the old me has died.' In my heart there was joy because I willingly laid these down for the Lord."[3] Later she told about the evangelical work on college campuses in Shanghai where "every college campus in Shanghai experienced great revivals. Many young people received the gospel and showed changes in their lives."[4]

In the Local Church, all ministries were centered around evangelism. There had been waves of voluntary out-migration to remote northwestern regions for the purpose of evangelism.[5] The church also encouraged young people to marry for evangelistic purposes: "Marriage means that after two people unite, they would face a serious calling, that is to preach the gospel and serve God."[6] Lily Hsu was impressed with many of these wedding ceremonies when the bride and the groom dressed plainly with no fancy reception. The whole emphasis was on starting a new mission together. Nurtured in this spiritual environment, Hsu was determined to live a puritanical lifestyle. She began to dress herself only in plain and drab colors. The atmosphere was that "Few sisters wore colorful clothes in church. That would be impious and one would feel uneasy. I paid too much attention to how pious I appeared. Without knowing it, I have heaped layer after layer of spiritual masks on myself."[7] Even when she was walking on the streets of Shanghai, Hsu forbade herself to indulge in any window shopping.[8] According to an old acquaintance of hers, Cao Shengjie (chapter 8), "she was not moved by anything in the world . . . for fear that her heart towards the Lord would become impure."[9] Although still in her twenties, Hsu became a well-known and respected figure in Christian circles due to her devotion and zeal.[10] In her memoir, Hsu described herself back then as "serious in speech and manner" and "inapproachable as a nun."[11]

By 1948, the church in Shanghai has grown to over 1,000 members. Its founder Watchman Nee has been influenced by accounts of the Plymouth Brethren since 1935. Ideas like plural eldership, disavowal of a clergy-laity distinction, and worship centered around the "Breaking of Bread" became marks of biblical piety. Nee's devotional book *The Spiritual Man* (1928) had a wide readership to make him one of the best known indigenous church leaders. In the 1930s, Nee traveled to Europe and gave sermons that later published as *The Normal Christian Life* (1938). By the early 1950s, the Local Church and Jesus' Family had become the two best known indigenous Christian sects. But with the intensification of political campaigns through the Three-Self Patriotic Movement, these groups became hardest hit by the storm of denunciation.

In 1952, Shanghai's Public Security Bureau set up a public exhibit to expose the crimes within the Jesus Family. Lily Hsu went but was unmoved by it: "The crime evidences were mostly caricatures drawn by propagandists. . . . The whole exhibit was about twisting facts and demonizing believers, eventually something disgusting."[12] Hsu returned to her church's Bible study on the book of Daniel, which gave her great encouragement during persecuting trials. She recounted, "We felt that the day for us to suffer for the Truth of God was drawing near. We took it seriously and were prepared."[13] The general response from the Christian community toward this kind of public exhibit was one of disbelief, because they considered communists as radicals who would be willing to say and do anything.

In 1954, Shanghai Local Church announced its decision to quit the Three-Self Patriotic Movement. In his late forties, Watchman Nee was soon arrested in Shanghai and faced charges of financial and sexual misconduct. In December 1955, when Lily Hsu was brought to a public exhibit of Watchman Nee's crimes, she realized that the followers of Nee had underestimated the impact of these public denunciations:

> They told me that Watchman Nee had lived a corrupt life. He raped two women co-workers who I knew and respected. Then they showed me the video record-ing that Nee made of one woman . . . those naked moving images and Nee's own signature was like a bolt of lightning from the sky. I was dumfounded and speechless. . . . I could not believe that this was true, especially when it involved two women co-workers I adored. Before, when I visited the Jesus' Family exhibit, I was only repulsed by the caricature and hyperbole. But this time is different. . . . My respect and reverence for Watchman Nee had in fact become a part of my Christian faith. I no longer knew how to face my own faith.[14]

The exhibit also had Nee's own written confession about multiple times of prostitution, including five instances with women who were virgins.[15] He also wrote a confession about the rapes of two women coworkers whose names were also revealed in the exhibit. To Lily Hsu, the world seemed to have turned upside down. "Why did Nee have to reveal the names of these two women? They were victims, and how cruel it was to make their names pub-lic?!" Hsu wrote in her book.[16] Hsu spent the next few weeks pondering over her own faith. She realized that the culture of the Local Church had turned her, a young woman, into someone rigid and alienated. Indeed, "Watchman Nee taught us young people to not love the world. Our hearts should not be moved by anything. But I realized that he and the church had turned me into someone utterly cold and indifferent towards the world."[17] She tried to make sense of what she had done in the past years, concluding, "I have lost the heart of a young person, and I tried to evangelize more young people to be like me."[18] Hsu did not leave the Local Church all at once. In 1956, she visited the survivors of sexual assaults (Sister Miao and Sister Zhang) by Watchman Nee, and she kept notes about the interview.

> Sister Miao, who was sixty-two years old, told us how it happened in Wuxi in 1931. "Brother Nee called me saying that he wanted to see me. Then he drove a car and picked me up. I was not prepared but I followed him. . . . That was the time when he video-taped me, naked. I asked him why. His answer was, 'For remembering you, because we won't have many opportunities to see each other.' . . . I don't know why he kept that tape."[19]

A few months later, when Watchman Nee's case was tried at the Supreme Court in Shanghai, Lily Hsu was among the twelve representatives from the Local Church.[20] She watched with her own eyes how Nee confessed the alleged crimes, including the rapes. Two days later, the Shanghai Local Church excommunicated Nee. But the response from congregants were divided, with some claiming that the evidence had been planted by the communists.

The dramatic change in Lily Hsu's attitude toward Watchman Nee was observed by many. When medical staff at her hospital were required to participate in political study sessions, Hsu had once strongly resisted. But after the exposure of Nee's crimes, Hsu also participated in the denunciation meetings.[21] Her article "I Denounce" was published on *Liberation Daily*, along with a list of Nee's crimes.[22] At the time of Watchman Nee's trial, Lily Hsu began working as a physician in a hospital. She prayed to God for future direction but experienced a dark night of the soul. Hsu decided to leave the God she vowed to serve. She even broke up with her fiancé, who had a strong Christian faith. She explained, "My faith has wavered, so the foundation in our relationship was lost."[23]

For the next twenty-four years, Lily Hsu stopped praying to God or attending church services. She moved away from Christianity, got married, divorced, and remarried. It was not until in 1980 that a visit from a Christian physician brought the topic of "God" back into her conversation. A year later, Lily Hsu immigrated to America to reunite with family. She passed medical exams and obtained qualifications to practice medicine. There, Hsu also met a few former members of the Local Church who, like herself, returned to the Christian faith after decades of spiritual exile.[24] Inspired by these testimonies, in her seventies, Hsu decided to write a history of the Local Church from her own experience. She then made trips back to China and interviewed people who were involved with Watchman Nee's activities.

After the publication of Lily Hsu's second edition in 2018, readers' passionate and divided responses to Hsu's book are revealing. Some church leaders listed Hsu's past record of "always standing on top of things" and accused her book as a similar gimmickry for public fame. They questioned her motive for writing such a book by spinning around conspiracy theories. They verbally attacked her as a modern "Judas Iscariot" and "Cain who shed the blood of Abel and persecute the Lord."[25] Even Hsu's prodigal spiritual journey was used to discredit her—they called her a traitor who had once denounced Watchman Nee and a longtime strayer who cannot be trusted with good judgment. Partly in response to these accusations, Hsu recalled in her 2018 book with genuine honesty that "through that denunciation [of Nee] I voiced the fact that I was deceived by Nee. Some people accuse me of not repenting my sins for denouncing Nee. But they ignore Nee's own lack of penitence."[26]

These controversial debates reveal something characteristic about the state of Protestant Christianity in China. Male leaders were elevated as persecuted martyrs, victims of the communist state. Even when allegations of sexual assaults against women were brought out, many Chinese believers refuse to acknowledge them as facts.[27] Instead, they use conspiracy theories to blame the authorities and even the women themselves for working with the government. The discrediting usually follows either a politicized approach or a spiritual one. Take Lily Hsu, for example. Her critics either politicize the discussion by claiming Hsu is complicit with the communists, or they characterize her as a spiritual infant for not having enough biblical maturity to forgive or to make sense of human failings.

The cognitive divide concerning the integrity of these Christian leaders may last for decades. For Watchman Nee, the English-speaking West continues to enshrine him as a spiritual giant and a mature Christian who was persecuted by a communist government in China. His spiritual writings were translated into English and became widely read in the West.[28]

In an interview with the media, Lily Hsu said: "Not very many Christians in the United States—or even in China—know he [Nee] was excommunicated by the Shanghai Christian Assembly [of the Local Church]. All the bad things have been covered up. The church leaders knew something, but they kept silent. I want to clear the fog."[29] Her critics such as Chris Wilde, director of communications for Living Stream Ministry, the primary publisher of Nee's writings, called Hsu's book "a re-statement of the old 'official' government charges."[30] Wilde also added that "prominent Christian and other religious leaders were accused by the Chinese Communists of all manner of nefarious deeds . . . and the credibility of the Party's allegations during that era has been viewed as highly dubious by most objective observers." On an English-speaking Local Church online forum in North America, a thread about what Lily Hsu's works mean to Western perception had hundreds of entries on with many reckoning the validity of the cover-ups. Some online commentators also took the opportunity to reveal a subculture of abuse in contemporary Local Church's North American congregations.[31] There is the same pattern of fundamentalist piety, patriarchal norms, and the persecution complex. Taking pride in the so-called house church tradition, which sums up all these layers, Local Church leaders consider themselves the guardian of true faith that had been tested under communism.[32] Historian Daniel Bays describes similar behavioral patterns among overseas followers of Watchman Nee. They devalue theological training and emphasized personal charisma to boost their own authority. Some centered on a narrative depicting the official churches and the Communist Party of China as the Red Dragon or anti-Christ of the Book of Revelations. These themes then feed into a martyrology that glorifies persecution at the hands of religious authorities in China.[33]

Among house churches, the anti-Three-Self polemics also gave rise to more radical sectarian groups in rural China such as the Established King sect (Beiliwang), the Three Grades of Servants (Sanban puren), the Eastern Lightning (Dongfang shandian), and so on. They are characterized by a wholesale anathema against religious and political authorities. Many took on folk religious practices and rituals, forming a kind of popular Christianity.[34] A few devolved into cult groups that brought social security hazards.[35]

Because ethnography is central to Lily Hsu's project of recovering suppressed voices, critics also tend to challenge her methodology. In fact, Lily Hsu's works pioneered an accessible ethnography based on women's "real" and "lived" religious experiences. In comparison, Three-Self theologian Cao Shengjie's textually based feminist theology imposes a sense of unreality and simplistic portrayals of women's experiences. "Lived experience" is a technical term used to signify "intentional, self-reflective, or valued activity, not merely anything that happens to a person."[36] As an ethnographer-historian, Lily Hsu analyzes and synthesizes the data about these lived experiences in order to construe the overarching, significant, or recurring themes of Local Church ethos and worldview. Hsu has adopted a research process that engages women as living documents. In collecting testimonies and data about oppressed women, her writings served as advocacy and agents in the distribution of knowledge in support of cultural change. Her books became the vehicle for particular Chinese women to develop their own voices. Moreover, in presenting women's stories, Hsu has been self-critical about the assumptions she inevitably brings to her research projects.

In 2016, Chinese American novelist Shi Wei published *The Apostates* (or *Renegades*) based on Lily Hsu's 2011 book.[37] Also a well-known Christian author and poet, Shi Wei's historical fiction rendition of Watchman Nee's scandals became very popular, earning her the reputation of "pioneering Chinese spiritual literature."[38] This book helped popularize the knowledge of Nee's scandals to an extent that it was no longer a taboo to discuss it publicly among Chinese Christians. Shi herself did receive hostile pushback from Local Church affiliates, but her adoption of fictional names for the main characters of this history largely fended off the attacks. That her book broke a taboo demonstrates that the prevailing narrative of Watchman Nee's sainthood has stubbornly dominated the public consciousness for over sixty years.

If Maoism posed the biggest trauma for the spirituality of the Chinese, then the second equally traumatizing moment would be the Tiananmen democracy movement in 1989. If the former tested the faith of Chinese Protestants through erasing their public visibility, the latter created preconditions for the Christian faith to be appealing again among a generation of educated Chinese who became disillusioned by the communist ideology. So by the 1990s, the spiritual wind has shifted, leading to an unprecedented mass conversion.[39] It was in this social context that a similar battle like Lily Hsu's emerged. This time the protagonists were Chai Ling (female) and Yuan Zhiming (male), both celebrity dissident-turned-Christians, who exiled to America after their leadership in the Tiananmen incident. Compared to Lily Hsu who wrote as an ethnographer-historian, Chai was herself the victim of an alleged rape incident, so she found it important to expose the details of how it happened. In 2014, Chai Ling released a public statement on her own website that again brought another storm of controversies.[40] She wrote that Yuan Zhiming, an activist-turned-pastor and leader in post-Tiananmen exile, had raped her in 1990, when they were both at Princeton University through its China Initiative. So Chai Ling's story came to the public eye twenty years later. By then, both "Yuan and Chai are two of the highest-profile Christian leaders among the world's 50 million overseas Chinese."[41] Before the release of this public statement, the diaspora Chinese Christian community considered Chai Ling and Yuan Zhiming to belong to the same camp. They both led the Tiananmen movement, later fled China and converted to Christianity. Both became famous representatives of God's work among Chinese dissidents.

According to Chai (then married), after having arrived in America as political refugees in 1990, Yuan (also married) invited her to his apartment to watch a film together.[42] Knowing that Yuan wrote *River Elegy*, a widely circulated documentary in China, Chai Ling agreed.[43] But she soon found that Yuan put on a pornographic movie. She then asked to leave but was assaulted by Yuan on the floor. "You grabbed me and physically pushed me to the carpet. You raped me right there and you covered my eyes with the jackets that fell during my struggle."[44] She also wrote, "My hatred turned you into lesser than a human in my memory. For all these years, whenever I heard your name, I utter 'Hypocrite!' in my heart. That is the only way I can live on."[45]

As Chai Lin explained, between 2011 to 2014, she has written to Yuan in compliance with the Bible's teaching on reconciliation, but he refused to apologize. In a face-to-face meeting between Chai and Yuan, accompanied by two pastors in November 2011, Yuan said that the incident was an "extramarital sexual iniquity," implying Chai's consent. He also quoted 2 Corinthians 5:17 ("If anyone is in Christ, the new creation has come. The old has gone, the new is here.") and taught Chai, a new convert, that if only she was familiar with biblical teachings then she would know one should start anew. Chai Ling was disappointed that after this meeting even the pastor who counseled her turned to believe Yuan's account. After that, Chai felt that she had to make this truth public "in order to protect other women from suffering the same abuse from Yuan." Chai explained that her purpose was biblical and that she just needed Yuan to confess about the past offense. In 2014 and 2015, Chai Ling wrote five open letters, exposing details about Yuan's assault on her. She wrote to Yuan in June 2014 about her trauma: "After I fled China, losing family, country, everything . . . my body, soul and mind shattered . . .

I never thought that I would be raped by you. What Satan did not accomplish in the fall [of 1989], you did in 1990."[46]

It is important to contextualize Chai Ling's personal story and her prolonged process of conversion to Christianity. The Tiananmen movement of 1989 marked a turning point for popular acceptance of the communist ideology, followed by widespread disillusionment and demoralization. It triggered a widespread spiritual and moral crisis as the CCP's moral authority collapsed. Social inequality, disenchantment with the official communist ideology, transiency in social relationships, and rising mental health problems all combined to create a deep spiritual crisis in the Chinese society.[47] There was an astonishing growth of all kinds of pseudo-religions, including Qi Gong (literally "Life Energy Cultivation") and the rise of Falun Gong groups.[48] It was in this climate when also mass conversion to Protestantism happened in mainland China. Not only did Tiananmen-affected conversions happened on a large scale, but common emotions, reflections, and discourses also emerged from individual accounts.[49] Post-1989 conversion took place across different cohorts, age groups, education levels, and occupations. Their conversion to the Christian faith was preceded by a gradual detachment from the official Communist dogma, which finally disintegrated after 1989. Many also mentioned a sense of betrayal and distrust of their earlier faith in the CCP as the savior of the Chinese people.

Many new Protestant converts after Tiananmen shared a "June Fourth Complex," characterized by a traumatized memory of the movement, a keen interest in China's political fate, a scorn for authoritarianism, and an idealistic desire. Consolidation in following Western democracy and constitutionalism. The happenings of Tiananmen and its post-crackdown cleansings defined their life trajectories, and the ideals and trauma of Tiananmen still haunt them today. Apathetic cynicism and activism are two post-traumatic symptoms going in opposite directions. Many among this June Fourth generation later entered the private economy. For those who worked in public universities, they willingly became marginalized. Nevertheless, they are more active in expressing opinions on political affairs. In the Chinese diaspora, especially North America, many new immigrants got baptized and joined churches, opening a new page for the previously Taiwanese-dominated Protestant demographic. Among the first generation Chinese clergy from mainland China background, many were in fact participants and activists in the Tiananmen movement.[50]

In 2003, Yuan Zhiming produced a documentary *The Cross: Jesus in China* via his U.S.-based charity, China Soul for Christ Foundation. A Pulitzer-winning journalist describes Yuan as "one of the country's most influential figures through his documentaries and videotaped sermons."[51] This four-episode documentary also included a public speech given by

George W. Bush at Qinghua University, China's top higher education institution. Bush mentioned that a majority of Americans believe in God. Remarks of this kind excited many Christian audiences in China who had been socially marginalized. Few were able to detect the blurring of line between Christian nationalism rhetoric and Christian spirituality. As American scholar Lee Marsden writes, the language of George W. Bush tends to "juxtaposes political concepts with religious metaphor. Freedom/democracy, just like 'saving faith,' calls to nations and individuals, a force that demands a response. The call of freedom/Jesus becomes apparent at the intellectual level of 'every mind' and at the spiritual level with 'every soul.' "[52]

Compared to Yuan Zhiming's fame, it is fair to say that Chai even had more controversies with regard to her involvement in Chinese politics and later advocacy work along the way. Here is a brief account of her life story. When Chai Ling was born in a fishing village in Shandong Province, her father was disappointed that his firstborn was not a son. As a young girl, Chai was "determined to overcome her gender deficiency" by bringing home good grades and prizes from school.[53] Chai's father was a young military officer with medical training. Sometimes when required by medical mission in the military, Chai's parents had to leave her to the foster care of a peasant family in the village. She remembered living in rural mud-brick dwellings and helpless poverty. Chai wanted to grow up and help people. Later Chai Ling's father was promoted to the head of a military hospital. Before she left for college in Beijing, Chai had an argument with her father about whether or not to join the Communist Youth League, the first step toward becoming a Communist Party member. By then, Chai Ling had adopted some liberal thoughts through the influence of a physics teacher. In 1983, Chai studied psychology at Beijing University. There she met a Christian who showed her an old Bible. Chai became very interested: "Through religion was outlawed in China when I was growing up, to me it was neither foreign nor intimidating."[54] After graduation, she got married and pursued a graduate degree.

In spring of 1989, when the Tiananmen movement broke out, Chao Ling became one of the three key student leaders and a commander of the Defend Tiananmen Square Headquarters. After the movement, both Chai and her husband were arrested by the Chinese authorities. In 1989 and 1990, she was twice nominated for the Nobel Peace Prize. A year later, she and her husband were exiled and arrived in France, then the United States. In 1993, Chai obtained a graduate degree in international relations and politics at Princeton's Woodrow Wilson School. She also earned another MBA from Harvard University and started a business in 1998. As Chai recalled, Americans who surrounded her wanted her to continue upholding democracy for China. Few people paid attention to her personal well-being. When a social worker talked with Chai about her first husband's domestic violence,

she heard the word "abuse" for the first time.[55] She explained: "In the culture
I grew up in, a woman must obey her father, and then her husband when she
marries . . . the social worker's words altered the way I looked at my past."[56]

In 1995, with the release of a documentary, *The Gate of Heavenly Peace*,[57]
Chai Ling's life was thrown into public controversy. The filmmakers claimed
that "the hidden strategy of the leadership she [Chai] dominated was to
provoke the Government to use violence against the unarmed students."
Chai even stated in her own words that "What we are actually hoping for is
bloodshed" and "only when the square is awash with blood with the people of
China open their eyes." The *New York Times* commented that "a central question for many in the student movement, and for some historians, is whether
moderation gave way to extremism during those six weeks and whether the
more radical student leaders spurned opportunities to declare victory by ending the demonstration and preserving, perhaps, the reformist trend that was
still a prominent feature of the Chinese leadership."[58] Chai Ling's words in
this documentary, as edited in a narrative by the producers, seemed to largely
confirm any doubt that her leadership resorted to extremism. In response,
Chai and many in the Chinese post-1989 exile community condemned it.
Chai protested that the filmmakers were "pro-communist."[59] Other scholars
also used Chai Ling's words as recorded in this documentary to affirm earlier
theories. "Her 'binary' approach and intolerant attitude of 'if you are not with
me, you are against me' is well documented in the film. . . . And it becomes
clearer in the debate over the film, when she attacked the filmmakers as co-
conspirators of the Beijing regime."[60] In 2007, Chai Ling brought a lawsuit
against the documentary website. In this process, Chai publicly denounced
the producers of this film as "tools of Satan."[61]

It was after this storm of public controversy that Chai began to search
for another worthy cause. Reggi Littlejohn, president of Women's Rights
Without Frontiers, influenced Chai toward accepting Christianity.[62] Littlejohn
shared with Chai Ling a book, *The Heavenly Man*, the story of a house church
leader named Brother Yun.[63] Chai's conversion to Christianity happened on
December 4, 2009, after a long conversation with Littlejohn. "My heart was
profoundly changed and my eyes were opened to all the dramatic events of
my life . . . the thirst I had is the longing for freedom placed in our hearts by
God. Only when I came to know God could I truly begin to comprehend his
unique purpose for my life."[64] Two months after Chai Ling received baptism
in 2010, she founded All Girls Allowed, a nonprofit organization whose
mission is "lifting up Jesus' name by exposing the human rights violations
caused by China's one-child policy"[65] When Chai gave a testimony in the
U.S. Commission on China's one-child policy, she confessed having had four
abortions. It was due to Chai Ling's new Christian faith that she gained the
courage to give this public confession.

In the years after her conversion, motivated by what she considered as biblical teachings, Chai Ling chose to deal with her past in a public way. In 2013, Chai released an open letter titled "I Forgive Them" in which she extended forgiveness to the leaders of China's communist regime.[66] As she wrote, "There could only be two futures for China: an outcome of continued fear, or a destiny that opens the door to true freedom—and forgiveness."[67] Chai then quoted a biblical story of how King David's son Absalom rebelled and took the throne. In the face of this betrayal, David forgave his son Absalom, but the king's generals continued the pattern of violence. Chai laments a similar vicious circle in the Chinese society. "Because of Jesus, I forgive them. I forgive Deng Xiaoping and Li Peng. I forgive the soldiers who stormed Tiananmen Square in 1989. . . . I pray that a culture of grace will arise in China, giving all people dignity and humanity."[68] Soon afterward, Chai's voice was soon drowned in a storm of criticism and attacks.[69] Many Tiananmen activists expressed their disappointment in Chai's change in outlook. Another Tiananmen student leader Wang Dan also released a public statement ending with this remark, "I hope she can distinguish between personal faith and factual judgement."[70] Mother of a Tiananmen victim accused Chai's action as "a betrayal to the '89 Tiananmen Spirit' that we Chinese are proud of" and "blaspheme on those who are dead on June Fourth."[71] Hong Kong Alliance in Support of Patriotic Democratic Movements of China decried Chai Ling for "spreading salt on the wound."[72]

Thus, by the time when Chai Ling went public with her story about Yuan Zhiming in 2014, her credibility had somewhat suffered because of these previous public remarks. Nevertheless, the alleged sexual abuse scandal of Yuan Zhiming became the most discussed topic in the Chinese diaspora. By then, evangelist Yuan Zhiming has become the most popular Chinese preacher in North America.[73] As media describes, "The accusations have roiled the Chinese Christian community."[74] In January 2015, eighteen Chinese American pastors wrote an open letter to Yuan Zhiming, calling him "to respond to Chai Ling's allegations responsibly in order to protect the image of the church."[75] An evangelical discipleship ministry, Chinese Christian Life Fellowship, convened a collaborative effort to commission a professional third-party investigative agency GRACE (Godly Response to Abuse in the Christian Environment) on Yuan's case.[76] According to the report, three other women also came forward with sexual abuse allegations. The incidents happened in France and Germany where Yuan Zhiming went for evangelistic meetings. A young college female student reported being invited to watch a pornographic movie in Yuan's hotel room followed by sexual misconduct by the evangelist.[77] The official voice of the China Soul organization responded by calling the fresh allegations "a deluge of rumors and malicious speculation" about Yuan.[78]

During this time, Yuan Zhiming denied all allegations but resigned from his position at China Soul for Christ Foundation.[79] The organization released a statement challenging the legitimacy of this independent report. A week later, Yuan released an open letter, which acknowledged his affair but denied other allegations.[80] Many Chinese American pastors also stepped up to support Yuan, claiming that discrediting Yuan was harming God's ministry. They also claimed that laws in America follow the principle of "innocent until proven guilty." Chai wrote in a response that "Truth is truth. God is God. Justice is justice. No matter how long the delay, it will surely come."[81]

Though these exchanges were highly visible among American Chinese Christian community, they became mere noises in mainstream American media. The two tales of Yuan Zhiming continued, just as Watchman Nee's contrasting images. The same pattern also happened to a Chinese house church leader Gong Shengliang, pastor of the South China Church, whose name means devotion and persecution in the English-speaking world but pops up sexual abuse in a simple Chinese language Google search. Daniel Bays offers an analysis:

[T]here was a tradition of agitated discourse with no lack of exaggeration and alarmist rhetoric in the American public discussion of China, especially concerning memories of the hopes for a Christian China. From the late 1970s, as news of surviving Christians trickled out of China, Hong Kong became an echo chamber for rumors about the reviving church in China, . . . This feeds the information machine of several groups in the US, mainly conservative evangelical groups. the message transmitted here to the public is usually that the unregistered churches are "persecuted," and the TSPM is hopelessly compromised, . . . Further, while the house churches are exemplary and noble in their martyrdom, the TSPM and the government are evil, intending to destroy the "real churches."[82]

These controversies also reveal much about a growing trend of celebrity power within Chinese churches since the 2000s. After a decade of growth, the diaspora Chinese church has adapted well to what America's religious freedom and consumeristic market have to offer. Multiple evangelical conferences registering thousands of Chinese Christians happen every other year in major cities like Chicago and Baltimore. Smaller conferences and newly registered ministry platforms mushroomed across North America. This submarket of diaspora Chinese evangelicalism has produced its own celebrity pastors, hymn-writers, and marriage counselors. Theologian Kwok Pui-lan once wrote that "As modernity mutated into postmodernity in the West, neocolonialism took a new form in the globalization of markets and capital."[83] Christian ministry also followed a market model, and with it comes branding. It is interesting to note that before the 2000s, churches in China have not developed a similar celebrity culture. But things gradually changed with the public visibility of urban churches and the wide range of Christian books and theological resources. It would take a few years for China's Christian bookstores to stock up books that was branded as popular and pious in America.

On the wide spectrum of opinions about the government in mainland China, a unified camp of diaspora Chinese leaders still favor using the persecution narrative to remind Chinese believers in a free land that their devotion and right to worship need to be taken seriously. These ministry leaders frequently travel back and forth to China, evangelizing urban-dwellers and leading rural Bible studies. They bring back idealizing tales about the pious but persecuted state of house churches with the intention of gently scolding North American congregants who grew too comfortable in a secular America. Sometimes they also invite church leaders from China to speak at their pulpits in America. During these exchanges, celebrity power is transferred across national borders. House church leaders who are good at telling stories about persecution and piety under communist regime accumulated enormous "reputational capital" in America.

At the same time, Asian patriarchal norms also factored into the discussion. As one popular theologian and commentator in this community observes: "Most Chinese churches are very pastor centered. . . . It's rare to see congregants openly challenge or question their pastor. Even minor disagreements can be seen as 'divisive' in the worst sense. Honor-shame cultures tend to be hierarchical. This is also a bedrock of Confucian ethics. . . . conflict is most frequently dealt with silence."[84] He also continues that "from a Chinese perspective, it's very unusual for Chai Ling to make this accusation so public."[85] Hinting a honor-shame culture especially for women in the church, this commentator applauds Chai because she was able to "convicts him in the court of public opinion."

For Chinese American evangelists like Yuan Zhiming, being in the diaspora did not change such tendencies. Since the 1980s, large-scale population movements have taken place across the globe. These new migrations created new diasporas. The notion of "diaspora" entails the shifting of regimes of power, which in history occurred as a result of conquest and colonization. Does Hsu's and Chai's social location in the Chinese diaspora have a connection with such advocacy? As Kwok Pui-lan has written, diasporic discourse may be "a fluid and challenging site to raise questions about the construction of the center and the periphery, the negotiation of multiple loyalties and identities, the relationship between the 'home' and the 'world,' the political and theoretical implications of border crossing, and the identity of the dislocated diasporized female subject."[86]

For the younger Chai Ling, her diaspora experiences in America continue to be politicized. Take her anti-abortion advocacy, for example. First, we need a context about abortion in China, where abortion regulations have much to do with its one-child policy between 1979 and 2015.[87] The draconian measure of family planning impoverished many rural families who paid huge fines for having multiple children.[88] Forced abortions by communist cadres harmed women's health and dignity. Social conflicts intensified over these disputes. Across the nation, it has profoundly reshaped the notion about Darwinian bioethics and what an ideal family is. In the long run, it has also prepared China's distorted demographics for an impending crisis. When natural disasters like the 2008 Sichuan earthquake struck, when tens of thousands of students died under the cement structures in poorly constructed schools, urban families that lost their only child experienced a deep collective trauma. After the state revised its policy to allow two children for married couples, the public propaganda system across China revised billboard messages condemning more than one child with encouraging slogans for families to have two.

In America, Chai Ling's anti-abortion activism has been dominated by a guilt-driven and shame-ridden component in her personal life. She told and retold about her regretted abortions. Doing so granted her a kind of sympathetic legitimacy, but the pressure of rhetoric from her right-wing American activist circle was also evident. The "third wave" of democratization has given American evangelicals new incentives and opportunities for expansion and influence in the global South. But on another level, Chai failed to overcome the guilt and reflect on how women's reproductive power has been controlled by patriarchal social norms. Discussions of abortion are detached from the issue of violence against women. While Lily Hsu lived through the disenchantment of her earlier Local Church faith, Chai Ling still finds advocacy for women and American right-wing politics on opposite sides. American scholar and evangelical leader Jennifer Butler insightfully points out that although the Christian Right supports rights for women, they are by no means for "women's rights."[89] She also adds that "Christian Right NGOs' views on homosexuality, abortion and religion are clearly shared by a large percentage of global civil society. These NGOs claim they are defending the developing world from a secular, libera, and feminist agenda that will tear families and nations apart."[90] Behind this observation was a whole other important topic, which deserves a separate volume.[91] To briefly summarize, I agree with Jennifer Butler who proposed that the globalization of the Christian Right in the early 2000s came after the revitalization of Christianity around the world, especially its conservative and fundamentalist camp. It is interesting but also concerning to observers that as the gravity of Christianity shifts to the global South, its leadership is becoming more conservative-leaning in these places. Having a president like George W. Bush who profusely used

Christian symbolism helped strengthen this trend. The right-leaning ideology of conservative evangelicals in America also reinforces itself by imagining themselves being victimized by secularism. As historian Philip Jenkins once puts it in a question, "What if a global North, secular, rational and tolerant, defines itself against the rest of the world as Christian, primitive, and fundamentalist?"[92] Swimming in this trend, Chai Ling and many Christian public figures in mainland China (as would be introduced in the next chapter) portray themselves as defending voices from the religiously reviving, family-oriented global South against the secular, liberal West who had forfeited its Christian heritage.

To conclude, Lily Hsu and Chai Ling broke the Chinese social norm of female silence in the sphere of public opinion about sex and sexual abuse. Chinese women in particular feel immense social pressure to conform to certain "patterned ways of expressing and negotiating socioemotional subtleties" in social interactions.[93] They are not entitled to anger. Even if they do, it is often expected that such emotions should be targeted at personal disputes, not public affairs. Both Hsu and Chai brought public attention to sexual abuse of women even before the #MeToo movement in America accelerated in 2017. In all these similar efforts, women wanted the same reckoning in public memory. As a #MeToo advocate later writes, "it's one thing for women to be privately plagued by reminiscences, to keep their memories secret. It is quite another for them to make their memories public and demand a collective revisiting of the past . . . efforts to bring sexual assault and rape into the public sphere, can be characterized . . . with the demand that we look at those stories with new eyes."[94] In many instances, like what Lily Hsu and Chai Ling had to endure, a cult of personality had grown around the perpetrator, making the public response to these women's speaking up mixed. Nevertheless, their efforts made a unique contribution to an increasingly globalized Chinese Christian community.

NOTES

1. Roberts, *Understanding Watchman Nee*. Secrets of Watchman Nee. Ka-Lun Leung, *Watchman Nee: His Glory and Dishonor* (Alliance Bible Seminary, 2003).
2. Lily M. Hsu, "Preface," in *The Unforgettable Memoirs: My Life, Shanghai Local Church and Watchman Nee* (Maitland: Xulon Press, 2011), v.
3. Ibid., 15.
4. Ibid., 31.
5. Ibid., 33.
6. Ibid., 34.
7. Hsu, 39.
8. Cao, *Oral History*, 70. More details about Cao Shengjie are in chapter 8.

9. Ibid.

10. Ibid., 28.

11. Hsu, "Preface," 39.

12. Ibid., 96.

13. Ibid.

14. Ibid., 105.

15. Ibid., 124.

16. Ibid., 125.

17. Ibid., 106.

18. Ibid.

19. Ibid., 135–38.

20. Ibid., 139.

21. Cao, *An Oral History*, 70.

22. Lily M. Hsu, "I Denounce," *Liberation Daily*, February 2, 1956.

23. Hsu, "Preface," 175.

24. The influence of Watchman Nee in the diaspora Chinese community has continued. See Eugene V. Gallagher et al., *Introduction to New and Alternative Religions in America, Volume 1, History and Controversies* (Santa Barbara: Greenwood publishing, 2006), 143–44.

25. "What Crimes Did Lily Hsu Committt?" Shi Dai Zhi Shi, a Chinese language Christian devotional site, July 8, 2019. http://nlsdzs.net/post/401.html

26. Hsu, *For Whom the Siren Wails*, 311.

27. Another example happened around 2003 when Gong Shengliang, founder of the South Church of China, was arrested by local authorities for financial and sexual misconduct. In 2019, a similar controversy about alleged sexual abuses in Early Rain Church led by a high-profile Chinese pastor also followed this pattern. See Ma, *Religious Entrepreneurism in China's Urban House Churches*.

28. See Amazon's author page about the translated works of Watchman Nee's spiritual writings.

29. Mark H. Hunter, "Book Challenges Watchman Nee's Legacy as Martyr: Former BR Doctor Publishes Memoir of Her Shaken Faith," *The Advocate*, September 1, 2012. http://theadvocate.com/features/fait...an-nees-legacy Retrieved on August 10 of 2020.

30. Ibid.

31. Online Local Church discussion forum: http://localchurchdiscussions.com/v Bulletin/showthread.php?t=3489

32. The pride in a socially constructed "house church tradition" is parallel to American fundamentalists' insistence on the heritage of "Christian America." On the façade, the former may seem apolitical, but it can also be argued that the "house church tradition" had been politicized from its conception. Only its form was manifested in reactive or resistance politics.

33. Ibid.

34. Xi, *Redeemed by Fire*, 222.

35. In 2014, members of Eastern Lightening (also known as Almighty God) killed a woman in a McDonald. See "Murder in Zhaoyuan City of Shandong Shocked

Chinese Netizens," *BBC News* (Chinese), May 30, 2014. https://www.bbc.com/zhong wen/simp/china/2014/05/140530_china_murder.shtml

36. Kamitsuka, *Feminist Theology and the Challenge*, 53.

37. Wei Shi, *The Apostates* (Montgomery: Dixie W. Publishing Corporation, 2016).

38. Jeshurun Lin, "Book Review: When a Celebrity Pastor Falls, Will There Be Apostates?" *China Source Quarterly*, 21 (2) (2019): 15–17.

39. See Ma and Li, *Surviving the State, Remaking the Church*, chapter 4.

40. Chai Ling, "We Can Always Find Truth, Are You Willing? A Letter to the Church about Yuan Zhiming," an open letter, December 23, 2014.

41. Timothy C. Morgan, "China Soul's Yuan Denies Rape Accusation, Resigns from Preaching," *Christianity Today*, March 9, 2015. https://www.christianitytoday.com/ct/2015/march-web-only/update-chai-ling-yuan-zhiming-rape-accusation-china-soul.html

42. Both of their spouses were still in China and reunited with them a few years later.

43. *River Elegy* (1988) was a documentary series about the failings of Chinese civilization. It was considered as a rallying cry for political reform. As one of its scriptwriters, Yuan Zhiming became famous in China even before the Tiananmen incident.

44. Quoted in Isaiah Narciso, "Tiananmen Dissidents: Chinese Pastor Yuan Zhiming Repents of Extramarital Affair, But Christian Activist Chai Ling Accuses Him of Rape," *Gospel Herald*, March 3, 2015. https://www.gospelherald.com/articles /54595/20150303/tiananmen-square-dissidents-chinese-pastor-yuan-zhiming-repents -of-extramarital-sex-but-christian-activist-chai-ling-accuses-him-of-rape.htm

45. Chai Ling, "Another Open Letter to Yuan Zhiming," January 3, 2015.

46. Quoted in Ian Young, "June 4 Student Leader Chai Ling Says Her Faith is Driving Her to Seek Confession of Alleged Rape by Fellow Dissident Yuan Zhiming in 1990," *South China Morning Post*, March 8, 2015. https://www.scmp.com/ news/china/article/1732100/june-4-student-leader-chai-ling-says-her-faith-driving-he r-seek

47. Hu Ping, "Cynicism: A Spiritual Crisis in Today's China," *Beijing Spring*, November 2011.

　　https://beijingspring.com/bj2/2010/280/20111121152948.htm

48. Cheris Shun-ching Chan, "The *Falun Gong* in China: A Sociological Perspective," *The China Quarterly*, 179 (September 2004): 665–83.

49. Ma and Li, *Surviving the State, Remaking the Church*, chap 3.

50. Teresa Wright and Teresa Zimmerman-Liu, "Atheist Political Activists Turned Protestants: Religious Conversion among Chinese Dissidents," *Journal of Church and State*, 57 (2) (Spring 2015): 268–88.

51. Ian Johnson, "Jesus vs. Mao? An Interview with Yuan Zhiming," *New York Review of Books*, September 4, 2012. https://www.nybooks.com/daily/2012/09/04/ jesus-vs-mao-interview-yuan-zhiming/

52. Lee Marsden, *For God's Sake: The Christian Right and US Foreign Policy* (London: Zed Books, 2008), 101.

53. Chai Ling, *A Heart for Freedom: The Remarkable Journey of a Young Dissident, Her Daring Escape, and Her Quest to Free China's Daughters* (Carol Stream: Tyndale Momentum, 2012), 39.

54. Ibid., 25.

55. Ibid., 588.

56. Ibid., 589.

57. Documentary website of the Gate of Heavenly Peace, http://www.tsquare.tv /film/

58. Patrick E. Tyler, "Six Years after the Tiananmen Massacre, Survivors Clash Anew on Tactics," *New York Times*, April 30, 1995. https://www.nytimes.com/1995 /04/30/world/6-years-after-the-tiananmen-massacre-survivors-clash-anew-on-tactics. html?pagewanted=all&src=pm

59. Chai Ling, "A Statement," *World Journal*, April 27, 1995. Also quoted in "The Rhetoric of Democratic Denunciation," on the documentary website of The Gate of Heavenly Peace.

60. Michael Sheng, "The Gate of Heavenly Peace," *The American Historical Review*, 1010 (4), (1996): 1150–116.

61. "The Long Bow Appeal: An Update," *China Heritage Quarterly*, No. 24, December 2010. An article in *The Guardian* titled "From Democracy Activist to Censor?" criticized Chai Ling's lawsuit. See Jeremy Goldkorn, "From Democracy Activist to Censor?" *The Guardian*, November 17, 2009.

62. Chai, *A Heart for Freedom,* 675–76.

63. Ibid., 683.

64. Ibid., 20.

65. Quoted in Young, "June 4 Student Leader Chai Ling." Also see Chai, *A Heart for Freedom,* 34–35.

66. Chai Ling " 'I Forgive Them': On the 23rd Anniversary of the Tiananmen Square Massacre in 1989," *Huffington Post*, June 4, 2012.

67. Ibid.

68. Ibid.

69. "Focus In: Why Was Chai Ling's Open Letter Controversial," *Voice of America*, April 25, 2014.

70. "Wang Dan Opposes Chai Ling's Forgiveness of the Communist Suppression of June Fourth," *BBC News* (Chinese channel), June 6, 2012.

71. Ding Zilin, "To Chai Ling: A Belated Open Letter," June 28, 2012. *Human Rights in China Bi-Weekly*, No. 81. http://biweekly.hrichina.org/article/1621

72. "Chai Ling Is Preaching God to Caesar," *Boxun News*, April 29, 2014.

73. By then the dissident-turned-evangelist Yuan has become arguably the first "celebrity pastor" in the Chinese Christian community. He has been a regular speaker at the Gospel for China Conference organized by Chinese Christian Life Fellowship in Chicago every three years. His evangelism conference in Hong Kong was ranked China's No. 3 Christian news story of 2014 by the *China Times*.

74. Ian Young, "Tiananmen Dissident Quits Church over Extramarital Sex; Denies Raping Activist Chai Ling," *South China Morning Post*, March 3, 2015. https://www

.scmp.com/news/world/article/1728273/christian-dissident-quits-ministry-amid-rape-claim-fellow-june-4-activist

75. Reposted in "Q&A about the Yuan Zhiming Incident," *Christian Life Quarterly*, Issue 80, December of 2008. Online resource. https://www.cclifefl.org/View/Article/5257

76. "Report on Chai and Yuan, Signed and Released by 18 Chinese-American Pastors," Chinese Christian Life Fellowship website, February 23, 2015. https://www.cclifefl.org/View/Article/3900

77. Timothy C. Morgan, "Prominent Chinese Christian Convert Accuses Another of Rape," *Christianity Today*, February 27, 2015. https://www.christianitytoday.com/news/2015/february/convert-chai-ling-accuses-yuan-zhiming-rape-china-soul-aga.html Morgan, "China Soul's Yuan Denies Rape Accusation, Resigns from Preaching." https://www.christianitytoday.com/ct/2015/march-web-only/update-chai-ling-yuan-zhiming-rape-accusation-china-soul.html

"Independent Investigation Reveals Sexual Abuse of a 23-year-old Female College Student by Yuan Zhiming," *Christian Times*, July 21, 2016. https://christiantimes.org.hk/Common/Reader/News/ShowNews.jsp?Nid=95319&Pid=5&Version=0&Cid=220&Charset=gb2312 Timothy C. Morgan, "Chinese Dissident-Evangelist Accused of Sexual Misconduct," *Religion News*, July 12, 2016. https://religionnews.com/2016/07/12/new-report-accuses-chinese-dissident-evangelist-of-sexual-misconduct/ Timothy C. Morgan, "Allegations of Sexual Misconduct by Famous Chinese Evangelist Span 24 Years," *Christianity Today*, July 15, 2016. https://www.christianitytoday.com/news/2016/july/more-allegations-sexual-misconduct-yuan-zhiming-china-soul.html

78. Young, "Tiananmen Dissident Quits Church over Extramarital Sex."

79. "Chai-Yuan Report Is Released. Yuan Resigned but Denied All Allegations," *Christian Times*, March 3, 2015. https://christiantimes.org.hk/Common/Reader/News/ShowNews.jsp?Nid=88205&Pid=5&Version=0&Cid=220&Charset=big5_hkscs

80. "Yuan Zhiming: A Letter to Brothers and Sisters," China Soul Foundation website, March 2, 2015.

81. Quoted in Young, "June 4 Student Leader Chai Ling."

82. Bays, *A New History*, 204.

83. Kwok, *Post-Colonial Imagination and Feminist Theology*, 19.

84. Jackson Wu, "Pastor Centered Chinese Churches," *Pantheos*, October 7, 2015. https://www.patheos.com/blogs/jacksonwu/2015/10/07/pastor-centered-chinese-churches/

85. Ibid.

86. Kwok, *Post-Colonial Imagination and Feminist Theology*, 45.

87. The "Second-child policy" was announced in October 2015 to "improve the balanced development of population." See "China to End One-Child Policy and Allow Two," *BBC News*, October 29, 2015. https://www.bbc.com/news/world-asia-34665539

88. The one-child policy was implemented unevenly in rural China where married couples were allowed to have a second child if the first one was a girl. Having more

than two children would result in huge sums of fines that equal the yearly household income.

89. Jennifer Butler, *Born Again: The Christian Right Globalized* (London: Pluto Press, 2006), 14. In her book, Butler proposes that the presence of a highly visible Christian Right coalition at the United Nations in year 2000 marked the culmination of this trend going global.

90. Ibid., 51.

91. The term "Christian Right" refers to leaders and organizations that actively promote a conservative social agenda which integrates religious values. Public religious figures like Jerry Falwell and Pat Robertson in the 1970s mobilized white conservative evangelicals around issues such as abortion, homosexuality, and traditional family values. They reacted to Supreme Court decisions over prayer in public schools and abortion. The theological roots of the Christian Right can be traced back to the modernist-fundamentalist controversy in the 1920s to 1930s when fundamentalists opposed the liberal interpretation of scripture. Since the 1970s, conservative evangelical forces began to build infrastructure institutions and actively engage in American politics. Problems created by this trend intensified during Donald J. Trump's presidency.

92. Philip Jenkins, *The Next Christendom: The Coming of Global Christianity* (New York: Oxford University Press, 2002), 160.

93. Miriam Johnson, *Strong Mothers, Weak Wives: The Search for Gender Equality* (Berkeley: University of California Press, 1988), 54.

94. Moira Donegan, "How Bertha Pappenheim Cured Herself," in Jessica Valenti and Jaclyn Friedman, eds., *Believe Me: How Trusting Women Can Change the World* (New York: Seal Press, 2020), 21, 23.

Chapter 10

Consumerism, Censorship, and Christian Celebrities

In May 2016, famous Chinese actress Yuan Li gave a public speech at Fudan University, one of China's top universities in Shanghai.[1] By then, Yuan had played roles in thirty-three TV drama series and ten movies. One of China's best-known actresses, Yuan started to be a household name as China's "Audrey Hepburn." She was also the spokesperson of China's Red Cross Society. Both fans and critics alike would chat about her acting roles, failed marriages, and outspoken personality in the public sphere. On the day she spoke as a guest at one of China's top higher education institutions, Yuan confessed that her once privileged life as a celebrity used to make her utterly indifferent to the suffering of the poor and marginalized in society. She also owned many pieces of expensive jewelry. After her conversion to Protestant Christianity, however, Yuan began to care about the misery of other people. She gave up her jewelry after recognizing the human cost in their manufacture. By the time of her public lecture in Shanghai, Yuan Li had been helping migrant workers suffering from pneumoconiosis for many years. Here is part of the speech:

> I used to be very very proud. I got famous fast, so many people held you very high, so high that you could not see the real world. You basically took airplane flights everywhere, and many people and cars surrounded you. It was impossible to ever eat at a small diner. You are out of touch with reality. I was an actress, but I rarely got in contact with the lowest class of people in society. . . . [Later] I realized that human beings are the most important, more valuable than a Mercedes. I knew that we are made in God's image, so we are precious.[2]

On this occasion and many others, Yuan Li unabashedly professed that she is a Protestant Christian and that Christianity has changed her life.

This lecture entitled "My Awakening and Redemption" and photo images of the famous actress hugging pneumoconiosis patients immediately went viral on the Internet. Yuan herself already had over 15 million followers on Weibo, China's equivalent to Twitter. In a media environment where Christianity has been one of the most censored terms, Yuan's story gained unprecedented publicity. The public buzzed about how Yuan Li left acting at the height of her career, suffered marriage failures, converted to Christianity, and has since advocated for poor migrant workers who are dying of pneumoconiosis, an occupational lung disease caused by working in high-dust environments, such as construction and jewelry manufacturing.

Yuan Li was born in Hangzhou of Zhejiang Province in 1973. In high school, she was targeted by a talent spotter and made many TV commercials. Gradually, she became interested in acting. She entered the Beijing Film Academy in 1992 and graduated as the top student of the class. Around 1997, Yuan Li met some Christians socially. She was critical of any religion and even stamped on the Bibles given by her Christian acquaintances. The more they tried to convince her, the harder Yuan tried to ridicule their faith. After one of these unpleasant encounters, Yuan went back to her job at filmmaking but fell from horseback the next day. She was not injured, and it made her more willing to take religion seriously. In 1998, Yuan's acting role in a popular TV drama *Never Close Eyes* won her great fame and a few national awards. In 2007, Yuan Li had her first transcendent experience when visiting the Notre Dame Cathedral in Paris. Light came down from the stained glass window, calling her heart to ponder life and God. She later recalled it as "the moving of the Spirit."[3] After she returned to Beijing, Yuan Li began to visit both Catholic and Protestant churches. The experience was disappointing as she found most sermons boring and church members too eager to make her say the "I Accept Jesus" Prayer.

The two decades between the late 1990s and 2008 (Beijing Olympics) were a golden age for exponential growth of unofficial churches. In urban China, the growth has been contingent on how much social space is allowed by the regime. In 2003, *Time* magazine Beijing bureau chief published a book titled *Jesus in Beijing*. He posited that China was becoming Christianized at such a speed that it was "in some ways like rolling thunder."[4] He even blew the future estimate out of proportions, claiming that in the next few decades 20 to 30 percent of the Chinese population would become Christians. By then, David Aikman thought that a Christian worldview would become dominant even among China's senior elites. During the same year, China specialist Carol Hamrin concurred with this assessment, also predicting "an unprecedented opening for Christianity to become the mainstream of belief in China."[5] Also writing in 2003, Huo Shui, a former Chinese government official, observes that the Christian faith has become indigenous:

"You can no longer say that Christianity is a foreign religion. Churches are led by Chinese. You see Chinese Bibles. You hear Chinese worship songs. You experience a Chinese style of worship. The church looks and feels Chinese. . . . Christianity has finally taken root in *Shenzhou* ('the land of God' meaning China in Chinese language)."[6] The optimism was shared by other historians:

> China has been opening to the world on two fronts, at home and abroad. Economic liberalization has opened China to the world market, but it has also created a vibrant diaspora, culture of Chinese immigrants . . . estimated at a total of 35 million people. It is likely that Chinese Christians in these and other diaspora communities will reconnect with the new religious developments in China and extend China's outreach.[7]

After private property rights were reinstalled into the Chinese constitution, and a housing market boom in the early 2000s, these economic restructuring practices led to the expansion of residential space that were not strictly surveilled by the state. More and more white-collar professionals, college faculty, and students who converted to Christian spontaneously formed faith communities that met in residential apartments and office buildings. Believers flourished in the private sector by owning businesses, working as technicians and professionals, establishing private education institutions, founding independent publishing companies, and so on. Fruits from four decades of market reform allowed Christians in urban centers to utilize economic opportunity structures to expand their professional presence and to secure worship space. In the realm of social life, individual Christian believers and even unregistered church groups enjoyed more social visibility and network connectivity. It is no longer unusual for common people in China to meet Christian believers in their personal and professional circles. This is largely because of the opportunity structures in the private economic sector.

Meanwhile, reentering foreign missionaries since the late 1990s, mostly Americans, have been influenced by a broader conservative evangelical resurgence. The vocal emphasis on marriage and family values was timely in a Chinese market of spirituality where the entire society has been witnessing higher divorce rates and growing public tolerance of premarital and extramarital affairs than ever before. Sexual immoralities also permeate Chinese politics as more and more cases of sex-related bribery and corruption were exposed by the media.[8] Party officials and the wealthy often have more than one mistress, nicknamed "second wives (*ernai*)." Some scholars call this "informal concubinage."[9] Against the backdrop of such prevailing immorality, public discourse has become largely cynical. Heavy censorship suppresses dissenting voices who present disciplined values.

It is important to explain how censorship works in contemporary China. The Chinese government uses censorship over all public media including television, print media, radio, film, theatre, text messaging, instant messaging, video games, literature, and the Internet. Subject matters of censorship include historical, political, and religious themes. The government issues directives on a regular basis as guidelines for public media coverage. Media organizations comply with self-censorship or run the risk of being closed down. Until today, there is no single publisher, TV station, newspaper or magazine funded purely by private capital in China. One reckons that the mainstream ideology in today's Chinese society is still official socialism. But both externally and internally, people seem to ignore the fact that this massive cultural enterprise has been infiltrated and intervened by transnational and private capital. The cultural enterprise has changed from mere propagandist tools to the current media and communication industry, rapidly gathering wealth, symbolism, and capital. Yet, the dominance of state media still produces a binary mode of thinking among the Chinese public that is typical of Cold War antagonism.

In the broader Christian community, believers now have full access to all the up-to-date technological tools, especially communication technology. The Internet nurtured a rare platform for expression in China. Thanks to new media technology, the sense of connectedness among Christians in China today has reached an unprecedented scale. The organizational dynamics of urban house churches in China have been embedded in the uneven distribution of opportunity structures in different societal spheres. While political-legal marginalization and discrimination remained unchanged from before, Christianity now faces less hostility in other spheres, especially in the economic and technological realms. If we understand these structures as different forms of "capital," Christianity in China can be said to have low political-legal capital but higher economic, technological, social, and cultural capital at its disposal. It is in this changing social context that the Western stereotypical impression that Christianity in China is entirely marginalized or "persecuted" no longer captures the reality. Christian groups now do have more informal social space facilitated by the growth of the private economic sector.

In media discourse, because the Chinese state has censored any mention of Christianity, some young people found the Christian message to be fresh and winsome. With conservative ministry brands such as Focus on the Family entering China, better still, Christianity seemed to offer hope for broken marriages and shattered families. In academia and on social media, Chinese Christian intellectuals continued to propose Christianity as a remedy for a demoralized society. Cultural pluralism and consumerism have enhanced an increased tolerance toward Christianity. Such cultural tolerance tends to fluctuate with seasonal campaigns of state nationalism.

While post-reform Chinese society as a whole was more welcoming toward Christianity, other competing ideologies were reviving too. A nostalgia for cultural conservatism either led to the resurgence of Maoism, neo-Confucianism, or other ideologies that might be helpful in counteracting the secularizing trend. In 2013, a Christian businessman funded a conference attended by a diverse group of Chinese scholars representing these different ideologies gathered at Oxford University and signed a statement known as "Oxford Consensus 2013."[10] The goal was to "work together to address challenges facing China and the world." After this conference, such interfaith dialogues continued on social media. But as the organizing pastors and Christian scholars increasingly showed lack of respect for other religions and traditions, the so-called consensus sowed even more divisions. In the sphere of churches, with a new discourse toward conservatism, Protestant leaders continued to encourage biblicism, conversionism, women to "return home" while denouncing extramarital affairs, abortion, and LGBTQ rights.

After her second marriage to a Canadian lawyer in 2014, Yuan Li spent three years traveling in North America. Quite early in this tour, she became a Jesus follower and received baptism in the Jordan River.[11] On her Weibo, Yuan retweeted Christian messages by Yuan Zhiming and other famous Christian personalities in North America.[12] She reminded the Chinese public that they should never forget Western missionaries who had sacrificed and contributed to the Chinese society. She also frequently visited holy sites such as Jerusalem and prayed for the conversion of the Jews. Her praises of Western civilization, the greatness of George Washington, and the spirit of Christ invited critics to comment that ever since finding a Western husband and a Western religion, Yuan Li has fallen completely for anything that is Western. Some even challenged that Yuan has squandered her popularity and lost her sanity after converting to Christianity. Three years later, after this interracial marriage ended in divorce, Yuan revealed the cause to be cross-cultural difficulties.[13] She also expressed regret about having married a foreigner and cautioned Chinese women to learn a lesson from her.[14]

Around 2014, China's entertainment industry went through a big change when South Korean-style reality shows dominated China's television screens. Yuan Li returned from North America only to find herself ill-adjusted to the new demands: "There were very few decent screenplays for me. Actors and producers now seem more keen on television competitions and games. I'm less than interested."[15] Since then, Yuan voluntarily became something of an "outcast" in the entertainment industry.[16] She did not like socializing with others in the same circle. In fact, Yuan grew uncomfortable with the label of "celebrity" many ascribe to her. After some travel in many Chinese cities and soul-searching, Yuan Li found a way to engage with the public through her Weibo presence. She began to actively comment on public affairs, which

Chinese celebrities rarely do for fear of political risks: "Even the most publicly involved actors would go no further than praying for peace after a national disaster, or writing a slogan-like call for justice on Weibo."[17] But for Yuan Li, Weibo became not only a public forum for her to find a voice, but also a place for Christian witnessing. As a media outlet *Christian Times* reports,

> She [Yuan] became a major voice for Christians in China's public sphere when officials in Zhejiang Province ordered over 200 churches to remove their crosses in a campaign to demolish and renovate what officials there consider to be dangerous buildings. . . . The campaign drew massive protests by Christians in the province. . . . Yuan felt an obligation to speak out and posted the chain of events closely on her Weibo, although her posts were often deleted by censors. "Normally, as an actress, I didn't like to speak out about public events. But I would question my faithfulness if someone is removing crosses in front of my home and I do nothing," she told [the media]. While her efforts won her support of some fellow Christians and allowed more people to know about the incident, they also led to vicious, nationalist comments insulting her motives and questioning her foreign religion.[18]

As the media comments, "In today's TV-movie boom when celebrities demand ever rising pay raises, Yuan plunged into philanthropy by visiting isolated elderly in mountainous areas, going down mine caves, looking out for abandoned children in poor villages, and comforting patients with lung diseases."[19] To better engage with this cause, Yuan Li stopped her acting career and retreated from the entertainment industry. She joined an NGO program called Love Save Pneumoconiosis which assists migrant workers with an occupational lung disease caused by working in high-dust environment like construction and jewelry manufacturing. It is also commonly known as the "black lung" disease. *Global Times* reported that "Among the numerous charity projects in China, Yuan picked this one after careful consideration. . . . She wanted to help those who are ignored and desperately in need."[20]

Initially, Yuan wanted to simply donate some money to help these people. When she visited mining families with this disease in mountainous areas in Hubei and Shaanxi Provinces, "[t]he poverty struck her so much that she soon began to hand out cash, withdrawing the bank machine's daily cap of 20,000 *yuan* every day."[21] But every visit deepened her burden for this particular group. She was shocked at how widespread the disease has become in China's poorest regions. In an interview, Yuan later told the media that she felt "calling of fate and God's will" for her connection with pneumoconiosis patients.[22] "Human life is more precious," she said.[23] Yuan also built deep relationship with local patients and even adopted a godson. Other volunteers shared their observation about Yuan Li's change during trips to villages. In the early days, she wore makeup and luxury brands. But toward the end of this program, she dressed plainly with no makeup and hugged villagers with tears streaming down her cheeks.[24] When Yuan Li started to befriend ordinary people, she paid attention to one of the most marginalized groups in China—migrant workers who had left rural hometowns to work in cities. They work in construction, mining, manufacturing, and service sectors, taking up the harshest and dirties jobs in the informal economy. Among these jobs, work hazards are highest for mining laborers. Once startled at seeing an X-ray picture of a migrant worker with pneumoconiosis, Yuan Li could not wave the images away. Her guilt and conscience awoke:

> This migrant worker needed an open-chest surgery so that he could prove to his employer about his "darkened" lungs in order to get compensation. That was 2015. I was thinking, what kind of time is this that people need to have their chests cut open to get compensation! . . . I did some online search and learned that there are six million pneumoconiosis patients in China, and many could never get compensation. . . . Our mines, jewelry, jade and stones, these can all cause pneumoconiosis.[25]

Since then, Yuan Li began to advocate for this marginalized group, connecting their plight to the twisted desires and greed of urban consumers, herself included. She also visited and lived with rural families with members suffering from this occupational disease. Before these trips, Yuan had no sense of what life is like in rural China. In the following years, she also donated large sums of money to help these people, including sponsoring a few lung transplants. In 2016, all these charity endeavors gave way to the formal registration of Yuan Li Foundation. Its mission statement says: "Occasionally heal, often help, always comfort." Yuan personally donated around 1 million *yuan* to assist patients. When people accused her of using philanthropy to preach Christianity, Yuan Li responded that "I offer no religion, but only faith and love."[26]

Yuan Li's voluntary downward mobility and strenuous emphasis on human dignity became a source of inspiration for the younger generation, which is living in a post-reform China with rising social inequality. By the 2010s, Chinese communism's developmental model has generated externalities, including serious environmental pollution. The problems of air pollution, soil erosion, and fouled water in China have become so grave that they are reported in the Chinese press all the time. Government plans to combat one ecological failing after another have not effectively solved the problems. Meanwhile, the tremendous human cost continues, borne especially by migrant workers who are the backbone of the nation's economy.[27]

Since the 1980s, China's massive rural-to-urban migration has brought sweeping social change. After agricultural de-collectivization and the collapse of communes in rural areas, the state deregulated control over the residential mobility of peasants, allowing them entry to nonfarming jobs in townships and cities. With deepening economic reforms since the 1990s, market incentives also encouraged enterprises, both state and private, to recruit cheap rural labor. In the following decades, China witnessed the largest peacetime wave of internal migration the world has ever seen. By the late 2000s, over half of the Chinese population became city-dwellers, compared to just 20 percent in 1985. During this time, however, the long-standing rural-urban income gap in China not only persisted but worsened. Remnants of socialist institutions, after the gradualist market reform, continue to stratify rural migrants and their next generation in disadvantageous ways. Some scholars compare the lot of rural migrants in China to that of illegal immigrants in the United States. In both instances, institutional discrimination and exclusion have barred these workers from obtaining equal rights. But unlike the situation of illegal immigration in the United States, where the second generation of migrants may obtain full citizenship by birth, China still enforced a system known as *Hukou*, which stipulates inherited status. Thus, the second and third generation of rural migrants are still not entitled to equal rights even when they were born in cities. These children are excluded from the urban public education system. As a result, migrant workers families experienced decades of separation, with adults leaving their children behind in villages. The drastic social inequality is thus perpetuated from generation to generation. Now making up two-thirds of the total labor force in China, rural migrants experience exploitation under China's market capitalism as well as repercussions from its socialist legacy.

American scholars and journalists have written about sweatshop laborers in China's factories.[28] The gender dimension of such inequality is hard to ignore. From massive state-owned enterprises' layoffs to rural migration to the cities, women have been a major part of structural socioeconomic injustice. In southern provinces and coastal areas, factories that rely on hiring nimble-fingered young female migrant workers in their late teens or early twenties function with a militaristic regime. They demand twelve hours of labor per day and calm emotions from the young women of rural China. First-timers consider the factory's package deal with free dorms and food a fair improvement compared to the lot of their peasant parents. Most of women leave factory work by their late twenties. They then seek work in the informal economy, either in small businesses or in the service sector; they form new families with other male migrants. In these cases, the children are often sent home to be raised by grandparents and relatives who tend to agricultural work. Most cities do not provide any education and welfare for the children of migrant workers. When these second or third-generation migrants come of working age in their late teens, they follow the same life trajectory. While Yuan Li is among the very small number of celebrities who has been focused on advocating for migrant workers, she has largely ignored the gender aspect, leaving many issues untouched, including alienated motherhood, conspicuous consumption among young women migrants, sexual harassment and abuses experienced by female migrant workers in urban workplaces, and so on.[29]

Among both Three-Self congregations and unregistered groups, church leaders tend to view believers who engage in charity work as a "social gospel" activity. Indeed, almost every church has its own charitable program, mostly small-scale operations. But these efforts are also oriented toward the final goal of evangelism. Because of the deep influence of a fundamentalist-pietistic theology that tends to draw a line between the sacred and the secular, between what is deemed as church ministry and what is not, issues like economic injustice are never a high priority for Christians. Despite widespread social tension and inequality in the broader post-reform society, very few sermons touch on the issue of migrant workers. White-collar professionals who buy newly renovated apartments do not see their role in advocating for the rural migrant workers who built them without fair compensation due to wage arrears. These urban elites may watch on the news about how wage delays and arrears caused climatic cases of "suicidal appeals" by rural migrants, but very few feel responsible to engage in advocacy. Even the Christian faith has helped little in challenging a social Darwinist outlook that has permeated the Chinese education system and state media for several decades.

With growing income disparities in China, a new rich class also emerged. In the 2010s, after Chinese Protestantism spread further into urban centers and with more white-collar professionals and educated Chinese converting to the Christian faith, a subgroup of Christian celebrities who became vastly popular on Chinese social media platforms became a new phenomenon. Actress Yao Chen was an example. With more than 80 million followers on Weibo, she is considered China's highest-profile celebrity, "Queen of Weibo," and the country's own Angelina Jolie.[30] As the media describes, Yao Chen is "one of the top five most followed micro-bloggers in the world after the likes of Lady Gaga and Justin Bieber, and ahead of President Obama."[31] Her wedding at Queenstown in New Zealand in 2012 became a way for the tourist industry of New Zealand to break into the Chinese market. According to a description by a news outlet, the tourist industry "could never afford to buy the same audience reach in a market like China."[32] In 2014, *Time* magazine included Yao Chen into its "Time 100" list.[33] *Forbes* magazine also listed her as the world's most powerful woman.

From time to time, Yao's Christian identity was revealed by her subtle tweeting Bible passages on Weibo. She does not hide the fact that she is a Christian believer. But neither has she been flamboyant about it. The tone of her Christian messaging has always been welcoming and inclusive. Her non-luxurious wedding in a church setting enhanced many young people's positive perception of Christianity. After giving birth, Yao Chen also advocated against the motherhood penalty in the Chinese entertainment industry.[34] She said that many actresses her age were offered lesser roles after returning from maternity leave. Thirty-nine-year-old Yao Chen was also aware that using social media can be a double-edged sword: "You are influenced by public opinion. . . . I try to use my popularity to share good values. . . . It's become a part of myself."[35] In the area of charity, Yao Chen was named the UN's Honorary Patron for China. In this capacity, she has visited refugees in places including the Philippines, Thailand, Somalia, Sudan, and Ethiopia. She was again named by the UNHCR as goodwill ambassador in China.[36] In 2016, Yao received the World Economic Forum's Crystal Award for raising awareness of the refugee crisis.

In China's entertainment industry, besides Yuan Li, there are other celebrity actors and actresses who have actively professed the Protestant faith. They make up a most vocal Christian community emboldening both a fundamentalist-evangelical theology to witness anywhere and the growth of Protestant influence in China. Husband and wife Sun Haiying and Lü Liping have been known for their bold and sometimes confrontational Christian witness as well-known actors. In 2001, after Sun Haiying won an award at the 15th Shanghai International Film Festival, he posted on Weibo, denouncing Maoist ideology and praising Christian values as manifest in the United States. Sun also commented that "you only know it after you are a believer of Christ."[37] In 2007, Sun Haiying made another controversial comment by labeling homosexuality "a sin against humanity."[38] In 2010, when Lü Liping received the Best Actress Award at the 47th Golden Horse Awards in Taipei, she gave a public speech laden with biblical passages and thanked God for the award. In 2011, outraged at New York State's legislations to legalize same-sex marriage, Sun's wife and actress Lü Liping posted and retweeted messages on Weibo that describe the gay and lesbian community as "shameful" and "sinners." She also encouraged her 125,000 followers to spread these biblical teachings. This led to a maelstrom of debate on Weibo. It even drew the attention of *China Daily*, an English-language media run by the Publicity Department of the Chinese Communist Party. It asked Sun and Lü to learn something from Lady Gaga who defended gay rights in a public speech to her fans in Rome. The same report continues:

> In a country where same-sex marriage is legal, such attacks on lesbians, often called "corrective rapes," are a frightening trend and . . . evidence of a deep

hatred for humanity that should never be nurtured or encouraged. Lu may feel that her utterings in cyberspace are far removed from the harsh realities of daily life for the Noxolo Nogwazas of this world, or for that matter any young gay or lesbian struggling in a society that makes it tough for them to be themselves. But if she believes that, she is kidding herself. . . . In blogging sentiments that fuel hatred for other human beings, good-Christian Lu couldn't have been less Christ-like if she tried.[39]

According to another CCP-run media outlet *Global Times*, more than ten gay rights groups have called for a boycott of the works of these two award-winning actors.[40] It also labels Sun and Lü as "fundamental Christians" who are influenced by U.S. fundamentalism through a Chinese American pastor in Rochester, New York. From 2011 to 2018, gay rights activists in Sydney, Australia, protested and boycotted a play in which both Sun and Lü will be performing. Due to mounting pressure against Lü Liping, the Golden Horse Awards did not invite her back as a presenter. Its chairman commented that the committee "cannot control what winners say. But we don't support or recognize any biased remarks."[41] This controversy regarding homosexuality continued well into year 2018. A Shanghai expat community media outlet also reported on the resistance against homophobia among Chinese Christian celebrities. It reports the remark of an LGBT advocate: "Homosexuality is not against any law in China. As a public personality, Lü Liping should not be passing such irresponsible comments. Her comments will only add to the discrimination faced by the LGBT community and exacerbate what is already a tough environment for sexual minorities in China."[42] It also quotes an openly gay director who challenged Sun and Lü by referring to Chinese tradition and other pro-LGBT celebrities:

Are Sun Haiying and Lü Liping of the opinion that we should censor the gay chapters of the *Dream of the Red Chamber*? Are they going to yell at Pai Hsien-yung, Kevin Tsai, Stanley Kwan, Ricky Martin, etc that they are sinners? Will they also start decrying the sin of actors who have played gay roles, like Liu Ye, Qin Hao, Chen Sicheng, Hu Jun, Tony Leung, Sandra Ng and Vivian Chow? Do they want a global ban of Lee Ang's *Brokeback Mountain*?[43]

Netizens became so angry that they even began to tweet anti-divorce Bible passages back at Sun Haiying and Lü Liping, calling them an "adulterous pair."[44] Before this, it has been widely known that Sun is Lü's third husband, and Lü is Sun's second wife. A renowned Chinese sexologist at the Chinese Academy of Social Sciences Li Yinhe commented that Sun's continued remarks about homosexuality as a "crime against humanity" to be "ignorant, cruel and without education."[45] Li also said that right-wing religious ideas filtering in from the West are clashing with tolerance toward the LGBT community.

It would be unfair to characterize Sun and Lü as not caring for the marginalized and vulnerable. When the Chinese government was tearing down crosses in Zhejiang Province in 2014, they protested vehemently for religious freedom. They have also been vocal about house churches. In fact, they have advocated for the same cause as Yuan Li did. In 2016, through a film *A Man's Classroom*, depicting the plight of left-behind migrant children in a poverty-ridden rural education system, Sun Haiying won "Best Actor" of the 49 WorldFest-Houston International Film Festival. Sun hoped that this film can help people in China "pay more attention to left-behind children and substitute teachers to make the society full of love."[46] The positive reporting, unsurprisingly, came from conservative Christian media in America, which did not mention any of Sun's controversial statements stated above.

Around 2005, a new conservative Reformed theological trend began to influence many churches in China.[47] Works and sermons by John Piper, Timothy Keller, and other American preachers who embrace male headship as the "order of creation" in family and church were widely circulated. By resorting to claims of true orthodoxy in its "complementarian" theology, churches under its influence require women to learn in all quietness and submission as marks of piety and biblical orthodoxy. In some extreme cases, churches matched impoverished male preachers with financially secure and successful career women. These women were encouraged to support kingdom work through their husbands who engaged in various forms of ministry.

It became a pattern that when conservative-leaning Christian celebrities in China spoke up publicly about their faith, mixed messages came out. While they have shown a rare humanitarian concern with the socioeconomically marginalized groups, this same set of principles have yet to be extended to all identity groups. With strong biblicism and doctrinal awareness, these boundaries led them to make immature absolutist projections and cultural exclusivism toward unbelievers in Chinese society. Take Yuan Li, for example. On her increasingly popular Weibo platform, she advocated for the weak and confronted abuse of power by state and industry. She showed admirable boldness and courage in rebuking government policies and state-sponsored nationalism. At the same time, however, Yuan's biblicist outlook on world affairs and a judgmental tone led her to comment on matters that stirred up anti-Christian sentiments. In April 2018, the United States, France, and the United Kingdom carried out a series of missile strikes against government sites in Syria. This news stirred up debate in China's social media. Yuan Li quoted a passage from the Bible to imply that this military action was predetermined by God:

Jeremiah 49:27 says that "I will set fire to the walls of Damascus; it will consume the fortresses of Ben-Hadad." Damascus is the capital, and Ben-Hadad was the king of Syria. This is a biblical prophecy. If you do not read the Bible, your perception about the world, within or without, can all be nullified. Give all things to God![48]

Many were shocked that the actress-philanthropist did not call for peace but rather endorsed war as "just" or divinely ordained. This gave her atheistic audience another opportunity to mock Christianity as outdated. Some of her Christian audience also questioned the wisdom of publicly associating every current event in the world with biblical prophecies. One commentator on Zhihu.com, the largest Chinese question-and-answer website, made the following observation:

Many Christians in China easily fall into a cognitive trap—they easily equate America with Heaven, the American military with the Heavenly Hosts, and consider every military action of the United States of America as practicing "the Mandate of Heaven" or a "Holy War" in accordance with God's will. They confuse the heavenly gospel with secular international politics. Doing this made unbelievers hostile towards Christianity. Just like before when unbelievers asked, when George W. Bush invaded Iraq, was that a "Holy War" between God and Allah?[49]

The eagerness of Christian voices in China's public sphere to speak Scripture into reality is reminiscent of what happened 100 years ago, before the Anti-Christian Movement. Whether it is influenced by progressive or fundamentalist theology, the discourse of using Christianity to save China from either dismemberment or moral depravity has not changed. Chinese Protestants have yet to tease out their nationalistic yearnings from their wholehearted reception of divine grace. Christianity, which has had only a minority status in China, has not only adapted to and challenged the sociopolitical status quo but has also been ironically shaped by its political culture. During a new Cold War climate between the United States and China, diaspora believers and mission work influenced by right-wing American political culture amplified this trend.

In 2018, China released a set of new religious regulations in the middle of a U.S.-China trade war. Observers noticed a "finer-tuning of control" on all details of religious life, including overseas funds transfer, education resources, and foreigners' participation. House churches with large congregations were subdividing into smaller groups. Anxiety over the uncertain political climate in China permeated among Chinese Christian leaders and foreign mission workers. Before churches could develop new coping strategies, a novel coronavirus began spreading. Quarantine further disrupted church life. The 2010s ended with Christianity's popularity declining and church growth plateauing.

NOTES

1. Heng'an Chu, "Christian Actress Yuan Li Gave a Public Speech at Fudan about Her Conversion," *Christian Times*, November 25, 2014.

2. Quoted in "Why Should Yuan Li Disappear?" *Radio Free Asia*, December 20, 2017. https://www.rfa.org/mandarin/zhuanlan/butongdeshengyin/jkdv-12202017114949.html

3. Zhang Yu, "Actress Yuan Li Turns to Activism after Successful Screen Career," *Global Times*, October 9, 2015.

4. Aikman, *Jesus in Beijing*, 285ff. Also see David Aikman, "Chinese Christianity: Turning the Nation Around," *China Source* 5 (1) (Spring 2003): 1–4.

5. Carol Hamrin, "History, Myth and Missions," *China Source* 5 (4) (Winter 2003): 4.

6. Huo Shui, "View from the Wall: China, the Greatest Christian Nation in the World?" *ChinaSource* 5 (4) (Winter 2003): 10.

7. Sanneh, *Disciples of All Nations*, 268.

8. Elaine Jeffreys, "Debating the Legal Regulation of Sex-related Bribery and Corruption in the People's Republic of China," in Elaine Jeffreys ed., *Sex and Sexuality in China* (New York: Routledge, 2006), 159–75.

9. Debby Chin-yen Huang and Paul R. Goldin, "Polygyny and Its Discontents: A Key to Understanding Traditional Chinese Society," in Howard Chiang, ed., *Sexuality in China: History of Power and Pleasure* (Seattle: University of Washington Press, 2018), 29.

10. "Full Text of the Oxford Consensus 2013," Sinosphere blog article, *New York Times*, October 18, 2013. https://sinosphere.blogs.nytimes.com/2013/10/18/full-text-of-the-oxford-consensus-2013/

11. Xinyi Wang, "'It Took God 17 Years to Turn Me Around': Actress Yuan Li Received Baptism and Remained Silent When Verbally Attacked," *Christian Times* (in Chinese), September 16, 2014. Hana Li, "Christian Yuan Li Wept over Cyber Bully due to Her Conversion to Christianity," *Christian Times*, October 13, 2014.

12. Wei Tian, "Chinese Actress Yuan Li Converted to Christianity and Liked Messages by Yuan Zhiming," *Gospel Herald* (in Chinese), May 6, 2013.

13. Ryan General, "Chinese Actress Reveals Why She Regrets Marrying a Foreigner," *Next Shark*, July 31, 2017. https://nextshark.com/chinese-actress-yuan-li-reveals-why-marrying-a-foreigner-caused-her-pain-and-suffering/

14. "Actress Yuan Li Discloses Why She Regrets Marrying a Non-Chinese," *The Borneo Post*, August 2, 2017.

15. Yu, "Actress Yuan Li Turns to Activism after Successful Screen Career."

16. Ibid.

17. Ibid.

18. Ibid.

19. "Why Should Yuan Li Disappear?"

20. Yu, "Actress Yuan Li Turns to Activism after Successful Screen Career."

21. Ibid.

22. Jianan Ge, "Actress, Patients and Hymns," *People* Magazine (in Chinese), no. 9, September of 2015. http://renwu.1she.com/3687/87211.html

23. Jingqian Xu, "Christian Actress Yuan Li: Human Life is More Precious, Pneumoconiosis Patients Are Yearn for Social Attention," *Christianity Today,* August 12, 2015. http://chinachristiandaily.com/news/culture/2015-08-12/christian-actress-yuan-li--human-life-is-more-precious--pneumoconiosis-patients-are-yearn-for-social-attention_84

24. Xinyi Wang, "Christian Actress Yuan Li: Volunteering in Helping Pneumoconiosis Patients was God's Will," *Christian Times,* September 24, 2015. http://www.christiantimes.cn/news/19273/. Also quoted on *Pu Shi Institute for Social Sciences* website, September 30, 2015. http://www.pacilution.com/ShowArticle.asp?ArticleID=6182

25. Ibid.

26. "Famous Actress Yuan Li: 'I offer only faith and love!'" *Herald Monthly,* April 2018. http://cchc-herald.org/hk/?page_id=25220

27. See Li Ma, *The Chinese Exodus: Migration, Urbanism, and Alienation in Contemporary China* (Eugene: Pickwick Publications, 2018).

28. See Leslie T. Chang, *Factory Girls: From Village to City in a Changing China* (New York: Random House, 2009).

29. Delia Davin, "Gender and Rural-Urban Migration in China," in Haleh Afshar, ed., *Women and Empowerment: Illustrations from the Third World* (London: Palgrave Macmillan), 57–66.

30. "Yao Chen Interview: Meet China's Answer to Angelina Jolie," *The Telegraph,* August 24, 2014. https://www.telegraph.co.uk/culture/culturevideo/filmvideo/film-interviews/11050458/Yao-Chen-interview-meet-Chinas-answer-to-Angelina-Jolie.html

31. James Beech, "Actress Marries at St Peter's," *Otago Daily Times,* November 23, 2012. https://www.odt.co.nz/regions/queenstown-lakes/actress-marries-st-peters

32. Ibid.

33. Daniel Eagan, "Chinese Actress Yao Chen on Motherhood and Her Career: 'I Couldn't Get the Same Roles Any More'," *South China Morning Post,* May 19, 2019. https://www.scmp.com/lifestyle/entertainment/article/3010664/chinese-actress-yao-chen-motherhood-and-her-career-i

34. Ibid.

35. Ibid.

36. Jane Onyanga-Omara, "Chinese Actress Yao Chen Uses Huge Weibo Following to Help Refugees," *USA Today,* January 21, 2016. https://www.usatoday.com/story/money/2016/01/21/yao-chen-refugees-davos-2016/79103072/

37. Frank Fang, "Santa Suppressed in China, but Regime Head Likes Him," *The Epoch Times,* December 29, 2014. https://www.theepochtimes.com/santa-suppressed-in-china-but-regime-head-likes-him_1168462.html

38. Kim Bowden, "Actress's Homosexual Slurs Unacceptable," *China Daily*, July 5, 2011. http://www.chinadaily.com.cn/opinion/2011-07/05/content_12835644.htm

39. Ibid.

40. Xuyang Jingjing, "Gay Bashing Actors," *Global Times*, June 30, 2011. http://www.globaltimes.cn/content/664057.shtml

41. "Awards Show Bans Actress for Anti-gay Remarks," China.org.cn, July 4, 2011. http://www.china.org.cn/arts/2011-07/04/content_22918886.htm

42. Fanhuang, "Gay Groups Urge Boycott of Movies by Lü Liping and Sun Haiying," *Shanghaiist*, May 5, 2018. https://shanghaiist.com/2011/06/27/gay_groups _urge_boycott_of_movies_b/

43. Ibid.

44. Ibid.

45. Quoted in Kenneth Tan, "God Hates China?" *Shanghaiist*, May 5, 2018. https ://shanghaiist.com/2007/09/25/god_hates_china/

46. Grace Zhi, "Chinese Christian Celebrity Wins 'Best Actor' of WorldFest-Houston International Film Festival," *China Christian Daily*, April 20, 2016. http: //chinachristiandaily.com/news/china/2016-04-20/chinese-christian-celebrity-wins- -best-actor--of-worldfest-houston-international-film-festival_1049

47. See Ma, *Religious Entrepreneurism in China's Urban House Churches.*

48. Yuan Li, a Weibo entry, April 14, 2018. https://www.weibo.com/yuanli. Also quoted in "Is Christian Celebrity Yuan Li Right about the Bible?" *Global Testimonies*, April 24, 2018. https://posts.careerengine.us/p/5ade3e4903172323fe6adbc1

49. Josiah, "What Is Problematic with Yuan Li from a Perspective of Christian Doctrines?" *Zhihu.com.* Online resource, https://zhuanlan.zhihu.com/p/73169341

Conclusion

The history of modern China changed drastically over more than a century of imperial collapse, nation-building, foreign invasion, civil wars, revolutions, Maoism, and neo-capitalist globalization supervised by the Chinese Communist Party. This book starts with the affirmation that during all these historical events, women were there too. In fact, the "Chinese woman" has been used as a flexible symbol, an epitome of social problems in China, ranging from national humiliation, political ideology to social diversity. Likewise, the history of Chinese Protestantism is not complete, or even comprehensible, without re-centering and understanding the role of women in it. As historian Gail Hershatter says, "In public discussion, the status of women was repeatedly invoked as a sign of China's crisis and was used to imagine alternative futures."[1] She continues:

> From the early nineteenth century to the present, the figure of Woman has been invoked repeatedly by state authorities and intellectuals of all political stripes and by people writing for elite and popular audiences, as they have sought to imagine and shape a new China. The question of what women should do and be was a constant topic of public debate during China's transformation, from empire to weak state to partially occupied territory to nascent socialist republic to reform-era powerhouse. Sometimes Woman was deployed as a symbol of a weakened culture; alternatively, Woman became a sign that China was entering the ranks of modern nations. Sometimes women were decried as ignorant and dependent drags on the national economy, and sometimes they were glorified as mothers who could save the nation or heroines who could hasten the achievement of socialism.[2]

This book delineates the role of Christian women in shaping the dynamics and boundaries of modern Chinese history. What this book has shown is that deeply embedded issues of gender consciousness, personal aspiration, social status, and geopolitical history often collectively help to shape the journeys of these Chinese women pioneers. These Chinese Christian women contribute to the conversation by asking different questions than do women from other social contexts in Chinese society. At the crossroads between their ancestral traditions and Christian identity, they ask questions about the relevance of China's past to God's work, missionary domination, nationalism, clergy abuse, and social activism. Although the sample of religious biographies contained within this book might be too small to shift the paradigm set by earlier histories of Chinese Christianity, they do suggest opportunities for future researchers to contextualize gender and Christianity in China.

A more important question concerning Christian women and modern China remains: Has China's embrace of modernity been problematic for or advantageous to Christian women? First, it is fair to summarize that the experiences of Christian women have been embedded in how gender has generally mattered in Chinese history. To a certain extent, what the perennial "woman's question" means to Chinese society is similar to that of racism to America. Time and again, debates about the role of Chinese women were at center stage in the nation's public life. Since the demise of the Qing dynasty, a nationalist and revolutionary impulse has guided China through many social and political change. Each time, movement leaders realized the effectiveness of putting forth women's issues to legitimate their call for change. As female scholar Meng Yanling describes the paucity of the Chinese tradition on feminist progress, "whether in reality or in literature, [women] had only two paths open to her, the same paths open to Hua Mulan: taking a male role, fighting the enemy, and acting as part of the feudal system, or going back home and waiting to become a wife."[3] Reformers and revolutionaries alike placed the fate of Chinese women at the center of their debates. But when these revolutions or reforms ran their course through history, decisions were made at the crossroads between granting freedom to women and bettering China's economic path and thus political stability. In almost every case, reformers and revolutionaries led China down a smoother road, avoiding the largely uncharted maps of gender equality. It was always assumed that once the path had been made straight, there would be time to address the women's question. However, a thorough reckoning of gender inequality and its remedy has never fully arrived. As historian Margery Wolf argues, "Though the revolution for women has never been repudiated, it has been postponed all too many times."[4] Or as Hannah Arendt puts it, "the most radical revolutionary will become a conservative the day after the revolution." Women's issues were used to strengthen each movement's need for legitimacy, but when the movement was consolidated, women were again being encouraged to double up the labor, both at home and work, and to sacrifice for the larger common good.

Here it is important to note how Chinese intellectuals prioritize women's issues when leading the public discourse. From time to time, educated Chinese have been simultaneously privileged and subordinated in society. This social location motivates them to specify causes or cultural factors and thus project a "subalternity" onto other marginalized subgroups. Through writing poetry and political treatises, these Chinese intellectuals, mostly men, expressed the passion for saving China using their expertise and ideals. But much of the vision they produced were proven to be illusions. A corporate narcissism has plagued their conflicting outlook on what role Chinese intellectuals should play in the Chinese society. Gail Hershatter's comment on Chinese intellectuals of the 1920s has perennial relevance:

> [They] were writing to and against a world in which they felt themselves to be (and were seen to be) profoundly subaltern with respect to Western governments and Western intellectuals. Their sense of their own subordination shaped the rhetorical uses that intellectuals made of subaltern groups. Rather than acknowledging their own social power over these groups, their complicity in oppression, they used that oppression as evidence for the indictment of Chinese politics and culture.[5]

A second summary to the question of whether China's embrace of modernity been problematic for or advantageous to Christian women is that almost at every turn of history, Christian women found their rights for equality come second to another more sublime goal. In the late imperial era, it was the mission of Christianizing China. In the Republican age, it had to be China's national independence. When a new hope rose on the horizon, the goal of proletarian revolution again became a priority. Just as feminist theologian Kwok Pui-lan puts it, "from late Qing to the 1940s, the women's movement in China evolved from initially a patriotic movement resisting the Manchus and foreign powers, then a suffragist movement during the first republic, and finally a mass movement demanding a radical transformation of the Chinese family and society."[6] Historian Gail Hershatter also argues that "the labor of women in domestic and public spaces shaped China's move from empire to republic to socialist nation to rising capitalist power."[7] All of these changes overthrew bits and pieces of bondage but also admitted new forms of inequality.

Chinese reformists since 1898 prepared the public discourse for advancing the cause of Chinese women. Many liberal-minded members of the local gentry class became catalyzing helpers. From late Qing to the early Republic,

"Segregation of space and control over the visibility of women were forms of patriarchal control which emphasized the need to channel and contain women's sexual power."[8] Meanwhile, women missionaries' participation reached an all-time high. Their conservative values and activism appealed to some educated local Chinese. Barbara Welter sums up in four traits a predominant ideology about women promoted by American missionary boards: piety, purity, submissiveness, and domesticity.[9] Meanwhile, drastically changing social structures provided Chinese women with new opportunities outside the home. Social modeling of Western women missionaries played a conducive role, initiating a series of further reforms. The lives of Shi Meiyu and Zeng Baosun testify how "Christianity drew Chinese women out of obscurity and seclusion, and stimulated them to develop their potential beyond the confines of home."[10] Born between the 1870s and 1900s, theirs was a special generation in modern Chinese history when families and individuals yearning for change still had Confucian mores etched into their memories yet also the first group to confront the "intrusive Western world forcing itself into Chinese territory and Chinese minds."[11] When even the word "feminist" was "associated with the dominant perspectives of white, middle-class, Western women," Zeng Baosun affirmed her unique cultural heritage.[12] Zeng also wrote that "For the modern Chinese woman, let her freedom be restrained by self-control, her self-realization be coupled with self-sacrifice, and her individualism be circumscribed by family duty. Such is our new ideal of womanhood and to realize this is our supreme problem."[13]

Shi and Zeng both advocated for egalitarian treatment of Chinese women with Western women and Chinese men as fellow believers in Christ who deserve their rightful place.[14] When it comes to society and culture, a paradigm shift means the radical critiquing and overturning of patriarchal ways of thinking and practices. As Daniel Bays writes, a few decades after missionaries set up regional Christian schools systems that provided upward mobility for many converts, by the early 1900s, China's coastal cities saw the concentration of many prosperous Chinese Christian communities.[15] He also adds that the missionary expansion phase from 1902 to 1927 was a time when "China seemed to be modernizing and Christianizing at the same time."[16] With regard to Chinese women, it did materialize for certain status groups in Republican China from the 1910s to 1930s when an androcentric, exclusively male-oriented perspective gave way to one that granted recognition to women's own experiences.

As ambassadors of the Christian gospel, Western women missionaries and their male counterparts played not a purely liberating role, as later biographers rosily present. Missionary women from America, despite their positive contributions, nevertheless "served to strengthen anti-colonial nationalisms and even to trouble missionary women's own racism."[17]

As a marginalized group within the missionary community, Western women missionaries shared in the tension and struggle from within. Western Christianity had yet to correct its own sexism, classism, and racial prejudice. When imperial China was making the transition from a closed social order, Europe or America were facing their own modernization problems. Protestantism's inability to confront institutional injustice also led to missionaries' complicity with militant colonialism. These ethnocentric practices sowed seeds of contention which continued to invite anti-foreign sentiments and resistance from indigenous Chinese. The same dynamic also happened in other "mission fields." Christianity sometimes creates a kind of "neo-colonial feminism," where missionary and church institutions intervened on behalf of women, claiming they were doing so on spiritual and progressive grounds. This has blindsided them and created harm ranging from cross-cultural insensitivity, utilitarianism to exclusion and spiritual abuse. For example, scholars in Japan point out how a kind of in-group homogeneity brought by Christian mission led to the exclusion of and disrespect for intergroup differences.[18] African biblical scholar and feminist theologian Musa Dube observes that indigenous women were often the "contact zone" for foreign missionaries.[19] Indian women, after having converted to Christianity, found themselves becoming the "excluded other" in the eyes of their fellow natives.[20] Womanist theologian Delores Williams claims that black women suffer from systematic double oppression—racial and gendered—by white men and women.[21] She also argues poignantly that "because the Bible is stamped by patriarchal oppression but claims to be the Word of God, it perpetuates an archetypal oppressive myth."[22]

More broadly speaking, the missionary movement cannot be separated from political and economic motives embedded within the expansion of global capitalism. Social inequality was its precondition. Philip A. Kuhn provocatively refers to China as one of "Capitalism's Asian victims."[23] Even in an age of Social Gospel, Protestantism's theological inability to address systemic injustice, mingled with its embrace of capitalism in Max Weber's sense, has largely contributed to an enlarging social divide.[24] Here a post-colonial lens is needed. African American scholar Beverly Lindsay writes that "Dependency relationships, based upon race, sex and class, are being perpetuated through social, educational, and economic institutions. These are the linkages among Third-World Women."[25] Female scholar Kumari Jayawardena once claims that "feminist movements in these societies were the products of economic and social changes set in motion by the forces of capitalism and nationalism. . . . If capitalism brought women into the social sphere and into economic production, nationalism pushed them into participating in the political life of their communities."[26] It is important to examine both the economic and political dimensions of structural suppression on

women. It is equally necessary to emphasize that Chinese women had different political pursuits in different phases of history.

The second contribution of this book is that it also resists this victimization narrative of China and Chinese women by providing more nuanced
understandings. The stories of Chinese women leaders also present their own
agency in making fair demands against the ethnocentrism of Western missionary women.[27] By the 1920s, Chinese Protestantism saw its first generation of indigenous women leaders contending with missionary power. The
independent spirit and cosmopolitanism of Ding Shujing and Wu Yifang
were examples. Asian missiologist Lin Meimei also points to the creation
of a "women's sphere" where cosmopolitan sisterhood could be built, networks could be strengthened, and the exploration of different roles was
encouraged.[28]

An enduring pattern in the history of Christianity is that the success of
spontaneous movements is followed by consolidation and institutionalization.
As Elisabeth Fiorenza writes, the latter brings about a "love patriarchialism"
that is "in contradiction to the conflict-producing ethical radicalism of the
Jesus movement."[29] When it becomes a success, often in revivalist terms,
Christianity began to attract the wealthy and the powerful. The movement
then builds institutions, and success strengthens authoritarianism. A process
of "gradual ecclesial patriarchialization" is followed.[30] This is true for early
Christianity, Puritan America, and reformist China after the 1920s. As a
result, the visible church internalizes "the status inequalities and structural
hierarchies typical of a patriarchal society."[31] By teaching a spiritual equality of "all one in Christ," this love-patriarchalism maintains the status quo of
social inequality (by class, race, or gender) by coercing codes of compliance
within the church. As a result, Fiorenza contends that the church is built "on
the backs of women, slaves, and the lower classes" rather than on prophets
and apostles.[32]

Prolonged warfare and foreign invasion from the 1930s to the 1940s
strengthened this discourse of women's victimization. For example, from
1931 to 1945, the Japanese military coerced hundreds of thousands of women
into "comfort stations," where these women were repeatedly raped on a
daily basis.[33] These traumatic stories left a painful imprint on the collective
memory and social psyche of the postwar Chinese community. It further
strengthened a nationalistic and anti-foreign passion. Compared to the early
Republic era, when discourse on gender oppression was held up as a mark
of modernity, these incidents of abuse by foreign powers reshaped Chinese
nationalism and the communist establishment, which later radicalized into
xenophobic warfare and violence.

The anti-capitalist victimization narrative has also dominated the communist historiography of Chinese Protestantism since 1949. It reinserted a

class-based analysis into a wholesale critique of Christianity. While doing this, it re-centered the "state" or "nation" and again pushed women to the margins. The life stories of Zhao Luorui and Gu Shengying illustrate this unfortunate trend wherein "Marxist theory seemed to offer a ready-made theoretical framework to evaluate Christianity's role in the imperialist era."[34] Historian Ono Kazuko once said that "Authoritarianism, according to the analysis of Chinese revolutionaries, was ultimately lodged in two major structures: the bureaucratic state and the family."[35] For a very long time, the battle has been fought in the family, because it is "where the convergence of these cultural imperatives reinforced in Confucian familial virtue ethics—the continuity of the family name, filial piety, and ancestor worship—serves as a powerful basis for generating, sustaining, and justifying the social abuse of women."[36] Although communist revolutions further abolished oppressive family structures, they also consolidated state power. That state power explains why gender equality was deferred to give way to the will of the nation-state, after 1949. As Chinese female scholar Nian Zhang writes, "Abstract egalitarianism became the source of legitimacy for the regime. But in the time of Proletariat Dictatorship, gender egalitarianism was interpreted as the eradication of classes."[37] Few Chinese Christian women pioneers dispensed with their nationalism because it is a powerful and totalizing ideology. Nian Zhang also offers another insightful analysis:

> In the genesis of modern nation-states, China is an unavoidable subject for observation. Since the appearance of "nation," an antagonistic logic was born into modern Chinese political life. Rhetoric about liberation and suppression were derived from national-ethnic ideals. From language to action, theory to praxis, the dual-track of national liberation and women's liberation were important characteristics of the modern Chinese narrative. Therefore, gender as a sensitive and symbolic interface also appeared with the rise of modern political themes such as nation, ethnicity, suppression and liberation.[38]

This phenomenon is shared by women leaders in other "Third World" countries. As South Korean female leader Sun Ai Lee Park puts it, "Third World women must prioritize national liberation together with their men. The women's issue is a secondary issue."[39] The difficulty of rewriting Christian women into history is the recurring subversion of gender inequality across different phases of time. Chinese activists, conservative or progressive, would endorse gender equality if it helped their agenda, but would not follow through on these promises. Asian feminist theologian Meng Yan-ling also writes that "because we have not transcended the influence of culture in our biblical interpretation, women are caught in conflicting interpretations."[40] Very few Chinese Christian women chose the path taken by Katharine

Bushnell, who returned to biblical interpretation for understanding women's role. Kwok Pui-lan reckons that "[t]he fundamental challenge of national salvation made Asian women more conscious of their responsibility toward society . . . Participation in revolutionary and political activities enabled women to explore new roles traditionally denied them."[41] She also adds,

> Christianity, as a foreign religion, had the iconoclastic effect of opening Asian women's eyes to deep-seated patriarchal traditions embedded in their own culture. By presenting a radically different worldview and a new set of rituals, Christianity helped to liberate our Christian foremothers from a kind of cultural anesthesia to question the legitimacy of those social and religious institutions which kept women in their inferior place. . . . This embedded liberation was like an enclave whose foundation, with no national or other source of legitimacy, would not exist.[42]

A social contract binds the Chinese nation and women through its new Marriage Law as if the latter has culminated gender equality. As historians comment, "The centrality of the 1950 Marriage Law and its subsequent revisions in 1980 and 2001 underscore the extent to which marriage, family, and gender roles have constituted key elements of China's revolutionary and reformist nation-building projects."[43] As a result, society has since re-centered family life, leaving the question of independent womanhood out of the discussion. Apart from communism as a civil religion, patriarchy has been restored to its prevailing cultural pedestal. Or maybe as Chinese revolutionary woman Ding Ling's experience reveals, although Marxist ideology did present new forms of freedom for women, the leadership of Chinese communism has at best-tokenized gender equality.

In the 1920s, the first generation of Chinese communists invoked the ideal of women's emancipation in order to legitimatize socialism as a new promising force in ending both traditional patriarchy and capitalist exploitation of women. Historians like Christina Kelley Gilmartin argues that "the temporal juxtaposition of the blossoming of feminism . . . during the mid 1910s . . . and the founding of the Chinese Communist Party in the early 1920s forged a greater compatibility between Marxism and feminism . . . than has generally been the case in other communist and socialist movements."[44] Marxism appealed to women's rights activists because it provides an ongoing critical theory of systemic economic injustice. Private property and class relations have been central to oppression of women. Its philosophical framework allows advocates to think systematically and historically. In practice, however, Marxist or communist regimes tend to create a new system of domination. They also tend to reduce social relationships to mere economic or materialistic features. The overwhelmingly male-dominated speakers of this discourse within the Chinese Communist Party did not integrate female representation as time progressed. Many of these early CCP leaders lived unhappily with arranged marriages, and it was this experience that motivated them to speak against feudalistic practices. But in the Yan'an era, when the voices of female activists joined in public speech and communal decision-making, male leaders reacted with sectarian politics, leading to the perpetuation of gender inequality.

Due to Marxism's progressive policies, Christian women were ambivalently positioned in relation to both Christianity and anti-Christian communism. Thus, Chinese Christian women struggled with legacies of colonialism while being accused of importing Western ideas. In short, during the 1940s, China's demand for indigenous control against missionary domination and China's role in the globalization of communism made Christianity a target on both fronts. As historian Lamin O. Sanneh writes, "On both issues Christianity yielded ground; first with respect to China's national interests, and next with respect to China's place in global revolutionary movements."[45] What remained was patriarchy in the family and in the state. Based on global women's experiences, feminist scholar Mary Daly said, "Patriarchy is itself the prevailing religion of the entire planet, and its essential message is necrophilia. All of the so-called religions legitimating patriarchy . . . from Buddhism and Hinduism to Islam, Judaism, Christianity, to secular derivatives . . . are infrastructures of the edifice of patriarchy."[46] While feminist theologians in the West rose to challenge patriarchy of the church and society in the 1960s, when the second wave of the feminist movement emerged, "they did not pay sufficient attention to how white women had colluded in colonialism and slavery."[47]

The post-reform era in China since 1978 unlocked opportunities for women's participation in social life. Educated professionals such as Lin Qiaozhi and Xie Wanying carved out their own space and established widespread recognition for their exceptional work in medicine and literature. Their contribution centered around healthy motherhood, which was a desirable agenda for the communist state. But as discussed before, motherhood in China was never purely "natural." Rather, it has always been shaped by religious systems and power relationships. During this time, the One-Child Policy has been strictly enforced among the Chinese in China's cities and townships with exceptions among ethnic minorities.[48] It has also reengineered China's reproductive culture and family values. Motherhood became an important building block in a post-communist belief system that defined the moral, social, and emotional mandates for women's lives in Chinese society. With it came many forceful ideologies that constrained Chinese women. In the 1990s, even the translation of the word "feminism" changed. The new term (*nvxing zhuyi*, or "feminine-ism") was used to intentionally "distinguish Chinese from western feminism."[49] By the 2010s, China has verified that communist ideology in the political realm, crony capitalism in its economy, and patriarchy in society can coexist. A woman's life is still circumscribed by her relationship to a man.

When it comes to re-centering Christian women in the history of modern China and Chinese Protestantism, there is a third difficulty: authoritarianism within the ecclesiastical church. Christian women have been struggling with a multilayered "otherness" due to colonialist, nationalistic, and ecclesiastical marginalization.[50] Over-relying on any one of these dimensions while neglecting the others would lead to an imbalanced understanding. This means that we must look into the power structures within the Chinese church and challenge dominant narratives that marginalize women. The parallel system of official Three-Self churches and unregistered house church groups continues to be characterized by an ideologically driven antagonism. Their respective expansion overseas, through the stories of Cao Shengjie and Lü Xiaomin, did not progress along gender lines. In each of their subsystem, Cao and Lü have, at best, been tokenized.

Equally important, the attempt to recover a women's history in Chinese Protestantism ought to include issues of abuse within the church. The advocacy of Lily Hsu and Chai Ling illustrate how Chinese Protestant churches fail the test, just as their American evangelical counterparts in the wake of the #MeToo movement. Often in the absence of a faith community, victims' experiences of sexual violence made them as questions about theodicy—the existence of evil in God's world. This also invites us to check for root causes within the Christian tradition. Re-centering abuse of women remains a challenge to biblical interpretation. As a hermeneutical analyst writes, "stories such as Hagar's disclose the patriarchal biases not only of the Bible but also of its would-be expositors."[51] When interpreting biblical texts or processing contemporary examples of sexual abuses against women, reformers and modern scholars tend to excuse men at any cost. Traditional theology has not offered a hermeneutical framework that center around violence against women. There is a lack of empathic identification with the suffering of women. Like the secular realm, there was also a "conservative obsession with women's believability."[52] Lily Hsu and Chai Ling remind us that understanding women's victimization is a necessary step toward healing and injustice. Chai Ling's story shows that it has always been "survivor leadership" from women who pushed for justice and dignity against tremendous resistance.[53]

Despite the racial barriers between feminist theologians, the topic of sexual abuse against women can become a significant experiential commonality that bridges the racial divide. For example, when African American theologian Katie Cannon and white lesbian theologian Carter Heyward began a dialogue on reconciling racial and sexual differences, in a poignant and candid moment, Cannon addresses Heyward's experience of being molested as a child—an experience Cannon also suffered.[54] Both of them were reading Alice Walker's *The Color Purple* in which the Black protagonist Celie has been sexually abused. Their connection to the story does not negate "race," but rather the opposite because "the discovery of this shared, very personal, and painful experience is also a discovery of racial differences."[55] This is probably how advocacy against abuse of indigenous women helped American woman missionary Katharine Bushnell overcome her own white privilege.

For Christian women, a further tormenting problem with regard to whether Protestant Christianity itself has anything inherently oppressive toward women. On the one hand, through the repeated recognition of female figures in the gospel and patristic commentaries, Christianity promised equal spiritual dignity to women. Jesus himself viewed women as spiritual equals to men. On the other hand, as Kwok Pui-lan writes, "the Bible does not speak in a single or monolithic voice, but is highly diverse and pluralistic: some texts show the indelible marks of imperialist ideology, while others challenge the dominant power and have liberating possibilities."[56] Symbols of Christianity, such as the cross and a male savior can empower but it can also render docile in the face of abuse and oppression. Feminist theologian Elizabeth A. Johnson even writes that "Christology in its story, symbol, and doctrine has been assimilated to the patriarchal world view, with the result that its liberating dynamic has been twisted into justification for domination."[57] There is a need for reinterpretation in this regard. Biblical scholar Elisabeth S. Fiorenza also challenges the Bible as "stamped by patriarchal oppression but claims to be the Word of God."[58] Early in her book *Bread Not Stone*, Fiorenza gives the following statements:

> In our struggle for self-identity, survival, and liberation in a patriarchal society and church, Christian women have found that the Bible has been used as a weapon against us but at the same time it has been a resource for courage, hope, and commitment in this struggle. . . . Certain texts of the Bible can be used in the argument against women's struggle for liberation not only because they are patriarchally misinterpreted but because they are patriarchal texts and therefore can serve to legitimate women's subordinate role and secondary status in patriarchal society and church.[59]

In church history, by the end of the second century, the main paradigm for women's status within the church had shifted from full inclusion to marginalization and subordination to the authority of men. As historian Elizabeth Schussler Fiorenza wrote, "the discipleship of equals was replaced by patriarchicalization of the church and ministry, as authority became vested in the local offices of the deacons and bishops in the second century."[60] Such an authoritarian and patriarchal feature has been intrinsic to the institutional establishment of Protestant Christianity. Meanwhile, Christianity has not been a consistently emancipating force for women. Its patriarchal religious and cultural patterns came from Greek and Roman philosophy and law as well as from the Hebrew world. Patriarchy rooted in these ancestral sources shaped a Christian worldview that took for granted the male hierarchical ordering of society and the church as the "order of creation" and the "will of God." In fact, as the biographies of some women pioneers show in this volume, sometimes the ideological and authority structures within the Christian community existed as forces that impose rules of submission on women.

Social analysis provides the framework for systemic thinking. It examines how different forms of suppression or domination—such as racism, sexism, or classism—operate along complex social dimensions: the cultural, socio-economic, symbolic, kinship, and religious spheres. Sociologists like Max Weber uses the word "domination," a form of power by imposing one's will on others. Weber offers a typology of domination: traditional, legal/rational, and charismatic. Based on the origins of the power wielded by those in the ruling position, these different modes of domination may be used by patriarchs, bureaucracies, and charismatic leaders. All of them entail the pursuit of legitimacy. The relationship between the rulers and the ruled can be complex, dialectic, and dynamic. Religions, including Christianity, may create their own forms of oppression. *The Dictionary of Feminist Theologies* offers this summary:

> The official rhetoric of most religious institutions conceals and reinforces the social logic of women's oppression, attributing it to the eternal order of nature and God's will. The religious principle of female inferiority has been sustained the face of social change. By devaluing women's bodies and exalting motherhood as a 'natural calling' that defines women's very identity, religious discourse and practice help organize and legitimate women's relegation to the home and become violent instrument for controlling women's sexuality.[61]

The same institutional change has happened to Christian women in the Chinese Christian community. As Chinese Christianity shifted from spontaneous growth to more institutionalized existence, women are marginalized from leadership positions. New relationships between gender and power had to be negotiated. Theologically speaking, time and again, Chinese Christian women also attempted to move from viewing God as a male protector to God as a liberator who empowers the most vulnerable.

Even in the twenty-first century, Chinese women's issues still matter as postmodernity has relegated religion to the private sphere. This is truer in communist China where state media strictly censor against messages of

Christianity. Meanwhile, rising social problems including marriage and family disintegration created a precondition that welcomes a comeback of conservatism. Theologically, nevertheless, the Chinese church has been influenced by fundamentalist theology. Writing in 2007, Marilyn French reflects on the major change affecting women during the past three decades being a "proliferation of fundamentalisms," such as "Christianity (the born-again Christian movement in the United States, the drive to criminalize abortion centered in the Catholic Church)."[62] She thinks that these movements were "not only responders to Western colonization or industrialization, but a backlash against spreading feminism." The stories of Yuan Li and other high-profile Christian celebrities in China show the powerful grip of theological conservatism and the limitations of this stance in an increasingly pluralistic society. At around 2017, the 500th anniversary of the Protestant Reformation, Protestant Christians in mainland China tend to elevate the sixteenth-century Protestant Reformation as a tradition of orthodoxy. Since the Reformation upheld a "high" view of the ministerial office, ordination became a special calling for men only. Most Chinese Christians are not familiar with the history that during the early church, women and men both served as key leaders and ordained priests. All these factors led to a revived theological discourse about the "order of creation" and "male headship" as spread by a new wave of conservative-leaning mission-sending and theological resources. Patriarchal values in church teachings helped perpetuate the sexist and stereotyped images by both women and men.

The biographies in this volume allow us to consider the contradictory aspects while drawing a preliminary, though provisional, set of conclusions about the relationship between Christian women and Chinese Protestantism. It shows Christianity's emancipatory potential for Chinese women, although not without its time-bound moral ambiguities. Chinese women are exploring what it means to be Chinese and Christian. They tend to draw on the wisdom found in their cultural traditions to reenvision what the Christian faith means for themselves and for the Chinese people. Usually, these include three principal sources such as the rituals of their own culture, their experiences of living in two worlds, and the Christian tradition transmitted through the missionary enterprise of their own time. In many instances, they have not given a name to that theological understanding, making it at best a synthetic and ambiguous effort. But at least we can come to a more nuanced understanding about the interplays of Christianity, gender, power, and modern Chinese history. Because "gender as an analytical category cannot be used in isolation from other social factors, including class, ethnicity, and religion,"[63] there are competing forces at work when it comes to the role of Christian women.

NOTES

1. Hershatter, *Women and China's Revolutions*, xiv.

2. Ibid., xv.

3. Meng Yanling, "Women, Faith, and Marriage: A Feminist Look at the Challenge for Women," in Pui-lan Kwok, ed., *Hope Abundant: Third World and Indigenous Women's Theology* (Orbis Books, 2010), 231.

4. Wolf, *Revolution Postponed*, 26.

5. Gail Hershatter, *Dangerous Pleasures: Prostitution and Modernity in Twentieth-Century Shanghai* (Berkeley: University of California Press, 1999), 28.

6. Kwok, *Chinese Women and Christianity*, 155.

7. Hershatter, *Women and China's Revolutions*, xiii, xv.

8. Sarah Graham-Brown, "The Seen, the Unseen and the Imagined: Private and Public Lives," in Reina Lewis, Sarah Mills, ed., *Feminist Postcolonial Theory: A Reader* (New York: Routledge, 2003), 503.

9. Barbara Welter, "The Cult of True Womanhood: 1820–1860," *American Quarterly* 18 (1966): 152.

10. Mary Keng Mun Chung, *Chinese Women in Christian Ministry: An Intercultural Study* (Bern: Peter Lang, 2005), 104.

11. John L. Sarri, *Legacies of Childhood: Growing up Chinese in a Time of Crisis* (Cambridge: Harvard University Press, 1990), ix.

12. Letty M. Russell, J. Shannon Clarkson, *Dictionary of Feminist Theologies* (Westminster John Knox Press, 1996), Xiii.

13. Baosun, "The Chinese Women," 344.

14. Tseng, Pao-Swen. "Christianity and Women," *The Chinese Recorder* 59 (4): 443, 1928.

15. Bays, *A New History*, 94.

16. Bays, *A New History of Christianity*, 92.

17. Mary A. Renda, "Doing Everything: Religion, Race, and Empire in the U.S. Protestant Women's Missionary Enterprise, 1812–1960," in Barbara Reeves-Ellington, eds., *Competing Kingdoms: Women, Mission, Nation, and the American Protestant Empire, 1812–1960* (Durham: Duke University Press, 2010), 368–69.

18. Hisako Kinakawa, *Women and Jesus in Mark: A Japanese Feminist Perspective* (Maryknoll: Orbis Book, 1994), 62.

19. Musa W. Dube, *Postcolonial Feminist Interpretation of the Bible* (St. Louis: Chalice Press, 2000), 58, 92.

20. Aruna Gnanadason, "Jesus and the Asian Woman: A Post-Colonial Look at the Syro-Phoenician Woman/Cannanite Woman from an Indian Perspective," *Studies in World Christianity* 7 (2001): 162–77.

21. Delores S. Williams, "The Color of Feminism: Or Speaking the Black Woman's Tongue," in Lois K. Daly, ed., *Feminist Theological Ethics* (Louisville: Westminster John Knox Press, 1994), 49, 50. This essay was originally published in 1986.

22. Ibid., 10.

23. Ibid., 2.

24. See Max Weber, *The Protestant Ethic and the Spirit of Capitalism* (New York: W. W. Norton & Company, 2008).

25. Beverly Lindsay (ed.), *Comparative Perspectives of Third World Women: The Impact of Race, Sex and Class* (New York: Praeger Press, 1983), 298, 306.

26. Jayawardena, *Feminism and Nationalism in the Third World*, 255.

27. Chung, *Chinese Women in Christian Ministry*, 119.

28. Lin Meimei, *Women in Missiology: The Episcopal Women Missionaries and Their Evangelical Work in Nineteenth-Century China* (Taibei: Liren, 2005), 92–111.

29. Fiorenza, *In Memory of Her*, 78.

30. Ibid., 80.

31. Ibid., 78.

32. Ibid., 79.

33. See Peipei Qiu et al., *Chinese Comfort Women: Testimonies from Imperial Japan's Sex Slaves* (New York: Oxford University Press, 2014). Even until today, the commemoration of "comfort women" who had been victims of military sexual slavery remains highly controversial in the Chinese society.

34. Kwok, Pui-lan, "The Emergence of Asian Feminist Consciousness of Culture and Theology," in Virginia Fabella M. M. and Sun Ai Lee Park, eds.), *We Care to Dream* (Maryknoll: Obis Books, 1989), 95.

35. Ono, *Chinese Women in a Century of Revolution*, 7.

36. Rosenlee, *Confusion and Women*, 121–22.

37. Nian Zhang, *Gender Politics and State: On Women's Liberation in China* (Beijing: Shang Wu Publishing House, 2014), 19.

38. Ibid., 17–18.

39. Sun Ai Park, "The Women's Movement and the Ecumenical Agenda," in Jennie Clarke, ed., *Weaving New Patterns: Women's Struggle for Change in Asia and the Pacific*, (Hong Kong: WSCF Asian-Pacific Region, 1986), 65.

40. Yanling, "Women, Faith, and Marriage," 233.

41. Kwok, "The Emergence of Asian Feminist Consciousness of Culture and Theology," 95.

42. Ibid., 94.

43. Sara l. Friedman, "Women, Marriage and the State in Contemporary China," in Elizabeth J. Perry and Mark Selden, ed., *Chinese Society: Change, Conflict and Resistance* (New York: Routledge, 2000), 148.

44. Christina Kelley Gilmartin, *Engendering the Chinese Revolution: Radical Women, Communist Politics, and Mass Movements in the 1920s* (Berkeley: University of California Press, 1995), 19.

45. Sanneh, *Disciples of All Nations*, 243.

46. Mary Daly, *Gyn/Ecology: The Metaethics of Radical Feminism* (Boston: Beacon Press, 1978), 39.

47. Kwok, *Post-colonial Imagination and Feminist Theology*, 18.

48. Early years of campaign in the countryside met with widespread resistance, giving way to a "one-son or two-children policy" in 1984: married couples whose first child was a daughter were allowed to try for another pregnancy. Tyrene White, "Domination, Resistance and Accommodation in China's One-child Campaign,"

in Elizabeth J. Perry and Mark Selden, ed., *Chinese Society: Change, Conflict and Resistance* (New York: Routledge, 2000), 176.

49. Kay Shaffer and Song Xianlin, "Unruly Spaces: Gender, Women's Writings and Indigenous Feminism in China," *Journal of Gender Studies* 16 (1) (2007): 17–30.

50. Marianne Kapoppo, *Compassionate and Free: An Asian Woman's Theology* (Geneva: World Council of Churches, 1979).

51. John L. Thompson, *Writing the Wrongs: Women of the Old Testament Among Biblical Commentators from Philo through the Reformation* (New York: Oxford University Press, 2001), 23.

52. Jessica Valenti, "Our Word Alone," in Jessica Valenti and Jaclyn Friedman, ed., *Believe Me: How Trusting Women Can Change the World* (New York: Seal Press, 2020), 16.

53. Sabrina Hersi Issa, "Survivorship Is Leadership: Building a Future for New Possibilities and Power," in Jessica Valenti and Jaclyn Friedman, ed., *Believe Me: How Trusting Women Can Change the World* (New York: Seal Press, 2020), 208.

54. Katie G. Cannon and Carter Heyward, "Can We Be Different but Not Alienated? An Exchange of Letters," in Lois K. Daly, ed., *Feminist Theological Ethics: A Reader*(Louisville: Westminster John Knox, 1994), 59–76. Also see Cannon and Heyward, "Alienation and Anger: A Black and a White Woman's Struggle for Mutuality in an Unjust World," *Stone Center Publication*, 54 (1992): 1–13.

55. Kamitsuka, *Feminist Theology and the Challenge of Difference*, 15.

56. Kwok, *Post-Colonial Imagination and Feminist Theology*, 8.

57. Elizabeth A. Johnson, *She Who Is: The Mystery of God in Feminist Theological Discourse* (New York: Crossroad Publishing, 2017), 160. The original version of this book was published in 1992. It won the 1992 Louisville Grawmeyer Award in Religion.

58. Elisabeth Schussler Fiorenza, *Bread Not Stone: The Challenge of Feminist Biblical Interpretation* (Boston: Beacon Press, 1984), 10.

59. Ibid., x, xii.

60. Fiorenza, *In Memory of Her*, 285–315.

61. Russell and Clarkson, *Dictionary of Feminist Theologies*, 195.

62. Marilyn French, *From Even to Dawn: A History of Women in the World, Volume IV: Revolutions and Struggles for Justice in the 20th Century* (New York: The Feminist Press at the City University of New York), 2.

63. Ibid., 26.

Epilogue

In the 1890s, for American woman medical missionary Katharine Bushnell, discovering Western missionary misconduct in China was a turning point for her to turn toward advocacy for Chinese women. This reckoning also motivated Bushnell to attempt something new, a reinterpretation of the biblical message for women. Personally, I went through a reckoning similar to that of Katharine Bushnell.

In the course of more than a decade of research on China's growing Protestant population, I have published on the growth, movements, and potential problems inside the church in China.[1] In 2019, I published a book titled *Religious Entrepreneurism in China's Urban Churches: The Rise and Fall of Early Rain Presbyterian Reformed Church*. It uncovers another side of a house church network which has gained immense reputation in the West through media publicity. As the church has drifted from its "city on the hill" mission, it has spawned a range of power abuses, the worst cases bring alleged sexual abuses of single women and single mothers by multiple predators. After the book's release, for more than a year, I faced both pushback and verbal attacks that most #MeToo advocates have typically experienced. Male colleagues within the field wrote of Chinese Protestantism lambasting reviews of the book.[2] Hidden in their critiques are persistent narratives that the story of Chinese Protestantism can only be told from a church-state perspective. Mentioning gender equality or abuse of women is not going along with the norm of this field. Below are two examples:

Li Ma clearly does not agree with the traditional views of the role of women in the church. She labels these as "anachronistic doctrines" (12). That is her right, of course. But the PCA Book of Church Order limits the offices of elder and deacon to men. This position was almost universally held in Christian churches

207

until very recently. It is still the rule among Roman Catholics, Eastern Orthodox, and many theologically conservative Protestant denominations. Proponents of this view base their position on a number of biblical texts that seem to deny certain offices and activities—such as preaching from the pulpit—to women. Ma also does not agree with traditional views of the role of women in the home. These ideas, sometimes called "complementarian" now, were the norm in most societies and Christian churches until very recently, and were also based upon biblical texts.[3]

It is precisely one of the book's most controversial claims that Ma's partisan tone and lack of direct evidence become particularly problematic, . . . It is significant and helpful, particularly in the #MeToo movement era when victims of sexual violence are gaining a voice, that Ma spoke directly with an alleged victim of rape, . . . On the other hand, Ma has not been encompassing enough, because she neglects to firmly situate her work in the scholarship on church-state relations in authoritarian China. . . . For many church-state scholars, the book may present an oddly inverted view of Chinese Christianity. . . . This is too bad, because Early Rain's trajectory is an important case of church-state relations and scholars need to learn more about the internal dynamics of how China's prominent house churches survive in hostile contexts by using international ties.[4]

These samples of discourse and their polemic style reveal two unwritten rules in this academic field. First, a male-headship theology continues to claim such a legitimacy that a female scholar's theology is at stake if she historicizes sexual abuses into a case study of the church. She needs to be put down with "conservative" spiritual jargons and her perspective with regard to gender inequality is questioned. In fact, the first reviewer later continued to sing praises of a celebrity pastor who allegedly cover-up sexual abuses against women, stating that his "history as a public intellectual and his clarion call to apply the Bible to all domains of life attracted people from all over China."[5]

Second, there is a dominant narrative framework which should not be interrupted. When it comes to Christianity under communism, it ought to center around church-state relationship. This binary approach necessarily places church leaders and communist authorities on opposing ends of the good versus evil moral spectrum. Activism by women against church institutions may inconveniently upset this analytical framework.

Apart from these findings, I also realized that with my approach re-centering women and gender equality into the picture, I have indeed stepped into a minefield with interlocking social relationships among these male scholars. They concertedly orchestrated some campaign similar to a treatment to Mary Trump's book. After a failure to stop the book's publication, they engaged in a campaign, together with some ministry leaders, to minimize my voice. There, of course, have also been voices of support which affirm the value of breaking from these dominant narratives. Below is one example from a female scholar:

> I have read . . . numerous forwarded rather biased and abusive reviews, which simply made me want to reach out to say that according to what I read, you made a great contribution and arguments with rarely presented data. . . . Protestantist elites saw themselves doing some greater enterprise (i.e., in Jesus name doing right in China, liberating Chinese from evil communism etc) and hence individual narratives were not allowed to disrupt their grandeur one, . . . I appreciate your integrity and sincerity . . . knowing it must be hard when all of a sudden, just because for once some English-written work unveiled some less disposed truth from the Chinese Christian community, so many criticisms came out, questioning you . . . without much reflecting of their own biases. . . . For the moment, . . . they were the powerful and the majority, but I don't believe human history as a whole is good at hiding. Bits and pieces from less powerful people and all individuals have a way of getting remembered. Such lingering forces run a long way down but will be seen and understood.[6]

By the time this current book titled *Christian Women and Modern China* came out, maybe I should thank both camps for helping me making a breakthrough in this line of research, that is, by recovering a women's history of Chinese Protestantism. So the story of a Chinese woman scholar's battle against male dominance behind this book may someday also enter into history.

NOTES

1. See Ma and Li, *Surviving the State, Remaking the Church*. Ma, *The Chinese Exodus*.

2. Wright Doyle, "A Missed Opportunity: The Failure of A Bold Project," *Global China Center* (May 6, 2020.) https://www.globalchinacenter.org/analysis/a-missed-opportunity-the-failure-of-a-bold-project

3. Ibid.

4. Carsten Vala, "Book Review: Religious Entrepreneurism in China's Urban House Churches: The Rise and Fall of Early Rain Reformed Presbyterian Church by Li Ma," *Review of Religion and Chinese Society* 7 (1) 2020: 149–52.

5. Wright Doyle, "What We Can Learn from Christian Entrepreneurism in China's House Church by Li Ma," a blog article, *Reaching Chinese World Wide*, April 29, 2020. https://www.reachingchineseworldwide.org/blog/2020/4/29/what-we-can-learn-from-christian-entrepreneurism-in-chinas-house-church-the-rise-and-fall-of-early-rain-reformed-presbyterian-church-by-li-ma

6. An email correspondence from a female scholar to the author, June 6, 2020.

Glossary

PERSONAL NAMES[1]

Ai Qing 艾青
Ba Jin 巴金
Cai Yuanpei 蔡元培
*Chai Ling 柴玲 (1966-)
*Cao Shengjie 曹圣洁 (1931-)
Chen Duxiu 陈独秀
Chen Mengjia 陈梦家
Chiang Kai-shek 蒋介石
Deng Xiaoping 邓小平
Deng Yingchao 邓颖超
Ding Guangxun (Kuang-hsun Ting, or K. H. Ting) 丁光训
Ding Ling 丁玲
*Ding Shujing 丁淑静 (1890-1936)
Ding Zilin 丁子霖
Eight Immortals 八大仙人
Fei Xiaotong 费孝通
Feng Xiaogang 冯小刚
Fu Lei 傅雷
Guo Moruo 郭沫若
Gong Shengliang 龚胜亮
Hu Shih (or Hu Shi) 胡适
*Hsu, Lily (Xu Meili) 许梅骊 (1931–)
Ji Zhiwen (Andrew Gih) 计志文

* Denotes a main character in this book, with detailed years of birth and death.

Jiang Qing 江青

Kang Cheng (Kang Aide) 康爱德

Kang Youwei 康有为

Lao She (Shu Sheyu) 老舍，舒舍予

Li Changshou (Witness Lee) 李常受

Li Delun 李德伦

Li Zhengdao (Tsung-Dao Lee) 李政道

Li Yinhe 李银河

Liang Qichao 梁启超

Liu Dezhong 刘德忠

*Lin Qiaozhi (Kha-Ti Lim) 林巧稚

Lin Zhao 林昭

Liu Shaoqi 刘少奇

Lu Xun 鲁迅

Lü Liping 吕丽萍

*Lü Xiaomin 吕小敏 (1973–)

Pan Hannian 潘汉年

Peng Zhen 彭真

Qian Mu 钱穆

Ma Geshun 马革顺

Mao Zedong 毛泽东

Ni Tuosheng (Watchman Nee) 倪柝声

Pan Hannian 潘汉年

Pearl Buck 赛珍珠

*Shi Meiyu (Mary Stone) 石美玉 (1873–1954)

Shi Wei 施玮

Song Meiling 宋美龄

Song Qingling 宋庆龄

Song Shangjie (John Sung) 宋尚节

Sun Haiying 孙海英

Sun Yat-sen 孙中山

Wang Dan 王丹

Wang Guangmei 王光美

Wang Mingdao 王明道

Wen Yiduo 闻一多

Wu Ningkun 巫宁坤

Wu Wenzao 吴文藻

Wu Yaozong (Yao-tsung Wu or Y. T. Wu) 吴耀宗

*Wu Yifang 吴贻芳

*Xie Wanying (or Bing Xin) 谢婉莹 (冰心, 1900–1999)

Xu Guangqi 徐光启

Xu Zhimo 徐志摩

Yan Fu 严复
Yan Yangchu (James Yen) 晏阳初
Yan Xishan 阎锡山
Yao Chen 姚晨
Yu Cidu (Dora Yu) 余慈度
Yu Yingshi 余英时
Yuan Shikai 袁世凯
Yuan Zhiming 远志明
*Zeng Baosun (Tseng Pao Swen) 曾宝荪 (1893–1978)
Zeng Guofan 曾国藩
Zhang Zhidong 张之洞
*Zhao Luorui (Lucy Chao) 赵萝蕤 (1912–1998)
Zhao Jingde 赵景德
Zhao Jinglun 赵景伦
Zhao Jingxin 赵景心
Zhao Zichen (T. C. Chao) 赵紫宸
Zhou Enlai 周恩来
Zhu Xiangyi 朱湘一

ORGANIZATIONAL NAMES

Christian Life Quarterly (*shengming jikan*) 《生命季刊》
Communist Youth League (CYL) 共青团
Gospel for China Conference 中国福音大会
House Churches 家庭教会
Little Flock (Local Church) 小群教会，地方教会
New Moon School 新月派
People's Liberation Army (PLA) 解放军
Three-Self Patriotic Movement 三自爱国运动

SPECIAL TERMS

New Youth 《新青年》
The White-Haired Girl 《白毛女》
The Christian Occupation of China (*zhong hua gui zhu*), 《中华归主》
Mi sai ya 《弥赛亚》(马革顺谱写)

Bibliography

Aikman, David. *Jesus in Beijing: How Christianity is Transforming China and Changing the Global Balance of Power.* Washington: Regnery Publishing, 2012.

Andors, Phyllis. *The Unfinished Revolution of Chinese Women, 1949–80.* Bloomington: Indiana University Press, 1983.

Bays, Daniel. *A New History of Chinese Christianity.* Hoboken, NJ: Wiley-Blackwell, 2012.

Bi, Lijun. "Bing Xin: First Female Writer of Modern Chinese Children's Literature," *Studies in Literature and Language*, Vol. 6, No. 2 (2013): 23–29.

Bickers, Robert. *Britain in China: Community, Culture and Colonialism, 1900–1949.* Manchester: Manchester University Press, 2017.

———. *Out of China: How the Chinese Ended Western Domination.* Cambridge, MA: Harvard University Press, 2017.

Brekus, Catherine A. (ed.). *The Religious History of American Women: Reimagining the Past.* Chapel Hill: University of North Carolina Press, 2007.

Cao, Shengjie. *An Oral History of Cao Shengjie.* Shanghai: Shanghai Bookstore Publishing House, 2016.

Chang, Leslie T. *Factory Girls: From Village to City in a Changing China.* New York: Random House, 2009.

Chen, Yongfa. *Seventy Years since China's Communist Revolution*, vol. 2. Taipei: Lianjing Press, 2001.

Chung, Mary Keng Mun. *Chinese Women in Christian Ministry: An Intercultural Study.* Bern: Peter Lang, 2005.

Cohen, Paul A. *China Unbound: Evolving Perspectives on the Chinese Past.* New York: Routledge, 2003.

Diamant, Neil J. *Revolutionizing the Family: Politics, Love, and Divorce in Urban and Rural China, 1949–1968.* Berkeley: University of California Press, 2000.

Du Mez, Kristin. *A New Gospel for Women: Katharine Bushnell and the Challenge of Christian Feminism.* New York: Oxford University Press, 2015.

Fairbank, John King (ed.). *The Missionary Enterprise in China and America.* Cambridge, MA: Harvard University Press, 1974.

Faries, Nathan. *The "Inscrutably Chinese" Church: How Narratives and Nationalism Continue to Divide Christianity.* Lanham, MD: Lexington Books, 2010.

Hershatter, Gail. *Dangerous Pleasures: Prostitution and Modernity in Twentieth-Century Shanghai.* Berkeley: University of California Press, 1999.

———. *Women and China's Revolutions.* Lanham: Rowman & Littlefield Publishers, 2018.

Hunter, Alan and Kim-Kwong Chan, *Protestantism in Contemporary China.* Vol. 3. Cambridge: Cambridge University Press, 2007.

Hsu, Immanuel Y. *The Rise of Modern China.* New York: Oxford University Press, 1999.

Hsu, Lily M. *For Whom the Siren Wails: Watchman Nee and the Local Church in China.* Maitland, FL: Xulon Press, 2018.

Hsu, Lily M. and Dana Roberts. *My Unforgettable Memories: Watchman Nee and Shanghai Local Church.* Maitland, FL: Xulon Press, 2013.

Janz, Denis R. *World Christianity and Marxism.* New York: Oxford University Press, 1998.

Jenkins, Philip. *The Next Christendom: The Coming of Global Christianity* (New York: Oxford University Press, 2002), 160.

Johnson, Elizabeth A. *She Who Is: The Mystery of God in Feminist Theological Discourse.* New York: Crossroad Publishing, 2017.

Jun, Xing. *Baptized in the Fire of Revolution: The American Social Gospel and the YMCA in China, 1919–1937.* Bethlehem, PA: Lehigh University Press, 1996.

Kane, Danielle and Jung Mee Park, "The puzzle of Korean Christianity: Geopolitical Networks and Religious Conversion in Early Twentieth-Century East Asia." *American Journal of Sociology,* Vol. 115, No. 2 (2009): 365–404.

Kennedy, Thomas L. "Preface," in Zeng Baosun, ed., *Confucian Feminist: Memoirs of Zeng Baosun, 1893-1978,* translated and adapted by Thomas L. Kennedy. Philadelphia, PA: American Philosophical Society, 2002.

King, Richard (ed.). *Art in Turmoil: The Chinese Cultural Revolution, 1966–76.* Vancouver: University of British Columbia Press, 2010.

Kraus, Richard Curt. *Piano and Politics in China: Middle-Class Ambitions and the Struggle over Western Music.* New York: Oxford University Press, 1998.

Kwok, Pui-lan, "The Emergence of Asian Feminist Consciousness of Culture and Theology," in Virginia Fabella M. M. and Sun Ai Lee Park, eds., *We Care to Dream.* Maryknoll: Obis Books, 1989.

———. *Chinese Women and Christianity, 1860–1927.* Atlanta: Scholars Press, 1992.

———. *Postcolonial Imagination and Feminist Theology.* Louisville: Westminster John Knox Press, 2005.

———. "Christianity and Women in Contemporary China," *Journal of World Christianity,* Vol. 3, No. 1 (2010), pp. 1–17.

———. (ed.). *Hope Abundant: Third World and Indigenous Women's Theology.* Maryknoll: Orbis Books, 2010.

Lindsay, Beverly (ed.). *Comparative Perspectives of Third World Women: The Impact of Race, Sex and Class.* New York: Praeger Press, 1983.

Lutz, Jessie G. *Pioneer Chinese Christian Women*. Bethlehem: Lehigh University Press, 2010.

Ma, Li and Jin Li, *Surviving the State, Remaking the Church: A Sociological Portrait of Christians in Mainland China*. Eugene, OR: Pickwick Publications, 2017.

———. *The Chinese Exodus: Migration, Urbanism, and Alienation in Contemporary China*. Eugene, OR: Pickwick Publications, 2018.

———. "Diverging Paths of Protestantism and Asian Nationalism: A Comparison of Two Social Movements in Korea and China in 1919," *International Bulletin of Mission Research*, Vol. 42, No. 4 (2018): 316–325.

———. *Religious Entrepreneurship in China's Urban House Churches: The Rise and Fall of Early Rain Reformed Presbyterian Church*. New York: Routledge, 2019.

———. *Christianity, Femininity and Social Change in Contemporary China*. New York: Palgrave MacMillan, 2020, 3.

———. "The Tragic Irony of a Patriotic Mission: The Indigenous Leadership of Francis Wei and T. C. Chao, Radicalized Patriotism, and the Reversal of Protestant Mission in China," *Religions*, Vol. 11, No. 4 (2020): 175. https://www.mdpi.com /2077-1444/11/4/175

———. *Babel Church: The Subversion of Christianity in An Age of Mass Media, Globalization and #MeToo*. Cascade Books, 2021.

Marsden, Lee. *For God's Sake: The Christian Right and US Foreign Policy*. London: Zed Books, 2008.

Ono, Kazuko. *Chinese Women in a Century of Revolution, 1850–1950*. Stanford, CA: Stanford University Press, 1989.

Perry, Elizabeth J. and Mark Selden (eds.). *Chinese Society: Change, Conflict and Resistance*. New York: Routledge, 2000.

Robert, Dana L. *American Women in Mission: A Social History of Their Thought and Practices*. Macon: Mercer University Press, 1996.

Reeves-Ellington, Barbara, Kathryn Kish Sklar, and Connie A. Shemo (eds.), *Competing Kingdoms: Women, Mission, Nation, and the American Protestant Empire, 1812–1960*. Durham, NC: Duke University Press, 2010.

Rosenbaum, Arthur Lewis. "Christianity, Academics, and National Salvation in China: Yenching University, 1924–1949." *Journal of American-East Asia Relations*, Vol. 13 (2004–2006), 27.

Sanneh, Lamin O. *Disciples of All Nations: Pillars of World Christianity*. New York: Oxford University Press, 2008.

Shaffer, Kay and Song Xianlin, "Unruly Spaces: Gender, Women's Writings and Indigenous Feminism in China," *Journal of Gender Studies*, Vol. 16, No. 1 (2007): 17–30.

Shemo, Connie Anne. *The Chinese Medical Ministries of Kang Cheng and Shi Meiyu, 1872–1937*. Bethlehem, PA: Lehigh University Press, 2011.

Spence, Jonathan D. *The Gate of Heavenly Peace: The Chinese and Their Revolution*. New York: Penguin Books, 1982.

———. *The Search for Modern China*. New York: W. W. Norton & Company, 1991.

———. *To Chang China: Western Advisers in China*. Westminster: Penguin Books, 2002.

Stacey, Judith. *Patriarchy and Social Revolution in China.* Berkeley and Los Angeles: University of California Press, 1983.

Wang, Zheng. *Finding Women in the State: A Socialist Feminist Revolution in the People's Republic of China, 1949–1964.* Oakland: University of California Press, 2017.

Wickeri, Philip L. *Seeking Common Ground: Protestant Christianity, the Three-Self Movement, and China's United Front.* Maryknoll, NY: Orbis Books, 1988.

Williams, Philip F (ed.). *Asian Literary Voices: From Marginalized to Mainstream.* Amsterdam: Amsterdam University Press, 2010.

Wolf, Margery. *Revolution Postponed: Women in Contemporary China.* Stanford: Stanford University Press, 1985.

Wong, Wai Ching Angela and Patricia P. K. Chiu, *Chinese Women in Chinese Society.* Hong Kong: Hong Kong University Press, 2018.

Wright, Teresa and Teresa Zimmerman-Liu, "Atheist Political Activists Turned Protestants: Religious Conversion among Chinese Dissidents," *Journal of Church and State*, Vol. 57, No. 2 (Spring 2015): 268–288.

Yan, Haiping. *Chinese Women Writers and the Feminist Imagination, 1905–1948.* New York: Routledge, 2006.

Yung, Judy. *Unbound Feet: A Social History of Chinese Women in San Francisco.* Berkeley: University of California Press, 1995.

Zhang, Nian. *Gender Politics and State: On Women's Liberation in China.* Beijing: Shang Wu Publishing House, 2014.

Zhou, Kate. *China's Long March to Freedom: Grassroots Modernization.* New Brunswick, NJ: Transaction Publishers, 2011.

Index

abortion, 153, 168, 174, 179, 194, 203
abuse, xiii, xvii, xviii, xx, xxv, xxvi,
   xxviii, xxixn31, 12, 15, 19n69, 23,
   34, 45, 100–101, 103–4, 145, 153–
   55, 157, 159, 164–66, 169, 170n27,
   173n77, 183, 186, 192, 195–97,
   200–201, 207–8
activism, activist, activistic, xviii, 5–7,
   28, 35, 40–41, 43, 46, 48–49, 62, 65,
   71, 106, 117, 123, 148, 154, 161–62,
   165, 168, 171n44, 172n61, 172n74,
   185, 188n3, 188n15, 189n20, 192,
   194, 197–99, 209
anti-Christian movement, anti-Christian
   sentiments, xi, 1, 14, 22n113, 30, 34,
   42–44, 46–47, 53n21, 54n34, 54n37,
   62, 79, 129, 186–87, 199
anti-foreignism, anti-foreign sentiments,
   1, 13, 46–47, 75, 195–96
Anti-Rightist, xii, 75, 83–84, 102, 136
authoritarianism, authoritarian, xxixn31,
   49, 124, 129, 145, 147, 162, 196–97,
   200–201, 208

bourgeois, bourgeoisie, 34–35, 48, 52,
   85, 90, 94, 98, 105–6, 109
Buddhism, 40, 199

celebrity, celebrities, xxiv–xxv, xxxn40,
   45, 127n58, 129–31, 140, 154,

161, 166–67, 171n38, 172n73, 175,
   179–80, 183–86, 190n46, 190n48,
   203, 208
Censorship, xxv, 115, 124, 175, 177–78
Chinese Communist Party (CCP), xi,
   33, 42, 45, 48, 54n33, 56n71, 60,
   64–65, 67, 69–70, 72n2, 79, 82, 85,
   99, 100, 104–5, 107n13, 111, 138,
   145, 162, 184–85, 191, 198, 199
Chinese diaspora, diaspora, xvii, xxi,
   xxii, xxiii, xxv, 129, 142, 148, 153,
   161–62, 165–68, 170n24, 177, 187
Christian Right, 148, 168, 171n52,
   174n89, 174n91
colonialism, colonial, colonialist, 15,
   41, 44, 83, 88, 94, 147, 166, 194–95,
   199–200
communism, communist, xvii–xxiv,
   xxviiin19, xxixn39, xxxn43, 1,
   21n105, 30–31, 33–35, 37n42,
   42–45, 48–49, 59–60, 64–65, 67–71,
   75, 78–79, 81–82, 84–85, 87, 89,
   94–95, 97, 98–100, 102–6, 107n13,
   111, 115–17, 119, 124, 129, 131–38,
   140, 145–48, 153–54, 156, 158–60,
   162–65, 167, 181, 196–200, 202
complementarian, 186, 208
Confucianism, Confucian, 8, 23–29, 31,
   33–34, 40–41, 43, 45, 49, 63, 86,
   102, 118, 167, 179, 194, 197

About the Author

Li Ma (PhD Cornell University) is a social historian and research fellow affiliated with Calvin University. She is the author of five books on Chinese Christianity, including *Surviving the State, Remaking the Church* (Pickwick, 2017), *Religious Entrepreneurism in China's Urban House Churches* (Routledge, 2019), and *Christianity, Femininity and Social Change in Contemporary China* (Palgrave MacMillan, 2020). Her other scholarly works also appear on journals such as *Religions, Journal of Markets and Morality, Logos & Pneuma: Chinese Journal of Theology, The International Bulletin of Mission Research*, so on. On issues of gender and social justice, Li Ma also contributes to public media in the Chinese-speaking world, such as the *Financial Times, Initium, Caixin,* and *Jiemian*.